AMERICAN LANDLORD

Everything U Need to Know... ™

about

PROPERTY MANAGEMENT

TREVOR RHODES, CEO OF AmerUSA

Mc
Graw
Hill

New York   Chicago   San Francisco   Lisbon
London   Madrid   Mexico City   Milan   New Delhi
San Juan   Seoul   Singapore   Sydney   Toronto

AUG

The McGraw·Hill Companies

1 2 3 4 5 6 7 8 9 0   FGR/FGR   0 9 8 7

ISBN-13: P/N 978-0-07-154976-9 of set
             978-0-07-154517-4

ISBN-10: P/N 0-07-154976-5 of set
             0-07-154517-4

(3|0|9|54|642|54)

Trademarks: Everything U Need to Know…, the Everything U Need to Know… horseshoe bar logo, AmerUSA, AmerUSA.net, and the AmerUSA swoosh logo are all trademarks or registered trademarks of the AmerUSA Corporation and may not be used without written permission. All other trademarks are the property of their respective owners.

Disclaimer: While the publisher and the author have used their best efforts in preparing this book, they make no representations or warranties with respect to the accuracy or completeness of the contents. Neither the publisher nor author shall be liable for any loss of profit or commercial damages, including but not limited to special, incidental, consequential or other damages. If legal advice or other expert assistance is required, it is strongly recommended that the services of a competent and experienced professional should be sought.

McGraw-Hill books are available at special quantity discounts to use as premiums and sales promotions, or for use in corporate training programs. For more information, please write to the Director of Special Sales, Professional Publishing, McGraw-Hill, Two Penn Plaza, New York, NY 10121-2298. Or contact your local bookstore.

For information about any of the other Everything U Need to Know… products, visit www.EverythingUNeedToKnow.com or write to: Everything U Need to Know…, AmerUSA Corporation, 3665 East Bay Drive, #204-183, Largo, FL 33771.

Available through book retailers nationwide.

CD-ROM Software: TailoredApplication.com
Index: ProfessionalIndexing.com

This book is printed on acid-free paper.

Acknowledgments

This being the first volume in the Everything U Need to Know… series, we would like to acknowledge and give proper thanks to the following people for their support and professional advice: Lisa Rhodes, Joseph & Deanne Spinazzola, Jacob & Brianna Smith, Jason & Kimber Ramage, Jeff Read, Joseph Casamento, Christopher Michael, Andrew Waggoner, Christopher & Nicole Rhodes, Josephine Rhodes, Glenn & Dawn Marie Humphreys, Sue Humphreys, Michael Rhodes, Paul Denker, Pegoty Lopez, Lyn Lopez, James Dennis & Linda Walsh, Kent & Glenda Petelle, Christopher Jones, Cameron Rhodes, Tyler Rhodes, Pamela Phillips, John Stalker, Kevin & Evan Petelle, Kara Petelle, Alex & Max Chudy, and the many thousands of AmerUSA clients who epitomize what it is to be a successful American Landlord.

A special thanks also goes to those responsible for bringing this series to market:

McGraw-Hill

Herb Schaffner - Publisher, Business Group
Mary Glenn - Director, Business Editorial
Janice Race - Senior Editing Supervisor
Maureen Harper - Production Manager
Anthony Landi - Senior Art Director
Staci Shands - Senior Publicist

Everything U Need to Know…/AmerUSA Corporation

Trevor Rhodes - Creative Director/President & CEO
Tomas Mureika - Managing Editor/Director, Media Relations
Ronald Rhodes - Vice President, Finance
Ross Dunkerley - Vice President, Production
Mary Rhodes - Vice President, Customer Relations
Nicole Février - Director, Legal Research
Nadine Smith - General Counsel
Laurence J. Smith - Senior Legal Counsel

Table of Contents

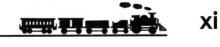

[Directory of appendices, including Section 8, on following pages]

Introduction

Whether you're getting started, getting frustrated or just not getting it all, becoming a successful landlord is not always easy.** Be it on account of the *maintenance*, the tenants, the *financing* or the remaining list of *unforeseen potential pitfalls*, owning rental property can often be downright frustrating – **however, it doesn't *have* to be that way!** Regardless of whether you're renting out a **single room in your home** or are responsible for **multiple property units**, *American Landlord* brings you the *collective personal experiences* of thousands of **professional and average American "everyday landlords,"** so that *you may learn in only a few hours what usually takes years to discover the hard way*.

American Landlord is meant to **simplify** and **clarify the complexities** of the real estate rodeo. **It is a book designed for anyone with the slightest interest in owning investment property**, *especially homeowners* who may (one day down the road) be confronted with the opportunity either to buy another property or to rent out their primary residence – perhaps to accommodate schooling, military, career, familial or other needs. **It doesn't matter if you consider yourself "in" the real estate industry or not;** *Everything U Need to Know... about Property Management* has *been carefully presented to educate the tenderfoot, as well as to enhance the seasoned wrangler's wealth of knowledge.*

Inside *American Landlord*, you will find **easy step-by-step instructions, simple examples, real-life experiences** of **genuine American landlords** – and even a **bonus CD-ROM** filled with *dozens of legal resources*, including **tenant screening forms, letters, lease agreements,** as well as a *handy reference guide on landlord-tenant laws for each individual state*, so **you can better understand your rights and responsibilities.**

In addition, **you are cordially invited to visit** and **join** the **American Landlord** website **(www.AmericanLandlord.com)** for *absolutely* **FREE** – an online forum where you can *chat with real estate peers and pros* and *share your stories with others just like you*. In addition, you'll receive **free news updates** and **gain access** to **numerous special features designed to help aid you further**. Premium products and services are also available directly through the website – including *credit reports, eviction records, criminal background checks* and *much, much more.*

I am confident you will enjoy *American Landlord* and its **light-hearted** – yet **extremely useful** – approach to learning from thousands of others who have tried and triumphed before you. There's no reason to wander blindly into foreign territory and repeat every one of the most common mistakes made by those that "didn't know." *Take advantage of the wealth of information and experience contained in this first edition from the* "**Everything U Need to Know**" *series*, so that you, too, can enjoy being an **"American Landlord"** and **reap the rewards** from what has *always* proven to be *the single best place* to invest your hard-earned money: the highly profitable world of *real estate*.

Consider this to be *your one-stop comforting guidebook to navigating this complex and confusing world*, affording you the **peace of mind** that you'll **never have to worry** about getting lost or misdirected along the way. Whether this is your first time venturing out or you're an old pro, **I wish you all the best** on your wonderful journeys into the great frontier of the **"American Landlord."**

Yours truly,

Trevor Rhodes
Chief Executive Officer
AmerUSA Corporation

Chapter 1

Becoming an American Landlord: To Be or Not to Be...?

This Chapter Discusses:

- ★ **Inheriting Property**
- ★ **Relocating Temporarily**
- ★ **Upsizing and Downsizing**
- ★ **Investing for the First Time**

"**T**o be or not to be..." an **American Landlord** – **that** *is* **the question**. For many, the answer has always been quite clear, but chances are good you've started reading this chapter because **you may be unsure about whether or not you *want* to become a landlord**. Possibly it's because you've heard *negative stories* or maybe the skeptic within you heard *too many "too-good-to-be-true"* ones – *or* perhaps you haven't heard *anything* at all and are quite **understandably overwhelmed** and lacking the confidence to tackle the great frontier of real estate on your own.

This first chapter will emphasize **the overwhelmingly positive rewards of being a landlord** and **why it's *well* worth your while to "be" one**. *The first rule of thumb to* always *remember is that most of the pitfalls encountered are seldom unforeseen and are often preventable* – if you **take a moment** to **carefully consider your options.**

It is important to thoroughly assess the situation *before* acting hastily or spontaneously. Although everyone wants to succeed, *many people do not have the patience, perseverance and basic knowledge to accomplish their goals.* So if you can muster up that patience and perseverance, *American Landlord* will provide you with the **necessary knowledge and support you need to see that you succeed.**

Inheriting Property

One of the more common scenarios in which people **unexpectedly** find themselves thrust into the position of becoming a potential landlord is by *inheriting property*. Just because it hasn't happened yet, **becoming the heir to your parents', grandparents' or other relative's home can easily happen to you.**

Regardless of the current state of the "FED" (the board that oversees the Federal Reserve Banks and ultimately determines national interest rates), people are unfortunately continuing to die at the same daily rate – and whether you inherit a property *in its entirety* or *as a percentage that is shared among other family members*, the first mistake that people invariably make is to liquidate the property for immediate cash without considering the long-term benefits of what would happen were you to rent it out.

If the interest in the property *is* divided, then *expect some friction from those "ever-friendly" family members* who exhibit no ability to reason when presented with the option of receiving immediate cash on hand, as opposed to foreseeing the property's greater value as an investment in their future.

This is when you will have to lasso everyone together with a great level of enthusiasm and some easily digestible facts and solid figures depicting the significantly larger pile of cash that awaits them. And while it is true that *not every property is worth holding on to*, it can be easily determined if there is more than just sentimental value or your family's heritage at stake.

Ask yourself this one simple question:

➤ *What is the condition of the property?*

If you feel neither confident nor skilled enough to answer this question on your own, then hire a *licensed home inspector*. It'll cost you only a few hundred dollars for *invaluable* knowledge as to whether you have a real investment opportunity or a money pit on your hands. Visit **www.AmericanLandlord.com** to find a licensed home inspector in your area.

---

12 (Months) x Proposed Rent Amount (Monthly) = Maximum Repair Allowance

As a general rule, *if the cost of the repairs or improvements doesn't exceed the equivalent of one year's worth of gross rental income, the property may well be worth retaining and renting if your intentions are to hold onto it for a while.*

TIP

It is generally accepted that if you *are* **short on cash, you may want to reconsider acquiring and rehabbing any property.** However, *there are ways of raising the extra money for repairs and improvements* – including *refinancing* the property and taking cash out of it – but **this chapter is intended to simplify the process** with a few basic guidelines as opposed to complicating it with complex and convoluted financial maneuvers. If you insist, **you are always encouraged to take a pencil and paper and do the numbers to see if you can add them up in your favor.**

Be sure to consider the following when taking additional risks:

➤ *How long do you reasonably expect to hold on to the property and in the end, would it have been worth the effort, time and money?*

> ➤ *Can you safely refinance and pull enough cash out of the property to make the necessary repairs and improvements without being severely penalized with a costly mortgage that you will live to regret?* [*See* **Chapter 17** *regarding tips on how to finance investment property and achieve the best program, term and rate.*]

> ➤ *Will the newly improved property be able to command enough rent to cover the new mortgage payment or can you stand to lose each month, hoping the property will appreciate enough over time to offset the monthly loss?*

You may be wondering why **only these three questions** were posed. Quite simply, all other issues you're likely to encounter are actually *very* easy to manage with the help of *American Landlord* and may just confuse and complicate the **basic decision-making process** at this point.

One such example is the logistics involved in *managing the inherited property if it's located out of state*. Even if you are an **"absentee landlord"** (one who lives a considerable distance from his or her property – i.e., several hours away or more by car), **you can still confidently take control of the unit, market it, repair it and continue to fill it with the best of tenants.** In fact, *thousands of absentee landlords do so every day with tremendous success,* all with the help of the **information contained in this property management volume**.

L. Nathanson
Wisconsin
Landlord

Living out of the area was a concern for me and my husband when he was offered a new job across the state, but didn't want to sell our current home. I didn't think we would get much sleep dealing with tenants at any waking hour, but surprisingly, it was no more of an inconvenience than being a local landlord; you just have to learn to screen your tenants and get to know reliable service professionals.

Aside from the sentimental value and family heritage, ***there are three wonderful things about rental property that need to be considered*** before making your decision regarding whether or not you should sell that inheritance or hold on to it and rent it out – they are as follows:

☆ Positive Cash Flow

As long as the ***remaining mortgage is minimal***, the ***property is in good condition*** and the ***taxes and insurance are not increasing exponentially every year*** (as they do in Florida and many other states), **never pass up the opportunity for extra monthly income**. If you do, you will assuredly regret that decision when you eventually stumble upon a calculator and do some elementary math. **Rental payments are like social security checks –** ***they'll continue to be there as long as the property is carefully handled and not mismanaged***. Granted, anything can go wrong with a property or a tenant at any time, but **in the long run, you can count on a solid return from your investment** – or at least a place to live if your personal life falls apart and you can no longer afford your primary residence... Sorry, it happens – and **your forethought suddenly becomes an absolutely priceless fallback**.

☆ Appreciation

Generally speaking, **property values will climb** – you will know if your area is ***too distressed*** or ***problematic*** to consider. **Some properties appreciate rapidly, others slowly –** ***the important thing is to stick with it for the long haul*** and you should do just fine. In fact, **most people that keep inherited property make out a heck of a lot better than those that cash out** and typically go on a spending spree. **Real estate is a great savings tool that also offers a valuable lesson in self-discipline**. If your money is tied up, you can't spend it – and if someone else is paying you for the use of your property, you might as well jump on and enjoy the yearlong hayride. **DON'T FORGET:** ***The only time you have to plan for the future is "now"*** – once the future becomes "now," it's already too late!

⭐ Income Tax Advantages

While this is not a volume on *American Accounting*, needless to say, **there are many creative ways to lower your income tax burden by correctly depreciating your rental property**. Any **Certified Public Accountant (CPA)** can help you on this matter; it is *strongly* recommended that you seek their advice. **It's well worth spending hundreds of dollars to save yourself** *thousands*, by taking full advantage of the elaborate and confusing tax code that was created specifically to protect those few individuals fortunate enough to own property of significant value. Visit **www.AmericanLandlord.com** to level the playing field by finding a local professional to help you navigate through the tax code.

So the next time you inherit a relative's property, *don't be quick to cash out until you've accurately assessed whether you might be able to bank upon your brand-new asset each and every month for years to come*.

Relocating Temporarily

For the purposes of this book, **"temporary relocation"** is defined as **"leaving a primary residence with the** *likelihood* **of returning one day** (usually between six months and a couple of years – or perhaps a little longer) **from the initial date of departure."** *If you're relocating out of the area* – whether for school, career development, military assignment or any other reason – *you should seriously consider renting out your primary residence as an alternative to listing your property for sale*. At the very least, **hold on to your home so you retain the option of returning one day**, should you wish to or – even more importantly – should you have the *need* to due to unforeseen circumstances.

In addition to leaving yourself a "safety net," it again just *makes good financial sense to take advantage of the opportunity to have someone else paying your mortgage for you while you're away*. Think about it – **your property is being maintained and cared for, while it does nothing more than appreciate in value**. Sure, there have been horror stories of bad tenants and property damage, but *don't let that scare you away*.

The *overwhelming majority* **of those that rent out their primary residence while away do quite well** – and are able to enjoy their extended hiatuses without worrying excessively about the home they left behind. It's simply a matter of *exercising good judgment* and *adopting a strict screening policy*. So **don't fret about long-distance landlord-tenant relationships**; later chapters will address in greater detail how to best screen and manage tenants – so that you can *ensure the odds are in your favor* by statistically distancing yourself from your own imagined horror story.

"I had to move out of state to pursue a Master's Degree and was unsure of what I should do with my home, which I purchased during my undergraduate years. It was a difficult decision to make, but I ultimately decided to rent it out.

Several years had passed and before I knew it, I found that I was never going to return – but luckily for me, the real estate market had escalated over the past four years while I'd been away and I was able to sell the property and pay the entirety of my student loans.

It was a fantastic decision as I am now debt free – well... except for my current mortgage, that is – but how many other graduate students can actually claim the luxury of having paid off their student loans?"

B. McPherson
Virginia
Former Landlord

Upsizing and Downsizing

When facing bad *or* **prosperous times** and the decision is made accordingly to **move into a more reasonable or lavish place**, you may want to *think about whether you are in a position to rent out your current residence*. The reason this question keeps recurring is because **the most difficult part about real estate has always been how challenging it is to buy it**. So, *if you already own something, use this chance to take full advantage of your opportunities, which may include converting it in to a profitable rental property*.

Obviously for those who have extra money and are in a position to upsize, this decision is much easier to make – but for those faced with difficult times and needing to tighten their budgets, *the decision requires careful attention:* **Make sure you are able to afford** owning two properties at once!

Okay – you may be asking: **"If I can't afford one, then how am I** *possibly* **going to afford two homes** – and **why would I want to move out of the more expensive one?"** Well, that comes down to a matter of common sense. The theory is that *the bigger the house, the more expensive the maintenance and the utilities – so let someone else take care of those expenses while you wait for your equity to grow*.

Before you jump the gun, you need to carefully consider two questions:

➢ *Will you be able to show enough income to qualify for a favorable mortgage on the second property? Most mortgage lenders will only calculate 75% of the monthly rental income toward your personal income, because they conservatively allow for a 25% vacancy rate.* [*See* **Chapter 17** *for more information on* **"non-owner occupied financing."**]

> ➤ *Will you be able to rent the property for more than what you'll owe each month?*

One final preliminary word of caution:

The emphasis here is to try to make the most of real estate that is already in your hands, by having it work to your advantage. If you feel that your financial situation will be too stressed or placed in jeopardy by keeping your previous residence, then – by all means – sell it! *However,* **you may be sitting on the market for an overly extended period of time while trying to sell it, so you may then want to rethink its use**. Either way, *the most important point is to always consider the option of renting out your current home* when either upsizing or downsizing to a new one.

Investing for the First Time

So maybe you've been thinking about it for a long time and have been **a little hesitant** to venture off into the great untamed frontier of real estate. Possibly you've dabbled in mutual funds, a few stocks and even a CD or two – but **there is nothing quite like the real estate market... and it always seems a little riskier for some reason**. Well, the reason it's riskier is *the number of hidden pitfalls*. This is where *American Landlord* comes in, as **there is no better time to begin than today**. So let's take that bull by the horns and ride it…

There is nothing like being in the right place at the right time. Most people have been there at some point over the course of their lives, but have *unfortunately failed to seize that moment*. So all you have to do is to reconstruct that moment and know when to seize it – and **it all begins with the search**. Whether it's the *lower-than-market price, owner-friendly financing, desirable location* – or anything else that appeals to your liking – **it's all good**...

Now that you're all amped up and excited to get started, **you need to understand the basics of what you're looking for** prior to breaking the bank on that geodesic dome you've been eyeing since your parents last took you to a drive-in movie. *It doesn't matter what you're looking for as long as it meets these three basic criteria*:

> ★ **The property must be in good condition or will be with minor repairs that you are qualified to perform yourself or can afford to have done for you without exhausting your cash reserves...**

> It is generally recommended that your *repairs be limited to no more than the equivalent of 12 months of the property's anticipated rental income* – which is actually quite a stretch for a beginner. **Wait until you get your feet wet before you start rehabilitating a property.** For those of you that are contractors or experienced flippers, you may skip ahead to the tenant screening chapters.

Before you submit an offer to purchase real estate, it is important to consider the following: **Does the property require repairs in excess of $1,000 *and* is it your intention to use a conventional mortgage lender (e.g., a bank) to finance the property?** If the answer is **"yes"** to *both* questions, *see* **Chapter 17** for more information on **"non-owner occupied financing"** because many lenders will *not* approve you if the property is subject to repairs or conditions.

> ★ **The property must have the potential to appreciate...**

> In other words, **the local market condition cannot be overly distressed** with *foreclosures, toxic waste, sink holes, radioactive fallout* or *anything else that can potentially lower property values*. Just **make sure these values have gone up over the years by consulting a** *local appraiser* or by simply **ordering a comparable sales report from www.USHomeValue.com** to see the difference in the property's two previous sales transactions.

✪ Your gross monthly rental income must at least equal your total monthly mortgage payment...

If the monthly rent does not cover your mortgage payment - including the principal, interest, taxes and insurance - then **your property must be able to appreciate at a *considerable* rate** (usually seen in coastal or high-demand areas, where developable land is scarce). **Unless you are a seasoned real estate investor, it is *not* recommended that you take a considerable monthly loss on your rental just yet.**

Remember, **this introductory chapter** was ***primarily intended to introduce the real estate "newbie" to a whole new world of doing business*** as an **American Landlord**. ***Take one step at a time and heed the conservative advice that follows*** before you and your posse embark on a real estate cattle drive all over town – which leads us to ***one final issue before continuing on to the next steps***: the concept of "**partnerships**."

Everyone wants to be a partner – but ***unless you truly need one*** (for **financial assistance** or **home improvement expertise, labor**, etc.) – ***be careful!*** **Money tends to spoil business relationships in a very short period of time** (even those with friends and loved ones). ***Know what you are getting into and with whom you are getting into it.*** **Simple agreements that spell out your relationship, responsibilities and contributions are always strongly recommended.** If serious money is at stake, then a serious attorney should be consulted to seal the deal.

Chapter 2

Preparing Your Rental Property: Tips to Entice the Herd

This Chapter Discusses:

★ Curb Appeal
★ The Kitchen
★ Bathrooms
★ Interior Painting
★ Flooring

There is a common consensus among landlords that tenants treat rental property like rental cars – and you know what that means – so ***don't spend a lot of money or energy trying to showcase your unit*** when **all you need to do is simply show it as a clean and comfortable place to live for a year or two** (or, if you're lucky, maybe more). There are some **easy, practical steps** you can take **to perform this makeover** without being ***too extreme***.

But before you start, **you need to determine what type of person will most likely be renting your investment** (e.g., college student, single professional, family, etc.). **Determining what type of tenant your property and its locale will attract is** *absolutely essential* to ensuring you're not wasting your resources.

A college student's needs and expectations are undoubtedly different from those of the working professional who's the head of a family of three. The student could probably care less about the overall **"curb appeal"** and **kitchen amenities**, while the family of three is more likely looking for convenience and a place to call home (at least for a little while). This is not to say that all college students have lower expectations and that they don't use kitchens – quite the contrary, many of them do... (well, at least they use the microwave). But seriously, *use your best judgment to tailor your unit to the general liking of the type of person who will most likely want to live there*.

Curb Appeal

Obviously, **not many people are attracted to a neglected home when looking for a place** to lease for the next year or two. As you will discover in the **next chapter on marketing your property,** *the most successful method is the sign in the front yard* – that is, **as long as you can see it clearly** through the overgrown lawn and shrubbery – or if you can even bother to focus upon it since you can't tear your eyes away from the obscene purple front door and pink shutters!

Like it or not, it's true: **People can actually have (without even realizing it) such incredibly bad taste that the exterior of their home will genuinely frighten prospects away!** *New landlords tend to forget that prospective tenants are not looking to buy*. **Therefore, they are not inclined to think about the changes they could make**.

On the next page, there are three items of improvement listed which are reasonable to attend to and will *only take a weekend* (or maybe two) **to help you attract** *substantially* **more prospects**...

Landscaping

Without wasting too much effort on plants and flowers that will most likely never even be tended to by the tenant, **it's best to simply make sure there is more grass on the lawn than weeds and sand**. *Pallets of grass cover about 500 square feet and can usually be purchased and delivered for about $200*. While laying it takes some effort, especially if you have old grass to remove, **inviting green grass is something difficult to pass by**. The **same premise applies to brown or naked shrubbery** – *replacing them is very affordable*. Finally, **let's not forget about the weeds** growing all over. *All it takes is about half an hour of your time to spray them with a long-lasting weed killer and the results are visible within 24 hours.*

☆ Painting

This is the easiest "do-it-yourself" home improvement. But **before you consider changing anything, take a couple steps back and think about the current exterior color scheme of your rental**. <u>Ask yourself</u>: *Does it work and will it appeal to other people?* Remember, now is not the time to make a political statement by mixing colors on the opposite end of the spectrum or by unifying the rainbow. *Calm, cool and neutral colors that do not go against the grain of the surrounding community typically work best*. This is not to say that people won't be attracted to your personal tastes – it just may take longer to find them if yours are a little *too* unique.

☆ Driveways and Walkways

Simple question: *Exactly how bad are they?* If the cracks are going to break your mother's back, then you need to do something about it. Otherwise, **you can always consider the latest craze of concrete stains, which enable you to add a subtle, even color to hide years of unsightly stains**. But don't forget that people will be continuing to walk and drive all over it, so *use your best judgment before you* *get too attached and start revisiting this issue every couple of years as new stains begin to appear*. If the rental happens to have brick or stone walkways instead of concrete, then **do your best to treat the ants and weeds and any uneven hazards that may increase your liability risk**.

Naturally, there are **many other items that were purposefully left out** because they were either too excessive or are perhaps just a given, using common sense – remember, **this is not a book** *for dummies*.

> Outdoor furnishings, lighting, fencing, etc. *These items don't need to be added, merely repaired or removed if they are not working properly or are too unattractive to look at.* The same applies to the **mailbox** – if it's so rusted that the neighborhood birds have found a way in to use it as their new nesting place… common sense would say replace it. **"Curb appeal"** is an **essential attribute in renting any property**, but *this does not mean the home has to appear brand spanking new in order to attract tenants*. **Just use a little good judgment** to make sure the property doesn't look like the mortgage is in default.

The Kitchen

Without a doubt, **the kitchen is key in attracting tenants**, *especially couples and families* – and, of course, those that are *Food Network* fanatics. However, *this does not mean you need to remodel it* using the latest and greatest granite, wood and steel. If anything at all is needed, the phrase **"minor makeover"** *needs to be stressed here*, as you could easily get carried away and spend thousands (if not *tens of thousands!*) of dollars performing a major makeover of a kitchen.

The goal is to make sure the appliances work safely and the entire area appears clean and not pest-infested. Here are some suggestions you may want to consider, depending on your kitchen's current condition:

Color

Try to avoid having a sterile white kitchen – *it showcases wear and tear like nothing else and it just doesn't feel like home for most people*. You can **add a little color by sanding and painting** the wood cabinetry or by simply painting the walls. **Wallpapering is *not* recommended** because it's hard to find two people that can agree on the same print. *You have a better chance of appealing to the majority of your prospects by choosing one universal paint color.*

⭑ Appliances

Only **if there are safety factors or known maintenance issues, should you consider replacing these**. If you must replace, **think about buying *"as is"* appliances** to save money. These are units sold at a reduced cost that are *fully guaranteed by the manufacturer and are still under warranty,* but which may have been scratched, dented, repacked or refurbished. *Thousands of landlords have saved money by purchasing these appliances and you can find them easily online or at major appliance showrooms across America*. In other words, **go for the deal wherever and whenever you can get it.** Just *make sure the original factory warranty is always attached* and – by all means – **try to avoid buying anything stainless steel except for the kitchen sink!** Stainless steel appliances require tender loving care – remember the rental car analogy?

⭑ Flooring

If you have to replace the kitchen floor, **go for (or stick with) a vinyl material**. It is the *least expensive and easiest thing to replace* when it eventually wears out and is *often under warranty for more than five years* when used in a residential setting. **Be careful** not to get too fancy though – **some vinyl costs more than ceramic tile**. *If you can afford to have tile* installed instead or you possess the talent to lay it yourself, *it's a good bet since its durability will definitely with-*

stand the test of time. **Wood and carpeting, of course, should be avoided at all cost** – *even commercial-grade carpeting* – **because where there is water, there should be tile** *just in case of a mishap.*

I was pretty gung ho with my first rental. Everything was upgraded and spotless; I even added brand-new stainless steel appliances. Needless to say, I had no problem renting the unit—the first time. The tenants ended up scratching the heck out of the dishwasher and refrigerator. I don't fault them or their kids as much as myself for not realizing that it really wasn't worth my effort to get the rental model ready, especially since I was charging only $1500 per month.

J. Harrington
Arizona
Landlord

Bathrooms

Unless your bathroom is on par with an outhouse off the old '49er Trail or today's typical interstate rest stop, **you needn't bother lifting anything except for a paint brush**. *As long as the plumbing works and the outlets and fixtures won't electrocute the occupants*, **it's not worth your money** to have somebody else defecating and spitting all over your newly-renovated bathroom.

The same rule of thumb applies to bathrooms as to kitchens: **Make sure that the bathroom appears clean and that all of the knobs, switches and plugs work**. But by all mcans, *if you have the skills necessary to perform most of the work and it won't cost you more than a few dollars to upgrade a few items* – such as a new faucet, sturdy towel rack or perhaps a new light – *go ahead and make your prospective tenant's day!* Otherwise, just be a friendly landlord and make sure your tenants don't travel too far back in time when they go in and depreciate your bathroom while enjoying their favorite reading material…

Interior Painting

Hands down, this is the best and most affordable solution to sprucing up your unit – *by giving it the fresh scent of latex paint.* Tenants love to walk into a newly-painted rental because it immediately tells them that this unit has been fully cleansed following the previous inhabitants. **It doesn't matter what brand you use, unless odor is truly a concern and you are limited on your aeration time**. If that's the case, then **Olympic** makes a great low-odor paint that can be found at **Lowe's** stores nationwide – and *for you pseudo-professional painters, the coverage is absolutely fantastic!*

But seriously, wherever you want to buy your paint or whichever brand you wish to use, it ultimately doesn't matter because **you will probably have to paint the unit all over again after the next tenant moves out**. So when it comes to interior design, *pick a single neutral color and roll with it.* Forget about accent walls, *faux*-painting and all the other nice ornamental flares you can add. **Give the tenant a blank canvas that they can make their own** by hanging pictures, paintings, memorabilia, mirrors, wall tapestries… and let's not forget about those pseudo-trendy velvet black light posters, still readily available at flea markets, thrift shops and novelty stores all across the United States.

I used to hire painters to go in after every tenant and spray the rooms down with "Summer Sage," a popular interior color until one summer, I decided to do-it-myself. I had some extra time and felt like saving a few dollars. After all, its not like I do this more than once a year, plus the reaction from people has always been positive. Everyone always remarks about how well the unit shows—that's because I paint over all the dirty handprints and the vacuum cleaner cord marks.

B. McPherson
Virginia
Landlord

Flooring

Okay, this is simple and has already been mentioned in reference to the kitchen, but still needs a little reiteration and elaboration. **The two best flooring products that are (conveniently) the least expensive and easiest to install, remove and replace are *vinyl and carpet*.** These materials are *so affordable; you could remodel every few years*, keeping the property **highly desirable**.

☆ **Unless your rental property commands a luxury rate, ignore the following temptations...**

Wood, marble, granite and tile – it's just a rental. *Wait until you are ready to move back in or to sell before upgrading your flooring.* If the unit came already equipped with a higher grade material, then you're a winner! **Keep it if it's in good shape;** *otherwise, replace it with a more affordable material.*

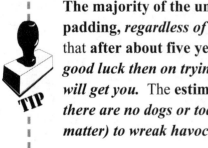

The majority of the unit should be carpeted with inexpensive fibers and padding, *regardless of what type of warranty is thrown your way.* The reason is that **after about five years, you'll invariably be replacing the carpet anyway** – *good luck then on trying to exercise your warranty rights, because the exclusions will get you.* The **estimated replacement time**, incidentally, takes into account that *there are no dogs or toddlers residing in the unit (or drunken party goers, for that matter) to wreak havoc on the carpeting.* Raspberry punch, anyone...?

What could possibly be wrong with wood flooring and pets? Well, I'll tell you—I've been having to refinish and treat my floors as best as I can because I made the mistake (twice) to allow some renters to keep their dogs inside so they could scratch and pee all over the place. You know—if you don't mop up urine right away on wood, then forget about it. The best part is the renters kept on reassuring me that they take care of their dogs. Unfortunately, retaining the pet deposit didn't do me much justice. What a mess!

S. Williams
Illinois
Landlord

It's well understood that every individual will have their own vision and tastes to bring to their rental property, but **keep in mind that your property is (at least, for the time being) just a rental property.** *Try to keep your amenities practical, not problematic, and your décor universal, not restrictive.*

No one else will ever appreciate your property and all your extra touches and tender loving care as much as you do, so **try not to set yourself up for disappointment** when you discover that some tenants exhibit no emotional attachment to the property *whatsoever* (i.e., they neglect it, because it is not their own). **Just do your best to make sure your rental vacancy "functions" completely safely and that it appears clean between tenants –** *this will definitely entice more cattle to graze, so you can pick the best of the herd.*

Chapter 3

Advertising Your Vacancy:
How to Avoid Spending a Fistful of Dollars!

This Chapter Discusses:

★ **Yard Signs**

★ **Flyers**

★ **Word-of-Mouth Referrals**

★ **Newspapers and Real Estate Publications**

★ **How to Write a Classified Ad**

★ **How to Use the Internet to Attract Tenants**

★ **Tenant Placement Agents**

Let's be honest here: There are **a million different ways to spend your money in seeking out tenants** – and **buying advertising just isn't one of them**. Okay, maybe just a little bit – but if you've ever been involved in owning or marketing a business, you've most likely already discovered this to be true. Some of you may disagree, but **when it comes to real estate, thousands of individual landlords, property managers and real estate agents agree that** *most advertising opportunities don't work* – **especially if you're only managing a handful of units.** So **grab a highlighter**, because this chapter will review *exactly what works and – more importantly – what doesn't!* We'll also provide you with some **examples on how to write and design an effective advertisement.**

It's important to note that – before you begin – you need to realize that *it is an undisputed fact that local market conditions will dictate your success.* **So don't feel compelled to add in everything including the kitchen sink** when trying to market your vacancy. *It ultimately won't matter how much you spend or where you advertise.* If the **local renter's market is flooded with vacancies or** – *even worse* – **the economy is too distressed** to care, **you'll have a difficult time getting** *anyone* **to apply regardless of what you do!** You simply **need to be patient** and just try your best to **pass the word along** *without* **having to pay for every word each time you run an ad.**

TIP

Yard Signs

Hands down, **there is** *no better way* **to advertise your vacancy than a simple sign stuck in the middle of your yard** *(not to mention it'll cost you all of $2).* That is, of course, *unless* **your property is located on the edge of town next to the landfill** – then you're gonna need a bigger sign!

Joking aside, **it's a given truism that a clear, uncomplicated sign prominently placed in your yard will usually do** *just fine* **in most areas.** Just be sure you splurge and actually *buy* **the sign from your local office supply store or retail giant** – *Don't bother trying to make your own* unless you can spell, have weather-resistant materials and can draw a straight line (this has the makings of a great redneck joke, Mr. Fox-worthy!). In all seriousness, *buy a sign (or even two!) and position it in your yard wherever the passing foot and street traffic have the best chance of seeing it* (e.g., front, back, corner, side, etc.).

In addition to the yard sign(s), **here are some other options that may make the whole vacancy experience much easier to endure,** by reducing the amount of time you'd normally end up spending on the phone, either taking or returning calls…

On occasion, I place classified ads in the local paper, but that's usually only when the market slows down. Most of the time, a simple sign stuck on the front lawn actually fills the majority of my vacancies. There's bound to be someone driving by through the neighborhood looking for a place to live. Ironically, everyone wants me to spend money—I can't begin to tell you how many times I receive emails and snail mail asking me to subscribe to some service or real estate publication to advertise my vacancies. I only have two duplexes and I keep them filled pretty much consecutively, but the mail keeps coming. I say, "if it works, don't fix it."

P. Edwards
New York
Landlord

★ Detailed Information Sheets

Be sure to include removable single-sheet brochures, which can easily be affixed to your sign in a tubular dispenser or any other type of standard vending device commonly used in the real estate industry. **This detailed information sheet can immediately answer many of those basic questions that prospects often have about a rental, all the while saving you time** on the phone repeating yourself over and over. **The following page shows an example of the type of detail commonly provided by real estate professionals**, which often includes the **rent amount and terms, square footage and room dimensions of the unit, included (*or* not included) appliances, and much more.** *Affordable word processing programs or publishing software (e.g., Microsoft Word or Publisher which are either sold separately or bundled together in the Microsoft Office suite) can easily assist you in making detailed information sheets - Microsoft even includes access to free, ready-to-use templates.*

Detailed Rental Property Information Sheet

Property Detail Report

1234 FANTASY DRIVE, ANYTOWN, USA 12345

For more information, contact:

**John Doe Landlord
(555) 555-555
Mon-Sat 9am-7pm**

**Pets Allowed Under 25 lbs:
$250 non-refundable deposit**

**Application Fee: $25 non-refundable
(credited towards first months
rent upon approval)**

Lease Term: 1 year minimum

Monthly Rent: $2,700

SAMPLE

Property Characteristics:

Gross Area:	5,654	Parking Type:	GARAGE	Construction:		
Living Area:	4,232	Garage Area:	690	Heat Type:	CENTRAL	
Tot Adj Area:		Garage Capacity:		Exterior wall:	BLOCK/STUCCO	
Above Grade:		Parking Spaces:		Porch Type:	FINISHED/OPEN PORCH	
Total Rooms:		Basement Area:		Patio Type:	DECK	
Bedrooms:		Finish Bsmnt Area:		Pool:	POOL	
Bath(F/H):	5 /	Basement Type:		Air Cond:	CENTRAL	
Year Built / Eff:	2002 /	Roof Type:		Style:		
Fireplace:	Y / 1	Foundation:	CONT. FOOTING	Quality:	EXCELLENT	
# of Stories:	2.00	Roof Material:	CLAY TILE	Condition:		
Other Improvements:						

Site Information:

Zoning:		Acres:	0.35	County Use:	SINGLE FAMILY (01210)
Flood Zone:	X	Lot Area:	15,300	State Use:	SINGLE FAMILY (01)
Flood Panel:	1251390057G	Lot Width/Depth:	100 x 153	Site Influence:	
Flood Panel Date:	09/03/2003	Res/Comm Units:	/	Sewer Type:	
Land Use:	SFR			Water Type:	

☆ Answering Machine

This option – which *could be used to replace the aforementioned information sheet* – involves **creating an equally detailed outgoing message on your telephone answering machine (or voicemail),** highlighting some of the same property characteristics. **A sample script has been provided below.**

Outgoing Answering Machine Script

"You have reached John Doe at 555-5555. ***If you are calling about the property*** *available for rent at 1234 Make Believe Street,* ***it's a fully carpeted 3-bedroom, 2-bathroom house, with approximately 1,300 square feet under central heat and air.*** *The unit* ***comes well equipped with*** *a washer and dryer, ceiling fans, fireplace and a newly remodeled kitchen, complete with garbage disposal, dishwasher, electric stove and refrigerator. The* ***area schools*** *are Huntington Elementary, Hathaway Middle School and Harrison High School. There is a* ***non-refundable $25 application fee,*** *which will be* ***credited towards the first month's rent upon approval.*** *If you would like* ***to schedule an appointment to see the unit*** *or* ***have any additional questions,*** *please leave your name and telephone number after the beep.* ***Thank you*** *for your interest in this rental."*

Flyers

At only 10 cents a copy, **this is another low-cost and effective way of advertising your vacancy – *especially if you have a computer with a word processor* ** to put together a simple design. **Your flyer should be limited on text – *Don't make it too busy to read for passing motorists!* – and get right to the heart of what your unit has to offer and for what price**. You may also want to consider creating **perforated phone numbers on the bottom of your flyer** so that prospects can easily tear one off and take it with them – this is **commonly seen on college campuses and community bulletin boards** (more on these below) and *it actually works very well*.

On the following page is a **sample of a basic layout that gets your message across**. (This flyer was created by modifying a free Microsoft Publisher template.)

C. Cox
Nevada
Landlord

I now have eleven units and my own color laser printer to do my marketing for me. Before taking the leap to spend $600 on my new HP, I used to go to Kinkos and spend more than 50 cents per page to have some flyers printed. Granted, I didn't buy the printer just for flyers—it saves me a lot of time and money, even more than an ink jet printer. I would highly recommend a color laser printer to anyone that prints a lot.

Rental Property Flyer

Only minutes away from the University and Downtown Shopping Plaza

Great Location, Newly Remodeled!

FOR RENT

1 Year Lease Minimum

- 3 Bedrooms
- 2 1/2 Bathrooms
- Wrap Around Porch
- 2 Car Garage
- Vaulted Ceilings
- Modern Kitchen
- Some Furnishings Included
- Central Heat and Air

Only $1,750 per month

1234 GHOST TOWN ROAD, ANYTOWN, USA 12345

Jane Doe Landlord

Mailing Address
1772 American Landlord Lane
Suite 100
Anytown, USA 12345
Phone: 555-555-5555
Mobile: 555-555-5555
Fax: 555-555-555
E-mail: someone@example.com

Come and enjoy the finest location in town while living at the best rental offered. Freshly painted and updated to bring you the comforts of home, you can't beat the rent for the amount of amenities that are included, such as a modern kitchen, utility room, dining room, master bedroom downstairs, walk-in closets, and even a washer and dryer included for your convenience. Contact Jane Joe Landlord to schedule a showing.

An Equal Housing Opportunity Landlord

The **next step** after designing your flyer is to **make copies and to decide where to optimally post them**. Obviously, *if you are near a college campus, that's a perfect place to start.* **Bulletin boards are commonly found** at the **admissions office, dining hall, library and even residence halls**, for those that plan on moving off campus next semester.

In addition to campuses, you can also consider **grocery stores, public libraries, community centers, churches** and **anywhere else that you can easily display it for the community to see**. However, it is *not recommended* that you *violate city ordinances by posting them on telephone, traffic or utility poles*. Although legal in some areas, **you do *not* want to aggravate the local community**; the **same goes for placing them on automobile windshields** throughout parking lots. Remember, *your phone number and address will most likely be on every flyer* – and nobody likes a nuisance… so **exercise your best judgment**.

Word-of-Mouth Referrals

How many times can you recall learning about a new restaurant, vacation destination or cool new product in the midst of a **casual conversation with a friend, relative, colleague**… or *even a complete stranger?* That's called *word-of-mouth* advertising and you've undoubtedly **experienced its success first hand** on many occasions.

The problem is: **How do you get your *own* words to travel down the grapevine?** Well, the **easiest way to begin** is by **having your friends, family, colleagues and even current tenants spread the word for you,** *in exchange for a referral fee* for any qualified applicant that signs at least a one-year lease agreement. **Referrals have been known to range anywhere from $25 all the way up to the equivalent of one month's rent** – commonly paid to real estate professionals.

If you think the offer would be better received if presented in a formal manner, then simply **put it in writing, so those to whom you are proposing this will take it very seriously**. Remember, **every day your property sits vacant, your cash stops flowing at a rate of $20 – if not $50 or more** *each and every day!* So **pass the word and share some of your proceeds**, because *it's better to pay for performance than to have no performance at all* – and **your potential outlay is substantially less expensive** than many of the other advertising strategies described in this chapter.

Newspapers and Real Estate Publications

Here is where you need to *begin seriously exercising caution* with your fistful of dollars, because **advertising space in print media can get very expensive** and *often yields little or no response.* Even among the nation's top *Times, Tribunes, Chronicles* and *Posts,* **you can spend hundreds of dollars for a single tiny ad, only to sit and watch the weeks go by with no calls at all**.

And let's not forgot about **the cost of display advertising** – frequently sold in those ubiquitous **free real estate publications** that are circulated around town at shopping centers and grocery stores. These are usually quarter-, half- or full-page ads – that are either in black and white or in color, accompanied with professional graphics and photos – and are *much* **more expensive**.

The best and simplest approach to print advertising is to pick a local community newspaper that you already know is **routinely circulated** *and actually read* every weekend. **Smaller, local papers often tend to work better than the majors,** because *your specific audience is targeted* and *you get more ad space for less money.* It is **suggested that you buy a "no-frills" classified ad** that *runs only on the weekend* (this is the primary time when most people look for rental notices in newspapers) and that you **take advantage of as many characters (or words) permitted for the lowest price.** *Choose your words very carefully, because each one is going to cost you!*

TIP

Don't be coaxed into purchasing extra-special characters, bolding, additional bells and whistles or the like, for the sheer and simple reason that **when someone is looking to rent in a specific area, most people will review** *every* **listing regardless of fancy letters and graphics** – which, typically, isn't a large amount to begin with anyway. The *only enhancement* (or "add-on") we would suggest is the use of the **Internet.** Many newspapers either will **post your ad online at no additional cost** or will **do so for a modest fee** – and if that's the case, you should *seriously consider paying the extra couple of dollars, as there are significantly more people surfing the Web for listings than looking through newspapers.*

If you own more than a couple of units and have to fill several vacancies throughout the year, it is *strongly recommended* that you **inquire about signing an** *annual advertising contract* with your local newspaper – especially if your initial campaigns have proven in past times to be effective. **Advertising contracts (even classifieds) can yield considerable discounts, beginning at around 10%.** As far as **real estate publications,** *only heavyweight landlords* that have several vacancies regularly *and* a substantial budget *are encouraged to explore those display advertising opportunities* – it just doesn't add up for the small landlord.

I've found that the Thrifty Nickel works for me when it comes to classified advertising. The ads run for pennies on the dollar—less than $20 per week per ad and it keeps the tenants knocking on the door. Even if there are no units available, I always keep at least one ad running just in case someone moves out early. There is a representative assigned to my account and she is great! She helps me customize my ads to be effective as possible within my contract limits.

M. Banning
Texas
Landlord

How to Write a Classified Ad

Okay, you've got **20 words or less** to get your phone to ring without lying about your luxurious beachside estate and its marble foyer that is only $500 per month. **The tricky part of classified advertising** is to **have the reader become excited about the property by painting a picture of its virtues through the use of rich colorful language** – *but without telling a tall tale.* **An ad sets up expectations** – and you can pretty much write off most of your prospects if your representation of the property doesn't match the actual digs.

So before you place an ad, **take a look at the most recent classifieds published in your local newspaper.** Although many of these ads change weekly, you should at least take a **look to see how many ads are running and what other landlords have written**, so you can do your best to **present something a little different** – *especially* if you discover vacancies are more plentiful than you expected.

You then need to ask yourself: *"What does my property have to offer that's unique and desirable enough to set it apart from the rest?"* **The most common amenities mentioned are** usually central heat and air, washer and dryer, fenced-in yard, pool, garage, pet friendliness and a newly remodeled kitchen… but **you should answer this question by making a list of *every* amenity you can think of** – and then sit back and **pick the ones you feel are most likely to tempt readers** *in 20 words or less.*

To better illustrate the effectiveness of a carefully worded classified ad, **there are two examples on the following page both written for the same property.** The first is a very simple, honest approach, the second is *sweetened with a little more dynamic enthusiasm.* **You can decide for yourself which one is likely to be more effective...**

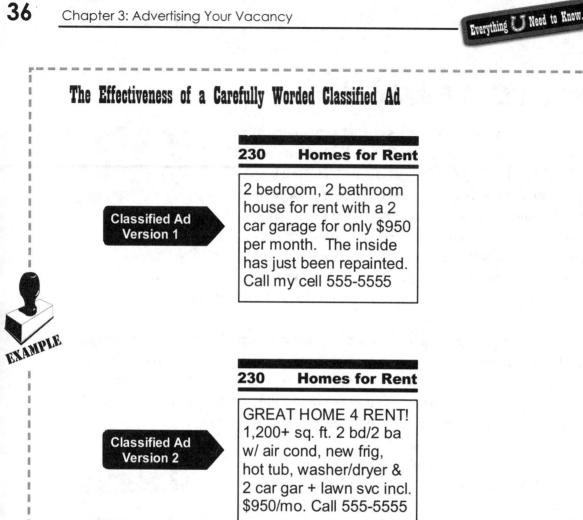

The Effectiveness of a Carefully Worded Classified Ad

Classified Ad Version 1

230	Homes for Rent

2 bedroom, 2 bathroom house for rent with a 2 car garage for only $950 per month. The inside has just been repainted. Call my cell 555-5555

EXAMPLE

Classified Ad Version 2

230	Homes for Rent

GREAT HOME 4 RENT! 1,200+ sq. ft. 2 bd/2 ba w/ air cond, new frig, hot tub, washer/dryer & 2 car gar + lawn svc incl. $950/mo. Call 555-5555

C. Smith
Florida
Landlord

Sell! Sell! Sell! That's what they taught me when I recently took an accreditation course for real estate agents. Every possible tool you can conjure up (as long as it's ethically and morally in line) needs to be used. Whether I'm selling homes or leasing one of my rentals, I throw the kitchen sink after everything in my ads. If the property has it, I flaunt it to the best of my ability. Just get your prospects to the door and the property will then do its best to get that lease signed for you.

How to Use the Internet to Attract Tenants

Who'd have ever thought that one day you'd be able to shop for a place to live *anywhere* in the world, able to view pictures and take virtual tours, from almost any home, office, canyon, plateau or mountain top – all from the comfort of *any online computer?*

Needless to say, this kind of extraordinary communications medium **should be exploited to the fullest extent possible.** As we mentioned before, many newspapers have already embraced this technology by offering it as a concurrent companion to their printed classified ads. Fortunately, it's precisely this type of implementation that makes it **easier for *everyone* to get their message online without much effort** at all. But for those that *really* want to tap into the massive reach of the new frontier, *there is much, much more available on the worldwide final frontier.*

There are basically **two types of Internet marketing that you will need to fully comprehend** before you saddle up with your credit cards and click on "submit." The two primary advertising opportunities that apply to the real estate industry are:

☆ Pay for Placement

This is when you **buy sponsorships, advertising space or even special keywords** (also known as **"pay-per-click"**) to ensure your ad is displayed. While this is similar to classified advertising, *don't expect to receive any guarantees regarding the success of this type of ad.* The **more notable pay for placement services** are **Google Adwords** and **Yahoo! Search Marketing**, which **allow you to bid on searched keywords or phrases** such as "Florida rental homes." *If you are the high bidder for the search term or phrase, your site comes up first in the search results in exchange for paying the service each time someone clicks on your ad and visits your website.* Unfortunately, the large number of unrelated ads these organizations have allowed to be placed on a consumer's search have diluted the quality of prospective tenant traffic. In addition, **the competition for** many of these keywords is so fierce that it is no longer worth it to **pay for placement** especially when just trying to rent your property. As an alternative, the ubiquitous **CraigsList.org** offers a similar, but **free** *classified-style website where you can post your vacancy and possibly receive a significantly greater response*.

Should you decide to use a popular posting board such as Craig's List, **you will want to be especially careful with your screening process**, as you are more likely to have to weed through more "shot-in-the-dark" inquiries from free ads. *(This is where the use of an application fee would prove particularly helpful.)*

★ Pay for Performance

This is exactly what the phrase suggests: **You only pay when the service performs for you.** In this instance, **if you place an ad for a rental and someone comes along and** *actually signs a lease*, **then you pay to the service their fee.** Probably the **most prominent service of this kind on the Internet** for rental properties is **Rent.com** – which happens to be an **eBay** company. However, the catch is that **the site reportedly requires a minimum of 20 units to be listed** – *which you might be able to circumvent, depending upon whether they actually verify and enforce this minimum requirement.*
The good thing is that **the finder's fee this site charges is very reasonable!** If the company secures for you a qualified tenant who signs a lease, you only have to pay a fee of $375 – about the cost of running a single classified ad for one week in a major newspaper. You can visit Rent.com for current terms, conditions and fees.

Back in the day (actually, only a few years ago), **there used to be many places on the Internet where you could submit your rental listings for free**. One of them was **Yahoo! Classifieds**, but it has **since changed to a paid service** (I know – big shocker, isn't it?) and now requires you to fork out around $35 for a basic ad for one month.

Fortunately, ***there is still a place you can go to post your vacancies for free*** – the ***American Landlord*** **website**, located at **www.AmericanLandlord.com**. It offers a forum for ***both landlords and tenants***, as well as **valuable resources**, many of which are ***completely free of charge*** **– unlike those of other sites!**

I challenge anyone to try online advertising for renting out a home. Especially the major advertising search engines. All it took was one deposit of $200 and that money was spent in less than a week. "Where did it go," I asked the search company. They said people clicked on my keywords and therefore, I was charged. This may be true, but the problem I figured out is that anyone can search and click on these keywords with no intention of actually doing anything. This can occur around the clock from teenagers to insomniacs just browsing for no apparent reason than just curiosity. One click—that's all it takes and you just spent 15, 20, 50 cents or more for nothing more that entertaining a web surfer.

P. Parker
Oklahoma
Landlord

Tenant Placement Agents

There are many licensed real estate agents that are experienced with rental property who will be glad to find qualified tenants for you. This is the *same premise behind* "pay for performance" *advertising*. In exchange for a signed lease agreement, the agent will usually charge a one-time fee ranging from $100-$600 for residential real estate. Granted, this seems expensive, however you need to do the math and consider the following carefully:

★ **U only pay for performance. In other words: no lease, no charge.**

★ **U can often reduce or eliminate additional advertising costs.**

★ **U save yourself a lot of time and aggravation, since the agent will usually handle the applicant from the initial inquiry all the way up to the lease signing.**

Visit **AmericanLandlord.com** to **find a local tenant placement agent** – or **contact a local real estate brokerage office that specializes in property management** – and inquire if this is a service they offer; most of them do. *Be on your guard,* though, because *the agency or office may try to suggest using it as a full-service management company* – which *can cost an average of 10% of your monthly proceeds plus incidental fees* for overseeing maintenance and repairs. So unless you are an "absentee landlord" (one who lives hours or more away from your rental), **you should be able to manage your own properties with the help of** *American Landlord* and companies such as **AmerUSA.net**.

Chapter 4

Tenant Screening, Part I:
The Information Roundup

This Chapter Discusses:

- ★ **The Rental Application**
- ★ **Asking the Right Questions**
- ★ **Acknowledgment and Authorization**
- ★ **Charging an Application Fee**
- ★ **Proper Identification**

Congratulations! So your marketing strategy worked and now you have a potential candidate for tenancy. Make no mistake—**this is a *great* first step!** But don't start your celebrating just yet… The next stage involves making what is—without a doubt—*the* **single most important decision in property management:** *deciding whether or not to approve a prospective tenant.* Merely handing the keys over to just any interested party, without ***thoroughly and knowledgeably* screening each and every one of them**, could result in your making a *huge* mistake—both financially *and* emotionally!

How could this have happened to me...?
* *They seemed like such nice people!*
* *They just had a new baby!*
* *They go to church every Sunday!*
* *They're my cousin's kids!*

The screening process is not a difficult one—you simply need to know how to do it *properly*. **Making a well-informed decision**—and **understanding all that is involved** in doing so—can be made much easier by *utilizing comprehensive screening resources,* such as **www.AmerUSA.net** or **www.AmericanLandlord.com**, an **informative forum website that connects landlords and tenants to answer questions and to share experiences.** There are countless stories of devastation and frustration in which landlords who have failed to take the proper precautions end up stranded in shock, disappointment and despair…

A friendly face or a referral may be a good start, but **neither one really offers an effective way of determining** if the rent will be paid on time, nor if the unit will be properly treated. <u>**Remember:**</u> **You are entering into a** *business relationship* **with another individual and both parties need to treat it as such!** Even if—actually, *especially if*—the **applicant is a friend or family member**, your **standard tenant screening protocol should still apply.** **Developing a** *consistent* **method** to use every time will not only prove to be **highly-effective**, but will also *ensure each applicant is treated fairly, reducing the chance of a possible discrimination claim against you.*

"Don't judge a book by its cover" has proven to be a **good rule of thumb to follow for a reason**—you may be pleasantly surprised who *actually* turns out to be your best tenant.

The Rental Application

It's hard to paint a masterpiece without a quality canvas. **The importance of a rental application is often misunderstood** and *cannot be stressed enough!* Don't think of it as merely a piece of paper to collect a name and a phone number. **It can be an invaluable tool, providing essential data and even offering legal protection… but** *only* **when used the right way.**

Rental Application

Instructions:
1. Insert your IMAGE or LOGO (optional)
2. Enter 'PROPERTY ADDRESS APPLYING FOR'
3. REPLACE ALL of this text with YOUR contact info
4. Click on 'PRINT FORM' when finished

Everything U Need to Know...

Click here to insert image/logo

Residential Rental Application

Applicant Information

Property address applying for:					
Name:					
Date of birth:		SSN:		Phone:	
Current address:					
City:		State:		ZIP Code:	
Own Rent (Please circle)	Monthly payment or rent:				How long?
Previous address:					
City:		State:		ZIP Code:	
Owned Rented (Please circle)	Monthly payment or rent:				How long?

Employment Information

Current employer:					
Employer address:					How long?
City:		State:		ZIP Code:	
Phone:		E-mail:		Fax:	
Position:	Hourly Salary (Please circle)		Annual income:		

Emergency Contact

Name of a person not residing with you:				
Address:				
City:		State:	ZIP Code:	Phone:
Relationship:				

References

Name:	Address:	Phone:

Have you ever been convicted of a crime? (yes / no) If so, please explain all offenses including where, when and why:

Have you ever been evicted? (yes / no) If so, please explain where, when and why:

I acknowledge that falsification or omission of any information on this rental application may result in the immediate dismissal or retraction of an offer of tenancy. I hereby voluntarily consent to and authorize the AmerUSA Corporation ("AmerUSA"), acting as the landlord's designated screening organization for the above referenced rental property, to obtain my consumer report and render a credit decision. I further authorize all persons and organizations that may have information relevant to this research to disclose such information to the landlord's authorized agent, AmerUSA. I hereby release the landlord and its authorized agent, AmerUSA, from all claims and liabilities of any nature in connection with this research, results and decision. A photocopy of this authorization will be considered valid. I understand that I have specific prescribed rights as a consumer under the federal Fair Credit Reporting Act ('FCRA') and have received a copy of those rights titled "FCRA Summary of Rights."

Signature of applicant:	Date:

This form provided by USLandlord.com

SAMPLE

Whether you intend to buy an existing template or create your own "homemade" rental application, **there are *vitally* important questions, acknowledgments and authorizations that you need to ensure are included** *for your own protection.* It is important to note that **many of these questions are often not included on standard rental applications –** *even the ones sold by those companies* which boldly assert their forms are created by attorneys or real estate industry professionals.

Along with each of these *"must-have"* questions, **there are other aspects associated with the rental application that you will also need to carefully consider**.

Asking the Right Questions

In order to get the right answers, you must ask the right questions. Sounds simple enough, but you'd be surprised just how **many rental applications fall short of their supposed duty.** Collecting *all of the important information* the first time around will **eliminate unnecessary delays and aggravation in screening** your "would-be" tenants—and will also *provide you the insight to be able to pick out the best prospects* before they have gone elsewhere.

> **Here is a list of essential questions that should be a part of every residential rental application:**

> ➢ *Have you ever been evicted? If so, where, when and why?*

You would think **the single most important question** would be an obvious inclusion, but—for some inexplicable reason—*most rental applications fail to ask it!* This question is **not just a great tool for pre-screening**, but *also serves as an opportunity for honest applicants to make themselves known.* If an applicant admits **"yes"** and **provides a reasonable explanation,** *that person's integrity speaks volumes* and **you may still want to keep them in serious consideration.**

Remember: The individual has **risked being *automatically disqualified*** by being honest with you, knowing full well a great deal of landlords never bother to conduct background checks. On the other hand, *if he or she knowingly makes a false statement on an application, this is solid legal grounds for immediately declining any applicant.*

You should always verify any claims made by an applicant with a reliable independent source, such as **www.AmerUSA.net**. *If an applicant admits to having had a prior eviction, it is then **very important** to ask them **in which state** this occurred, as **eviction records are usually checked by individual state**. Having all of this knowledge in advance will undoubtedly **save you a lot of time and money** in screening your applicants.*

➢ *Have you ever been convicted of a crime? If so, where, when and why? Please explain all offenses.*

Most of the time – if it is asked at all – you will see this question inquiring only about felony convictions. **A criminal record, whether misdemeanor or felony, is nothing to take lightly** – and **unless you ask for an explanation of *all offenses,*** you will most likely get a flippant or evasive response.

Once again, this is an instance where you have an **opportunity to assess an applicant's integrity**, with the option of granting that second chance should their explanation hold water. **Otherwise, he or she has actually just committed another act of indiscretion** and *you shouldn't even be considering them for tenancy at this point.* Seriously – if the applicant has already blatantly lied to you at this early stage of the game, do you *really* want to enter into any relationship in which you'll be relying on them financially *each and every month?*

"*Honesty is one of the most important qualities for me in tenant screening. I will always give an applicant additional consideration for being upfront with me before submitting his or her application. It's all a matter of mutual respect, which I've found usually leads to a very good landlord-tenant relationship.*"

B. Ross
California
Landlord

> ### *Who will be residing at the property? Please list all occupants and their ages.*

This may not seem all that necessary, but it's **actually *very* important! If there is no clear disclosure of *all* prospective *adult and minor* occupants, then you might as well just post a permanent vacancy sign** – and install a revolving door while you're at it! *Having a list of every potential occupant who is going to be living at your property will enable you to screen accordingly,* as well as to **draft your lease agreement to legally protect your investment,** *by reserving the right to approve any additional residents.*

> ### *Do you own any pets or animals? If so, please list all breeds and weights.*

This question speaks for itself: If you fail to include it, you may be in for a mighty unpleasant surprise! **Having a list of every pet allows you to consider the risks associated with each individual breed of animal** – *you can even require a pet interview* to be certain that the animal itself, regardless of breed, is amiable. *You should never agree to accept any pet or animal unless you understand completely its potential for property damage and for bodily injury* (for obvious personal *and* legal reasons).

"I rented out my house while away at college. It was a tough time financially and I was glad I had a tenant. I was aware they had a dog, but I didn't think much of it until I returned home to find the carpeting, door knobs and most of my wooden deck destroyed. Over $10,000 in damage and I never saw the tenant again—or her little dog!"

Dr. D. Rhodes
North Carolina
Landlord

Acknowledgment and Authorization

Credit reporting agencies, which are governed by the **Federal Trade Commission** and the **Fair Credit Reporting Act** [For more on this topic, *see* **Chapter 6**] **require that every landlord obtain a proper** *Acknowledgment* and *Authorization* from a prospective tenant – **prior to being** *legally* **able to acquire his or her consumer credit file**.

Most rental applications sold online or in office supply stores do not contain the necessary language required by law! So unless you intend on having all of your applicants each signing separate forms to cover your legal requirements, *you must add a standard Acknowledgment and Authorization to your rental application* **to ensure you are compliant** with *both* the credit reporting agencies and the Federal Trade Commission.

My application already has some fine print on the bottom, isn't this sufficient?

The *Acknowledgment* has an **applicant agree that he or she has received a copy of the** *FCRA Summary of Rights* (*see* **Chapter 6**). This is an *essential federal disclosure, informing the applicant they have certain rights* under the **Fair Credit Reporting Act**, while **also having them acknowledge that—***should they have falsified or omitted any information you have requested of them***—they may very well forfeit any offer of tenancy**. The *Authorization,* on the other hand, **gives the landlord a** *clear legal approval* **by the prospective tenant to conduct a background check** in order to verify all information contained on the rental application.

The following is an example of a standard *Acknowledgment* and *Authorization* **declaration**, which should appear *above the signature lines, at the bottom* of a rental application:

> *I certify and declare under penalty of perjury under relevant state and federal law that the information contained in my rental application is complete, true and accurate. I acknowledge that falsification or omission of any information may result in the immediate dismissal or retraction of an offer of tenancy. I hereby voluntarily consent to and authorize the landlord to obtain my consumer report. I further authorize all persons and organizations that may have information relevant to this research to disclose such information to the landlord. I understand that I have specific prescribed rights as a consumer under the Fair Credit Reporting Act (FCRA) and have received a copy of those rights titled FCRA Summary of Rights.*

Charging an Application Fee

Relax—it's okay! **Asking someone to pay to apply for tenancy is not only okay, it's an established, industry-accepted practice in most states.** *Every landlord should consider charging a modest, non-refundable application fee* **to at least cover the costs associated with conducting a sufficient background check.** Otherwise, you may find yourself more likely to approve an applicant you would ordinarily think twice about, simply because you've passed on all the previous applicants and your pockets are running on empty.

Keep in mind that an average background check usually costs around $25. Application fees collected by landlords, depending upon where the property is located, range from $25 all the way up to $75 (sometimes seen in higher-rent areas, such as San Francisco). **And if you're worried that asking for an application fee will discourage applicants from applying**—*don't be!* First of all, you may discover this

to be a constructive—and, indeed, very valuable—**way of weeding out (pre-screening) those that already think they may not qualify.** Secondly, **you can always consider offering the cost of the application fee as a credit toward the first month's rent** – *contingent upon approval of course.* This type of gesture is always greatly appreciated and **helps establish a good-will landlord-tenant relationship** from the get-go.

> *"I used to think that only large apartment communities could get away with charging an application fee. I was always afraid that no one would apply for my little rental if I were to ask for one. One day, I finally started requesting the fee and—as it turns out—my suspicions were wrong. Most people don't have any problem paying an application fee to help cover my screening costs."*

L. Stalker
Florida
Landlord

> ➤ *How much should I charge someone to apply?*

The best way to determine anything in real estate is to perform a comparable analysis—which, in this case, means snooping around and *checking out the competition*. Open up your local **newspaper or apartment guide** or visit your **favorite rental website** and place a few phone calls. *Find out what the competition charges to apply for a lease*—and then *calculate your own personal screening expenses* and base your fee within a comparable range.

A word of caution concerning the law: While most states permit application fees, **there are a few that have stringent requirements (e.g., Wisconsin - where** *you are not permitted to charge an application fee if the applicant provides you a current copy of his or her credit report*). Note: You can still pull it yourself, you just can't charge for it. If the applicant fails to provide you a current copy obtained within the past 30 days, then you can charge for the cost of obtaining your own report (up to $20) if you perform your own credit check. *For a detailed look at your legal rights and responsibilities, see the* **American Landlord Law** volume.

CAUTION

Proper Identification

Before you accept a rental application, *it is imperative that you ask to see some type of government-issued photo identification* (e.g. a driver's license or passport) *and a Social Security Card*. And **photocopies should immediately be made for your records**. If you do not have convenient access to a copy machine, **you should** *definitely* **copy down the identification numbers, names, addresses and date of birth**, *exactly as they appear on each individual ID card.*

Do not accept a photocopy of any identification made by the applicant! You should always ask to see the originals. Personal computers, high-tech scanners and printers have made it **far too easy to be able to manipulate virtually any type of government-issued identification**. This is **especially true** if the end result is intended to appear as if it was a photocopy of the original. *Be on alert!* **Identity theft is the primary reason why credit bureaus and the federal government are constantly changing their policies and laws** with regard to the tenant screening industry.

The purpose of the photo identification is to verify that **Jane Doe** *really is* **Jane Doe** – and not Ms. Ima Fraud. *If you accept an application without ever seeing the applicant's photo ID for yourself, you will never know…*

⭐ **Asking for the applicant's Social Security Card is also critical!**
The most common problem encountered when screening tenants is an incomplete credit check, the result of an inaccurate credit report. Oftentimes, **that can spring from just a *single* incorrect digit in a Social Security Number.** Whether an intentional error or simply a

case of bad handwriting (or even poor vision for that matter), **Social Security Numbers are commonly transposed.** Asking to **see the applicant's actual Social Security Card** not only **improves the reliability of your tenant screening results,** but also **deters the applicant from attempting to assume another person's identity** for (at the very least) the purpose of renting your property under false pretenses. This is **just one example of the many unseen pitfalls that landlords *must* be aware of in order to protect themselves** from disasters the likes of which you can't imagine…

JOHN Z DOE

000-00-0000

But **there's no need to be scared of the process -** *as long as you follow these and other steps outlined in the upcoming chapters, you'll prevent yourself from falling prey to these* **"hidden traps"** set by identity thieves and a small number of deceitful tenants. Just relax and be sure to never stray from your tenant screening protocol.

Chapter 5

Tenant Screening, Part II:
The Dreaded Credit Report

This Chapter Discusses:

★ Getting Access to a Tenant's Credit Report

★ How to Read and Interpret a Credit Report (sample included)

★ Personal Information

★ Employment Information

★ Scoring (Credit Score)

★ Credit Summary

★ Public Records

★ Collections

★ Revolving Accounts

★ Installment Accounts

★ Mortgage Accounts

★ Inquiries

As if you didn't know this already, a **credit report** is used in almost every business-to-consumer transaction today that involves *any* extension of credit. More often than not, every time you need to borrow, lease or finance, you will undoubtedly be asked to produce your Social Security Number so that a consumer credit file can be pulled to determine how much of a credit risk you are prior to approving your request.

Everything U Need to Know...

A credit report contains a detailed historical record of virtually all of your financial obligations from the past seven to ten years – *debts that have been reported by banks, credit card companies, mortgage lenders, utility companies, collection agencies and anyone else with whom you may have had any financial transactions.* In addition, **a credit report can also reveal a list of reported addresses, employers and public record filings, such as bankruptcies, civil judgments and tax liens.** So it is **really difficult for an applicant to hide a questionable past** – *which is a good thing*… at least for landlords…

Over the past 30 years, **the data and algorithms used to determine risk factors and credit scoring have improved immensely**, to better assist in the decision-making process. *When used correctly, there is no better way for a landlord to assess an applicant's ability and willingness to satisfy a lease agreement than with a personal credit report* – which is precisely why the entirety of this chapter is dedicated to **making sure you understand how to use the most important tool in tenant screening *before* you ever have to approve an applicant**.

Getting Access to a Tenant's Credit Report

Now that you know the most important tool in tenant screening is a credit report, you're doubtlessly wondering: **"So how do *I* get access to one?"** Well, **it used to be really easy until the end of 2006 – before the credit bureaus changed their requirements.** In the past, you could get a credit report in mere minutes, but *now it can take days just to set up an account with a company that is licensed to provide you with a report!* Fortunately, **there are some possible solutions to help you should you be in a hurry to screen an applicant and don't have time to comply with the many steps now required by the consumer credit bureaus.**

To learn more about your different options for screening your tenants, visit **AmerUSA**, located online at **www.AmerUSA.net** to set up an account (or you can always call toll-free at **1-800-488-7730** if you have any questions). Established in 1999, **AmerUSA** is the **leading provider of credit reports to small landlords throughout all fifty states**. *Thousands of professional and "everyday landlords" rely upon* **AmerUSA** *for their tenant and employee screening needs.* **There is no cost for setting up an account**; it's a "pay-as-you-go" service that can be billed monthly or to a major credit card.

Any landlord who requires access to another individual's credit report will have to be *inspected,* in accordance with the latest credit bureau guidelines. **Inspections are now the biggest hurdle to overcome**, *especially as an "everyday landlord."* **A real estate agent or credit reporting agency** (such as **AmerUSA**) arranges for **a third-party source to verify** to the credit bureaus that **wherever you claim to operate from** (either out of your home or from a commercial office) **is – in fact –** *a real location*… and not some anonymous mail drop box or an abandoned warehouse.

☆ **Don't worry – inspections are not a big deal!**

They occur only once (unless you relocate) and are a one-time cost of only $75. Unfortunately, *there is no way around this mandatory requirement if you want to view someone's credit report* – well, there is, but you have to be either a 501(c)(3) nonprofit organization, a local, state or federal government office or a company listed with the **U.S. Securities & Exchange Commission**. *If not, then you have to be inspected.* **On the positive side, you receive online access that enables you to pull credit reports instantly 24 hours a day, 7 days a week –** *and that's a definite plus when processing applications on the weekend!*

How to Read and Interpret a Credit Report

Okay, so you finally took the time to setup a tenant screening account and you've just pulled your very first credit report – Nice shootin', Tex! Now you're undoubtedly wondering what to do with it. **Credit reports (while appearing to be somewhat overwhelming or even intimidating at times) are actually not terribly difficult to read or understand,** *as long as you know what to look for and where to find it.*

Fortunately, you can receive an **entire credit file** in an *easy-to-read format* that is conveniently *broken down into sections*. **The following pages depict an actual sample of a tenant's credit report in its entirety,** courtesy of **AmerUSA.net,** annotated with important items to note, **as well as frequently asked questions following immediately thereafter**...

The information contained in this chapter is for informational purposes only *and* **is not intended to address every element of a consumer credit report.** While some of you may be able to render a decision based upon this information, *all readers* **are encouraged to download and review** *- for free -* **the complete guide to understanding credit report results which can be found at the AmerUSA.net resource center (www.AmerUSA.net/resources.html).**

Credit Report

SAMPLE

AMERUSA®

Exact Match between SSN on input and SSN on file.

Personal Information Since 12/1/1985 FAD 1/1/2008	
	Reported
Name DOE, JOHN Z **SSN** 123-45-6789 **DOB:** 01/01/1965 **Address** 1234, MAKE BELIEVE ST, ANYTOWN, USA, 12345 **Address** 30100, MAKE BELIEVE AVE, ANYTOWN, USA, 12345 **Address** 3420, MAKE BELIEVE DR, ANYTOWN, USA, 12345 **Phone** 555-5555 Personal	10/31/2004 1/01/2008

Employment		Date Hired	Date Separated	
Employer	ACME PUBLIC SCHOOLS			Reported 9/1/2002
Employer	ABC EDUCATION			Reported 8/1/1994

Add-On Products Summary

Product: Score Model - FICO CLASSIC 98
Status: Default product delivered

Scoring

Score Model: FICO CLASSIC 98 +514

Factor: 038 Serious delinquency, and public record or collection filed
Factor: 002 Level of delinquency on accounts
Factor: 020 Length of time since derogatory public record or collection is too short
Factor: 010 Proportion of balances to credit limits is too high on bank revolving or other revolving accounts

+514

Credit Summary From 12/1/1985 To 6/15/2007

Public Records	1	Collections	2	Negative Trades	8
Hist Neg Trades	5	# Trades	39	Revolving	12
Hist Neg Occurr	15	Installment	25	Mortgage	2
Open Trades	0	Inquiries	9		

Type	High	Limit	Balance	Past Due	Payment	%Avail
Revolving	$1,500	$14,300	$1,269	$0	$99	91%
Installment	$57,586	$0	$31,584	$0	$609	-
Closed	$0	$0	$29,483	$2,833	$464	-
Totals	$59,086	$14,300	$62,336	$2,833	$1,172	-

Public Records

Reported/ $Amount	ECOA/ Subscriber	Assets	Type/ Plaintiff/Attorney	Docket/ Paid	Court/ City, State
04/03	C A 00000000	$0	Chapter 7 bnkrptcy discharged Pltff: JOHN AND JANE DOE	BK00000000 08/03	Federal District

Credit Report

Collection Accounts

Firm/ID Code	Paid/ ECOA	Placed/ CLSD	VRFD/ CS(MOP)	$PLCD/ BAL	Acc#	Creditor Name	Remarks
ARROW FINCL Y 00000000	I	01/07	04/07A O9B	594 827	00000000	A F S ASSIGNEE OF FIRST PREMI	Placed for collection
FIN CR NETWK Y 00000000	I	10/06	11/06A O9B	187 147	00000000	10 AT T SOUTHWESTERN BELL	Placed for collection

Revolving Accounts

Acc Name/Address	Rptd DLA ECOA	Opened Clsd/PD	High Limit	Pmt Term	$Bal	$Past Due	Mths 30 60 90	Rating
CAPITAL 1 BK 50000000000000 **Subscriber:** B 00000000 **Loan Type:** Credit Card **Remarks:** Canceled by credit grantor	05/07A 03/06 I	11/05 11/06F	856		977	977		R9
FST PREMIER 50000000000000 **Subscriber:** B 00000000 **Collateral:** SLDTO ARROW FINANCIAL SERVICES **Loan Type:** Credit Card **Remarks:** Profit and loss writeoff	04/07A 05/04 I	03/04 04/04F	594 400		0			R9
HSBC NV 50000000000000 **Subscriber:** B 00000000 **Loan Type:** Credit Card **Remarks:** Purchased by another lender	10/05A 12/04 I	02/04 10/04F	1002		0			R9
HSBC NV 60000000000000 **Subscriber:** B 00000000 **Loan Type:** Credit Card	05/07A I	05/07	0 300		0			R1
USA CREDIT 70000000000000 **Subscriber:** F 00000000 **Loan Type:** Credit Card	10/05A I	10/05	0 12.5K		0		01 1	R1
PROVIDIAN 10000000000000 **Subscriber:** B 00000000 **Loan Type:** Credit Card **Remarks:** Canceled by credit grantor **Max Del:** 11/01/00; MOP-03	05/02A 04/99 I	11/96 04/99C	10.6K 9900		0		24 02 01 00 111111211111 111113211111	R1
GTWY/CBSD 60000000000000 **Subscriber:** H 00000000 **Loan Type:** Combined Credit Plan **Remarks:** Account closed by consumer	10/01A 05/01 I	03/01 05/01C	1591 3500		0		08 11111111	R1
CHASE/CC 10000000000000 **Subscriber:** H 00000000 **Loan Type:** Credit Card **Remarks:** Closed	06/00A 10/94 I	08/94 08/99C	5 600		0		02 11	R1

SAMPLE

Credit Report

	Rptd DLA ECOA	Opened Clsd/PD	High Limit	Pmt Term	$Bal	$Past Due	Mths 30 60 90	Rating
CITI 50000000000000 **Subscriber:** B 00000000 **Loan Type:** Credit Card **Remarks:** Canceled by credit grantor	07/99A 04/99 A	04/90 11/97C	0		0			R1
GOODYEARCBSD 70000000000000 **Subscriber:** A 00000000 **Loan Type:** Charge Account **Remarks:** Chapter 7 bankruptcy	12/06A I	01/03 05/03C	1154 1200		0			RUR
Revolving Totals					$0	$977		

Overdraft/Reserve Accounts

Acc Name/Address	Rptd DLA ECOA	Opened Clsd/PD	High Limit	Pmt Term	$Bal	$Past Due	Mths 30 60 90	Rating
CENTR OK FCU 50000000000000 **Subscriber:** Q 00000000 **Loan Type:** Unsecured	04/07A 04/07 I	12/06	1500 1500	99 MIN	1269		04 1111	C1
TINKER FCU 40000000000000 **Subscriber:** Q 00000000 **Loan Type:** Line of Credit **Remarks:** Closed	01/06A 04/03 I	12/02 04/03C	1500		0		48 02 00 00 X11111XXXXXX XXXXXXXXXXXX XXXXXXX2X21 1X1111111111	C1
Overdraft/Reserve Totals					$99	$1,269		

Installment Accounts

Acc Name/Address	Rptd DLA ECOA	Opened Clsd/PD	High Limit	Pmt Term	$Bal	$Past Due	Mths 30 60 90	Rating
THE BANK NA 90000000000000 **Subscriber:** B 00000000 **Loan Type:** Deposit Related **Remarks:** Profit and loss writeoff	05/07A I	08/04 09/04F	927	84MO	927	927		I9
CHASE AUTO 50000000000000 **Subscriber:** B 00000000 **Remarks:** Repossession	04/03A 01/03 C	09/02 04/03F	27.2K	464 84MO	27.5K	929		I8
AMERICAN LNS 10000000000000 **Subscriber:** F 00000000 **Loan Type:** Note Loan **Remarks:** Closed	02/07A 02/07 I	08/06 02/07C	192	48 4MO	0		05 01 00 00 21111	I2
SECURITY FIN 40000000000000 **Subscriber:** F 00000000 **Loan Type:** Unsecured **Remarks:** Closed	01/07A 01/07 I	07/06 01/07C	700	100 7MO	0		06 01 00 00 211111	I2

SAMPLE

Credit Report

Acc Name/Address	Rptd DLA ECOA	Opened Clsd/PD	High Limit	Pmt Term	$Bal	$Past Due	Mths 30 60 90	Rating
TINKER FCU 40000000000000 **Subscriber:** Q 00000000 **Loan Type:** Automobile **Remarks:** Closed	09/02A 09/02 I	12/99 09/02C	14.0K	285 60MO	0		03 X11	I1
TINKER FCU 40000000000000 **Subscriber:** Q 00000000 **Loan Type:** Secured **Remarks:** Closed	12/00A 11/00 I	04/99 12/00C	10.6K	275 42MO	0		03 X11	I1
TINKER FCU 40000000000000 **Subscriber:** Q 00000000 **Loan Type:** Automobile **Remarks:** Closed	11/00A 05/02 I	11/00C	1860	111 18MO	0		07 X11111	I1
SM SERVICING 40000000000000 **Subscriber:** B 00000000 **Loan Type:** Student Loan **Remarks:** Transferred to another lender	01/00A 01/00 I	03/94 01/00C	7768	101	0			I1
BANCFIRST 50000000000000 **Subscriber:** B 00000000 **Loan Type:** Secured **Remarks:** Account closed by consumer	12/99A 12/99 I	11/96 12/99C	15.8K	263 61MO	0			I1
WM FINANCE 30000000000000 **Subscriber:** F 00000000 **Loan Type:** Secured by Household Goods **Remarks:** Closed	11/98A 11/98 C	08/97 11/98C	662	55 12MO	0			I1
AMQUEST BANK 10000000000000 **Subscriber:** B 00000000 **Loan Type:** Automobile	10/98A 10/98 I	11/96	15.8K	263 61MO	0			I1
ARVEST BANK 60000000000000 **Subscriber:** B 00000000 **Loan Type:** Secured **Remarks:** Closed	11/03A 09/03 C	05/02 11/03C	3761	137 30MO	0		01	IUR
SM SERVICING 40000000000000 **Subscriber:** B 00000000 **Loan Type:** Student Loan **Remarks:** Student loan not in repayment	09/01A 07/01 I	03/94	7768	101	5071		17 111111111111 11111	IUR
Installment Totals				$609	$60,090			

Mortgage Accounts

Acc Name/Address	Rptd DLA ECOA	Opened Clsd/PD	High Limit	Pmt Term	$Bal	$Past Due	Mths 30 60 90	Rating
							Current Status	Hist Status
ARVEST BANK 70000000000000	08/04A 07/04	05/02 08/04C	67.5K	594 360MO	0		09 111111111	M1

SAMPLE

Credit Report

Subscriber: B 00000000 **Loan Type:** Conventional RE Mortgage **Remarks:** Closed	C								
SUPERIOR FED 10000000000000 **Subscriber:** B 00000000 **Loan Type:** Conventional RE Mortgage **Remarks:** Transferred to another lender	11/03A 11/03 P	05/02 11/03C	67.5K	572 360MO	0		17 11111X111111 11111		M1
Mortgage Totals				$0	$0				

Inquiries

Date	Name/Address	Code	MKT	Type Inq/Loan	Amount
06/15/07	AMERUSA.NET	Z 00000000	FLA	I	
02/14/07	TRUELOGIC FI	Y 00000000	IND	I	
02/01/07	ARROW FINANC	Y 00000000	IND	I	
11/03/06	NCO GRP	Y 00000000	IND	I	
09/30/06	ELITE RECOVE	Y 00000000	IND	I	
05/04/06	CENTRAL OKL	Q 00000000	SCT	I	
12/21/05	ENCORE RECEI	Y 00000000	IND	I	
11/04/05	CAP ONE BANK	B 00000000	NTL	I	
09/17/05	FIN RECOVERY	Y 00000000	WIS	I	

Serviced By:

AMERUSA.NET
800-488-7730

END OF REPORT

SAMPLE

Personal Information

The information displayed here is exactly what it appears to be: **the subject's name** *(including any known aliases),* **date of birth, social security number** and **up to three of his or her most recent addresses, as reported by creditors** (banks, mortgage lenders, credit card companies, etc.).

Personal Information Since 12/1/1985 FAD 1/1/2008		Reported
Name DOE, JOHN Z		
SSN 123-45-6789 **DOB:** 01/01/1965		
Address 1234, MAKE BELIEVE ST, ANYTOWN, USA, 12345		10/31/2004
Address 30100, MAKE BELIEVE AVE, ANYTOWN, USA, 12345		1/01/2008
Address 3420, MAKE BELIEVE DR, ANYTOWN, USA, 12345		
Phone 555-5555 Personal		

> ➤ *What if my applicant's current address isn't listed? Does this mean the applicant(s) are lying about where they live?*

Chances are, probably not. *While this section can corroborate the information found on an application, it is not a lie detector* or a "Magic 8-Ball." Unfortunately, **there are too many variables to even list as to why an applicant's current address may not appear** (e.g., creditor statements sent to a different address, the applicant hasn't applied for credit since moving to their last address, etc.). *You should really only become concerned when* an applicant proclaims that they have only lived in one state their entire life and another one pops up – or if they claim to have lived at the same place for the past ten years and three different addresses were reported in the past five. *Situations like that should be seen as pretty clear red flags.*

If you feel uncomfortable with your credit report findings, don't hesitate to ask the applicant (*politely* – it's not an interrogation) *for an explanation and for any supporting documentation to back it up*. Always give the applicant the benefit of the doubt and an opportunity to clarify any discrepancies – *there may very well be a reasonable explanation.*

Employment Information

Only if available, up to three current and previous employers will be listed here and the data *may or may not include* city and state, position and date the applicant's employment was verified, reported or date on which they were hired.

Employment			Date Hired	Date Separated	
Employer	ACME PUBLIC SCHOOLS				Reported 9/1/2002
Employer	ABC EDUCATION				Reported 8/1/1994

> *There was no employment information listed – what should I do?*

Actually, **don't be surprised to find most credit reports missing this information**. One theory is that consumers change jobs too often to have an up-to-date file – it's not as if people continue to work for IBM for 20 years the way they used to back in the day… Remember, **creditors usually report this information when you apply for credit** – *and a lot of the time, they don't even bother asking for this information or report it.* So don't worry if the current employer is not reported.

If you are *truly* concerned, the obvious recommendation is to contact the current employer directly – a **Verification of**

Employment (VOE) form has been included on the enclosed **CD-ROM** for your convenience *if you'd prefer getting a written response*. Simply **fax over the VOE to the Human Resources manager at the applicant's current place of employment, along with a copy of your applicant's authorization to release information** – and then hope for a timely response.

Now **if the employer appears to be in any way suspect (***possibly a friend or relative of the applicant's***), you may then also wish to verify the existence of the business** itself – **this is easy to do using directory assistance** (such as **411.com**) **or by searching for an** *occupational license* or *business filings* through the applicable city, county or state department websites.

In order to open up a business account, most banks usually require some type of formal documentation – *so you can expect to find something on public record about the employer*. You could even settle for a **Better Business Bureau** listing, for that matter.

NOTE: If your prospective tenant's friend or relative actually owns a business, there is nothing you can do to verify the employment history *independently* **unless you want to start pulling previously filed tax returns from the IRS** – possible, but a little too extreme for even an **American Landlord**.

Scoring (Credit Score)

This area lists the applicant's infamous *credit score*, **which purports to predict the likelihood a consumer will become delinquent within the next two years**. Proprietary algorithms developed by the **Fair Isaac Corporation** (known as the **FICO Score**) are **the most commonly used when generating an applicant's credit score**. In addition to the *actual* **score number**, the *top four components* which influence the score (called **"score factors"**) *are also included in this section* – **these are listed in their order of importance from top to bottom**.

<table>
<tr><td colspan="2" align="center">Scoring</td></tr>
</table>

Scoring	
Score Model: FICO CLASSIC 98 +514	
Factor: 038 Serious delinquency, and public record or collection filed **Factor:** 002 Level of delinquency on accounts **Factor:** 020 Length of time since derogatory public record or collection is too short **Factor:** 010 Proportion of balances to credit limits is too high on bank revolving or other revolving accounts	+514

> ### *How low and how high can a credit score get?*

The **most popular and commonly used** credit score **(FICO) ranges from 300 to 850 – statistically speaking, the lower the score, the greater the credit risk**.

> ### *What's a good credit score for rental agreements?*

Generally speaking, **you want to strive for applicants that score a minimum of 600 or higher**. As soon as a credit score drops to **599 or below**, there is a *much greater risk that the person will become delinquent within the next two years*. However, **any decision-making criteria that you decide to adopt should not be based on scoring alone, as you will soon discover**… This will be discussed in greater detail in the next chapter on **Determining Credit "Worthiness."**

Credit Summary

This section provides a **quick snapshot of all the fine detail you will discover throughout the rest of the credit report**. Instead of having to perform your own calculations to determine the number of **public records**, **historical negative trades** (accounts that were paid late at least once in the past seven years – abbreviated **"Hist Neg Trades"**), **historical negative occurrences** (total number of times accounts were paid late in the past seven years – abbreviated **"Hist Neg Occurr"**), **open trades** (number of open accounts), **collection accounts, trades** (total number of closed and open accounts), **installment accounts, inquiries, negative trades** (accounts that are now past due), **revolving accounts** and **mortgage accounts**. This section also **summarizes the total amount of debt** and the **available percentage on the revolving accounts**, so you can *immediately* assess the applicant's activity.

Credit Summary From 12/1/1985 To 6/15/2007						
Public Records 1	Collections 2	Negative Trades 8				
Hist Neg Trades 5	# Trades 39	Revolving 12				
Hist Neg Occurr 15	Installment 25	Mortgage 2				
Open Trades 0	Inquiries 9					
Type	**High**	**Limit**	**Balance**	**Past Due**	**Payment**	**%Avail**
Revolving	$1,500	$14,300	$1,269	$0	$99	91%
Installment	$57,586	$0	$31,584	$0	$609	-
Closed	$0	$0	$29,483	$2,833	$464	-
Totals	$59,086	$14,300	$62,336	$2,833	$1,172	-

> ➤ *Can I stop at this point and make an informed decision – or do I need to review the rest of the information that appears on a credit file?*

> It ultimately depends on you – after all, you're the one that gets to decide what you are willing to accept. However, *unless you have had enough experience in evaluating credit reports, it is strongly recommended that you take your time to review the entire file and fully understand all of its components.*

Public Records

This information is **obtained from county, state and federal courts** and **includes bankruptcies, civil judgments and tax liens**. The data reported will vary, but *typically includes* a **file date, case number, case type, jurisdiction, amount** and **other relevant details**.

Public Records					
Reported/ $Amount	ECOA/ Subscriber	Assets	Type/ Plaintiff/Attorney	Docket/ Paid	Court/ City, State
04/03	C A 00000000	$0	Chapter 7 bnkrptcy discharged Pltff: JOHN AND JANE DOE	BK00000000 08/03	Federal District

 How long do public records remain on a credit report?

The length of time varies for each type of public record so a list has been provided below:

- ◆ **Bankruptcy Chapters 7 and 11 stay on for 10 years** (7 years if voluntarily dismissed)
- ◆ **Bankruptcy Chapter 13 filings stay on for 10 years** (7 years if discharged or dismissed)
- ◆ **Tax liens that are *unpaid* stay on *forever***
- ◆ **Tax liens that are *paid* stay on for 7 years** (from the date paid in full)
- ◆ **Civil judgments that are *unpaid* stay on for 7 years**
- ◆ **Civil judgments that are *paid* stay on for 7 years** (from the date paid in full)

Collections

Any accounts listed here are ones that have been **assigned to collection agencies because the original creditor was unsuccessful in getting the applicant to completely satisfy their outstanding obligation.** Some creditors have their own internal collection division, so **you may only see the name of the original creditor listed.** Other types of data reported here include the **account number, ECOA (Equal Credit Opportunity Act) designation** – which simply indicates whether it's an *individual or joint* account, *DLA* (date of last activity) – when the last payment was made – the *balance owed* and the *current account status* (whether or not the debt has been paid, is being paid or remains unpaid).

Collection Accounts							
Firm/ID Code	Paid/ ECOA	Placed/ CLSD	VRFD/ CS(MOP)	$PLCD/ BAL	Acc#	Creditor Name	Remarks
ARROW FINCL Y 00000000	I	01/07	04/07A O9B	594 827	00000000	A F S ASSIGNEE OF FIRST PREMI	Placed for collection
FIN CR NETWK Y 00000000	I	10/06	11/06A O9B	187 147	00000000	10 AT T SOUTHWESTERN BELL	Placed for collection

➤ *Why is there sometimes a difference in the "reported amount" versus the "balance amount?"*

When this occurs, it's usually with a *larger* amount appearing in the balance field because collection agencies are entitled to add on their own penalties and interest. However, **if payments have been made since the debt was transferred to the collection agency, then you should see a** *lower* **adjusted amount** between the current balance and when it was last reported.

➤ *How long do collection accounts remain on a credit report?*

The **Fair Credit Reporting Act** *only* allows collection accounts to stay on a consumer's credit report for **seven years from the date of last activity**. Now this isn't the *American Credit Repair* volume, but here is **A FRIENDLY TIP**:

If you were not to make a single payment on a collection account for seven years, it would have to be removed (usually automatically) *from your credit report as if it never existed*, **as long as there continues to be no activity**. You may still legally be responsible for the debt, but it will no longer negatively impact your credit score or be seen by any other creditors you decide to do business with in the future. *How's that for a consumer-friendly l'il loophole?*

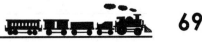

Revolving Accounts

The **"tradelines" (accounts)** that are listed under this heading *revolve*. In other words: **when you charge against the account, the balance goes up and the available credit goes down. Then when you make a payment, the balance goes down and the available credit goes back up.** This *revolving* cycle **continues to repeat itself for the life of the account.** Examples of **revolving accounts** include **credit cards, department store cards** and **gas cards** and *often have the greatest impact on an applicant's credit score*.

Interpreting this section is very easy. It begins with the **name of the creditor**, followed by **when the account was reported or updated, the date of the last activity, when the account was opened, how much credit was ever used, the estimated monthly payment required to keep the account current, the balance, the number of months being reported, the historical status** (showing how many 30-, 60- and 90-day late payments were recorded during those months) and – *most importantly* – **the account's current rating. The rating system is as follows**:

"R" – stands for **revolving** – and the **number appearing after** shows the **manner of payment.** For example: **"R1"** means the account was last reported as paid on time, **"R2"** signifies 30 days' late payment, **"R3"** – 60 days' late payment, etc. The *three most recent late payments* (if any) *will be reported underneath the current rating*.

Revolving Accounts											
				Current Status			Hist Status				
Acc Name/Address	Rptd DLA ECOA	Opened Clsd/PD	High Limit	Pmt Term	$Bal	$Past Due	Mths	30	60	90	Rating
CAPITAL 1 BK 50000000000000 **Subscriber:** B 00000000 **Loan Type:** Credit Card **Remarks:** Canceled by credit grantor	05/07A 03/06 I	11/05 11/06F	856		977	977					R9
PROVIDIAN 10000000000000 **Subscriber:** B 00000000 **Loan Type:** Credit Card **Remarks:** Canceled by credit grantor **Max Del:** 11/01/00; MOP-03	05/02A 04/99 I	11/96 04/99C	10.6K 9900		0		24 02 01 00 111111211111 111113211111				R1

> ➤ *What is a charged-off account?*

When an **applicant stops paying an outstanding obligation,** the **creditor has the right to assume that debt can no longer be collected** and **writes it off as a loss** – also known as a **"charge-off."** The rating for this type of an account is listed as an **"R9"** and has *a very negative impact on an applicant's credit score*.

> ➤ *When an account has a remark stating that it was closed by the credit grantor, is this necessarily bad?*

There could be many reasons why a **credit grantor** (or **creditor**) has chosen to close an applicant's account and *the reasons are not always negative.* So **it's not recommended that you act upon this information alone.** It's always *more important to focus on the account rating and historical payment status* as opposed to any remarks.

Installment Accounts

Unlike credit cards, these tradelines do not revolve. They are **opened with a fixed loan amount** and **come with a set monthly payment that is paid until the balance reaches zero.** Then **the account is closed and cannot be used again.** Examples of *installment accounts* include **student loans, personal loans** and **automobile loans.**

The formatting of this section is similar to the one covering revolving accounts – the primary difference is that *the monthly payment is usually fixed* and *does not fluctuate like a credit card* – which has its monthly payment based upon whatever the outstanding balance is at the end of the statement period. **You'll notice that the rating system is exactly the same,** however: an **"I" for installment** is used instead of an "R" for revolving.

Installment Accounts											
				Current Status			Hist Status				
Acc Name/Address	Rptd DLA ECOA	Opened Clsd/PD	High Limit	Pmt Term	$Bal	$Past Due	Mths	30	60	90	Rating
TINKER FCU 40000000000000 **Subscriber:** Q 00000000 **Loan Type:** Secured **Remarks:** Closed	12/00A 11/00 I	04/99 12/00C	10.6K	275 42MO	0		03 X11				I1
SM SERVICING 40000000000000 **Subscriber:** B 00000000 **Loan Type:** Student Loan **Remarks:** Transferred to another lender	01/00A 01/00 I	03/94 01/00C	7768	101	0						I1

➢ *What does "secured" or "unsecured" mean when it appears next to the loan type?*

When an applicant opens an account, it is sometimes **guaranteed with some type of collateral** – such as an automobile for a car loan or even a certificate of deposit for a personal loan. If this is the case, then **the account has been "secured,"** which means that – *should the applicant default on the account, then the creditor has every right to claim the collateral*, as is commonly seen with vehicle repossessions. If there is *no collateral attached to the loan*, then it is **"unsecured."**

➢ *What does "deferred" mean should it be notated under a student loan account?*

Students are commonly allowed to **defer (put off until a later date)** their payment obligations **regarding a student loan** while they are either still in school, unemployed or seeking new job placement upon graduating. This allows students an opportunity to take full advantage of the education they financed, so they can **more adequately prepare themselves financially before having to pay back this obligation.**

Mortgage Accounts

All obligations that are secured by a mortgage are provided here, so **you can easily see how the applicant's payment history has been in terms of real estate obligations only**. Accounts reported in this section include *purchase and refinance mortgages*, as well as *home equity loans* and *lines of credit*.

As you can see, **this section is formatted the same way as the fields for revolving and installments accounts**, except an **"M" for mortgage** is used for the account rating as opposed to the "R" or "I."

Mortgage Accounts									
				Current Status			Hist Status		
Acc Name/Address	Rptd DLA ECOA	Opened Clsd/PD	High Limit	Pmt Term	$Bal	$Past Due	Mths 30 60 90		Rating
ARVEST BANK 70000000000000 **Subscriber:** B 00000000 **Loan Type:** Conventional RE Mortgage **Remarks:** Closed	08/04A 07/04 C	05/02 08/04C	67.5K	594 360MO	0		09 111111111		M1
SUPERIOR FED 10000000000000 **Subscriber:** B 00000000 **Loan Type:** Conventional RE Mortgage **Remarks:** Transferred to another lender	11/03A 11/03 P	05/02 11/03C	67.5K	572 360MO	0		17 11111X111111 11111		M1

> ➤ *When does a mortgage begin to face foreclosure and how is that displayed?*
>
> When an applicant **fails to make a payment for three consecutive months**, the mortgage **lender will usually begin initiating foreclosure proceedings**. This means the account rating would most likely be **"M4" or higher** for this to happen – at which point a **remark would also be placed under the creditor's name** stating *foreclosure process started*.

Inquiries

Every time a creditor or collection agency pulls an applicant's credit report (this includes landlords too) **the inquiry is recorded and reported for other creditors to see for two years** – after which the inquiry will simply fall off the record.

Inquiries					
Date	Name/Address	Code	MKT	Type Inq/Loan	Amount
06/15/07	AMERUSA.NET	Z 00000000	FLA	I	
02/14/07	TRUELOGIC FI	Y 00000000	IND	I	
02/01/07	ARROW FINANC	Y 00000000	IND	I	
11/03/06	NCO GRP	Y 00000000	IND	I	

> ➤ *How much of an impact do inquiries have on an applicant's credit score?*

First of all, **only the inquiries that an applicant voluntarily initiates (when applying for some type of credit) will be taken into account**; all **other inquiries requested by the applicant** *for personal review* – or for an employer or existing creditor performing an account review – **will not be considered.** An **initiated inquiry (pulled for the purposes on obtaining credit)** *may or may not* have **an impact on an applicant's score**; it all depends on the condition of the current file at the time of each pulling. *If it does have an impact, one inquiry could take as much as five points off a credit score.*

Unfortunately, **the score is a complex proprietary calculation** that the **Fair Isaac Corporation** does not disclose. However, it is safe to say that having an *excessive amount of inquiries in the past two years* (e.g., double digits) *could have a major negative impact on a credit score*.

Now that you have completed this chapter, **you should have a basic working knowledge of how to read a credit report.** Regardless of which of the three major credit bureaus (**Equifax**, **Experian** and **TransUnion**) provides the report, **the manner in which data is presented is very similar.** The **industry consensus,** however, is that **TransUnion** – the preferred credit report of **AmerUSA** – is *the best for tenant screening*. (If you find yourself needing a **more comprehensive guide to understanding credit report results**, visit: **www.AmerUSA.net** to see the **official guide that experienced landlords and professionals rely on everyday.**)

And now that you have a basic understanding of *how* to read a credit report... well, **what the heck do you *do* with the danged thing...?**

Chapter 6

Tenant Screening, Part III:
Determining Credit "Worthiness"

This Chapter Discusses:

★ **The Importance of the Credit Score**

★ **The Credit Summary (including How to Deal with Identity Theft)**

★ **The Fair Credit Reporting Act (FCRA)**

★ **FCRA Definition of a Consumer Report**

★ **FCRA Definition of an Adverse Action**

★ **The Adverse Action Notice (Statement of Credit Denial)**

★ **Non-Compliance with the FCRA**

★ **The FCRA Summary of Rights**

★ **How to Get Your Own Free Credit Report—*For Real!***

Before beginning, it is important to understand that the topic of **"credit worthiness"** is **completely subjective** and has been debated for decades – **while one landlord may accept an applicant based upon their payment history, another landlord could just as easily reject the same applicant**. *Only years of experience will ultimately make you comfortable with making this determination*, as you will begin to discover **what type of historical credit profiles you, yourself, deem permissible**. So, in the interim, **this chapter will serve as a basic guide for assisting you in evaluating** your applicant's **"credit worthiness."**

Everything U Need to Know...

The Importance of the Credit Score

As soon as you obtain a credit report, *the first thing you should look at is the credit score.* This **will tell you in a split second whether or not you have an immediate credit approval**. *The minimum threshold for an immediate credit approval on an average residential rental agreement is 650 or higher unless there is evidence of an eviction which will be explained later in* **Chapter 7.** Applicants that have a credit score of 650 or above have a *significantly lower rate of delinquency* than those that are 649 or lower. If you are screening roommates or married couples, *at least one of the applicants that will be guaranteeing the lease should score at least a 650 or greater;* **otherwise, you should review all applicants' files in their entirety.**

Once again, **this is intended for those landlords just starting out** –those who need a basic threshold from which to work without having to worry about picking apart a credit file. Please keep in mind that **scoring is** *not* **an absolute almighty factor**, but **most real estate professionals will agree** that **650 or above is an immediate credit approval** – after all, you can actually *buy* a home with zero money down if you use a sub prime lender and score 50 points lower.

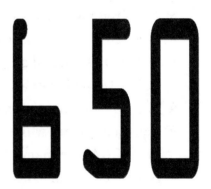

So what do you do when someone is **649 or below? The first thing you need to look at** is the **score factors** located under the *"Scoring"* section **to determine what is causing the lower score** – *the factor causing the worst damage will appear right at the top*. **From here, you can then determine what in particular needs to be reviewed within the report** – whether it's because there are **too many inquiries affecting the score** or **delinquencies** or **public records** – or perhaps **the proportion of outstanding balances to available credit is too high on the revolving accounts** (i.e., the prospective tenant has almost maxed out his or her credit cards).

The Credit Summary

After learning what the primary score factors are, you can then begin your investigation by visiting the *"Credit Summary."* Remember, **this section will give you a snapshot of all the activity on a credit report**. *Don't let yourself get discouraged or confused at this point* – all you're trying to determine is where the problems lie, and the **credit summary** is the best place to look before you go any further.

Once you determine if there are **public records, collections, negative trades, historical negative trades, etc.,** then you can continue to move down the report to each applicable section and see exactly *what* is being reported, *when* it occurred, *how much* is owed or past due, etc.

Here are some frequently asked questions concerning tenant credit profiles:

 My applicant says that he experienced hard times about four years ago, but that everything they have has been paid on time since then. How do I verify that?

> In the **Credit Summary** section, you need to look for *negative trades* and *historical negative trades*. **If there are no negative trades and only historical negatives, then that means all of the late payments occurred in the past.** If you want to see the actual dates of the last three late payments for each account, you can find and view the detail under the **Account Rating Column**. **Remember:** *Any rating greater than "1" is a late payment!*

 My applicant said she was a victim of identity theft, which caused her credit score to go down. How should I approach this situation?

This has always been a difficult subject because **it definitely does happen** – but you also need to be aware that *there are those that use this as an excuse for their bad credit*. Normally, **if the applicant is aware that they have been a victim of identity theft, there should be a consumer alert notice on their credit report informing anyone who pulls the report to call a phone number for verification** – *this notice will appear at the bottom after the* **"Inquiries" section**. In addition, there should be a **consumer dispute notice** listed **next to each account they claim was opened without their authorization.**

If none of these notices appear, then you need to look at all of the derogatory accounts under the "Account Rating" column to see when the late payments occurred. *If the late payments have occurred scattered throughout several different years* (e.g., 2001, 2003, 2006, 2007) *as opposed to a narrower point in time, then chances are the applicant is not telling the truth, since the credit report shows a historical trend of bad payments.* As a last resort, **you could always ask for a copy of the police report they filed to have their identity theft investigated**, but if they didn't bother to have an alert placed on their credit file, they probably also forgot to call Wyatt Earp.

> ➤ *All of the applicants that have applied have low credit scores! To whom do I rent?*

If your local demographics breed bad credit consumers or your rental simply attracts this model of clientele (if so, you should review **Chapter 2** again), *then you'll need to start looking at the credit reports a little differently*. Your approach should be to **weed out those applicants that have negative trades** until you're left with the last applicant standing. **Historical negative trades are okay;** *it's the negative trades (the ones that are past due right now) that you need to avoid!* If all the remaining applicants *still* have negative trades, then you need to **whittle down the next group by rejecting those applicants that didn't pay their utilities**. *You do not want to see utility collection accounts!* **This is bad news** – *especially when everything else is bad on the credit report as well.*

By the way, if you ever encounter an applicant with no credit, always remember: *No credit is usually better than bad credit.*

So now you should only have applicants remaining with negative trades. At this point, **your final step should be to** *get rid of those with the worst negative trades*, such as car payments. *You do not want applicants that are late on their car payments right at the point when they'll be renting your property*. Otherwise, how will they get to work to pay the rent? And while there *is* always public transportation, you need to be realistic – if the car payments are late, chances are the rent will also be late. *Believe it or not, it's better to start off with an applicant that has no car than one with a late car payment.*

Obviously, you can only lower your standards so far to accommodate even the *worst* of demographics. **In the end, if you still cannot find an applicant, you've got to hang in there and keep looking for** *the one* **that rises just above the rest**... or roll the dice and take your chances – *you may even consider collecting more for a security deposit* (up to as much as your state permits) *or requiring more rent to be paid in advance*.

The Fair Credit Reporting Act

Officially known under the United States Code as 15 U.S.C § 1681, the **Fair Credit Reporting Act (FCRA)** was *designed to protect the privacy of the consumer* and to *ensure the information contained on a consumer credit file is as accurate as possible*. The **government agency that enforces the FCRA** is the **Federal Trade Commission (FTC)**, located in Washington, D.C.

The FCRA allows landlords to use consumer credit files for tenant screening provided they follow their provisions – all 86 pages of which have been included on the enclosed CD-ROM for your late-night reading pleasure. In the meantime, we've provided the highlights for you below:

FCRA Definition of a Consumer Report

A **"Consumer Report" contains information about a person's credit characteristics, character, general reputation and lifestyle**. A report also may include information about an individual's rental history, such as information from previous landlords or from public records – like housing, criminal or eviction files. **To be covered by the FCRA, a report must be prepared by a Credit Reporting Agency (CRA)** – *a business that assembles such reports for other businesses*. **The most common type of CRA is a credit bureau.**

Landlords often use consumer reports to help them evaluate rental applications.

★ Examples of consumer reports include:

- ◆ A **credit report from a credit bureau**, such as **TransUnion**, **Experian** or **Equifax**, or a licensed reseller (e.g., **AmerUSA.net**)
- ◆ A **report from a tenant screening service** that **describes the applicant's rental history**, based on reports from previous landlords or housing court records
- ◆ A report from a tenant screening service that describes the applicant's rental history and **also includes a credit report that the service obtained from a credit bureau**
- ◆ A report from a tenant screening service that is **limited to a credit report the service obtained from a credit bureau**
- ◆ A **report from a reference-checking service that contacts previous landlords or other parties listed on the rental application** on behalf of the rental property owner

Landlords often ask applicants to give personal, employment and previous landlord references on their rental applications. **Whether verifying such references is covered by the FCRA depends on who performs the verification.** *A reference verified by the landlord's employee is not covered by the Act; a reference verified by an agency hired by the landlord to do the verification is covered.*

FCRA Definition of an Adverse Action

An **"Adverse Action"** is **any action taken by a landlord that is unfavorable to the interests of a rental applicant.**

 Common adverse actions by landlords include:

- **Denying the application**
- **Requiring a co-signer on the lease**
- **Requiring a deposit that would not be required for another applicant**
- **Requiring a larger deposit than might be required for another applicant**
- **Raising the rent to a higher amount as compared with another applicant**

The Adverse Action Notice (Statement of Credit Denial)

When an adverse action is taken – that is based solely or partly on information in a consumer report – *the FCRA requires the landlord to provide a notice of the adverse action to the consumer.* The **enclosed CD-ROM contains** a **"Statement of Credit Denial" template,** ready-made for you to use. **The statement of credit denial is required** *even if* **information in the consumer report was not the main reason for the adverse action.** In fact, even if the information in the report plays only a small part in the overall decision, *the applicant must still be notified.* While oral adverse action notices are allowed, *written notices provide proof of FCRA compliance.*

★ Here are situations that require a Statement of Credit Denial:

♦ **A landlord orders a consumer report from a CRA** – information contained in the report **leads to further investigation** of the applicant; **the rental application is denied because of that investigation.**

Since information in the report prompted the adverse action in this case, a statement of credit denial *must* be sent to the applicant.

♦ **An applicant with an unfavorable credit history** – such as past-due credit accounts – **is denied tenancy.** Although the credit history *was* considered in the decision, the applicant's poor reputation as a tenant in his current location played a more important role.

The applicant is *still* entitled to a statement of credit denial, because the credit report played a part – no matter how minor – in the denial process.

♦ **A person with an unfavorable credit history**, like a bankruptcy, but with no other negative indicators, applies for an apartment. **Rather than denying the application, the landlord offers to rent the apartment, but requires a security deposit that is double the normal amount.**

The applicant is entitled to a statement of credit denial because the credit report *influenced the landlord's decision* to require a higher security deposit from the applicant.

♦ **A landlord hires a reference-checking service to verify information included on a rental application.** Because the service reports that **the applicant does not work for the employer listed on the application, the rental application is denied**.

The applicant is yet again entitled to a statement of credit denial. The report is a consumer report from a **CRA** (the agency serving to check the references provided by the consumer on the application), and its report influenced the landlord's decision to deny the application.

♦ **A landlord rejects an applicant because of insufficient income *and* a bad credit report.**

Even though income was another important factor, **the applicant is entitled to a statement of credit denial because the credit report still influenced the denial**.

Non-Compliance with the FCRA

Landlords who fail to provide required disclosure notices face legal consequences. *The FCRA allows individuals to sue landlords for damages in federal court. A person who successfully sues is entitled to recover court costs and reasonable legal fees.* The law also allows individuals to seek *punitive damages for deliberate violations of the FCRA.* In addition, the **Federal Trade Commission,** *other federal agencies and even individual states can sue landlords for non-compliance and prevail in civil penalties.*

However, **a landlord who *inadvertently* fails to provide a required notice in an isolated case has legal protections –** *so long as he or she can demonstrate* **"that at the time of the… violation, he maintained reasonable procedures to assure compliance"** with the FCRA.

If you have questions about the FCRA, you can call the Federal Trade Commission toll-free: 1-877-FTC-HELP (1-877-382-4357). You can also **visit the FTC online** at **www.ftc.gov** or mail a letter to:

Federal Trade Commission
600 Pennsylvania Avenue, N.W.,
Washington, D.C. 20580

The FCRA Summary of Rights

To ensure consumers understand their rights under the Fair Credit Reporting Act, the Federal Trade Commission requires a summary of one's rights under the FCRA to be given to all consumers at the time they apply for credit. *This is especially important if the creditor intends on using a consumer credit report to assist them in rendering a decision.* A sample of a standard **FCRA Summary of Rights for tenant screening** appears on the next page; **one is also included on the enclosed CD-ROM.**

FCRA Summary of Rights

AmerUSA Corporation
3665 East Bay Drive #204-183
Largo, Florida 33771
Ph 727.467.0908 Fx 727.467.0918

FCRA Summary of Rights

A Summary of Your Rights - Under the Fair Credit Reporting Act

The federal Fair Credit Reporting Act (FCRA) is designed to promote accuracy, fairness, and privacy of information in the files of every "consumer reporting agency" (CRA). Most CRAs are credit bureaus that gather and sell information about you -- such as if you pay your bills on time or have filed bankruptcy -- to creditors, employers, landlords, and other businesses. You can find the complete text of the FCRA, 15 U.S.C. §§1681-1681u, by visiting www.ftc.gov. The FCRA gives you specific rights, as outlined below. You may have additional rights under state law. You may contact a state or local consumer protection agency or a state attorney general to learn those rights.

- **You must be told if information in your file has been used against you.** Anyone who uses information from a CRA to take action against you -- such as denying an application for credit, insurance, or employment -- must tell you, and give you the name, address, and phone number of the CRA that provided the consumer report.

- **You can find out what is in your file.** At your request, a CRA must give you the information in your file, and a list of everyone who has requested it recently. There is no charge for the report if a person has taken action against you because of information supplied by the CRA, if you request the report within 60 days of receiving notice of the action. You also are entitled to one free report every twelve months upon request if you certify that (1) you are unemployed and plan to seek employment within 60 days, (2) you are on welfare, or (3) your report is inaccurate due to fraud. Otherwise, a CRA may charge you up to eight dollars.

- **You can dispute inaccurate information with the CRA.** If you tell a CRA that your file contains inaccurate information, the CRA must investigate the items (usually within 30 days) by presenting to its information source all relevant evidence you submit, unless your dispute is frivolous. The source must review your evidence and report its findings to the CRA. (The source also must advise national CRAs -- to which it has provided the data -- of any error.) The CRA must give you a written report of the investigation, and a copy of your report if the investigation results in any change. If the CRA's investigation does not resolve the dispute, you may add a brief statement to your file. The CRA must normally include a summary of your statement in future reports. If an item is deleted or a dispute statement is filed, you may ask that anyone who has recently received your report be notified of the change.

- **Inaccurate information must be corrected or deleted.** A CRA must remove or correct inaccurate or unverified information from its files, usually within 30 days after you dispute it. **However, the CRA is not required to remove accurate data from your file unless it is outdated (as described below) or cannot be verified.** If your dispute results in any change to your report, the CRA cannot reinsert into your file a disputed item unless the information source verifies its accuracy and completeness. In addition, the CRA must give you a written notice telling you it has reinserted the item. The notice must include the name, address and phone number of the information source.

- **You can dispute inaccurate items with the source of the information.** If you tell anyone -- such as a creditor who reports to a CRA -- that you dispute an item, they may not then report the information to a CRA without including a notice of your dispute. In addition, once you've notified the source of the error in writing, it may not continue to report the information if it is, in fact, an error.

- **Outdated information may not be reported.** In most cases, a CRA may not report negative information that is more than seven years old; ten years for bankruptcies.

- **Access to your file is limited.** A CRA may provide information about you only to people with a need recognized by the FCRA -- usually to consider an application with a creditor, insurer, employer, landlord, or other business.

- **Your consent is required for reports that are provided to employers, or reports that contain medical information.** A CRA may not give out information about you to your employer, or prospective employer, without your written consent. A CRA may not report medical information about you to creditors, insurers, or employers without your permission.

- **You may choose to exclude your name from CRA lists for unsolicited credit and insurance offers.** Creditors and insurers may use file information as the basis for sending you unsolicited offers of credit or insurance. Such offers must include a toll-free phone number for you to call if you want your name and address removed from future lists. If you call, you must be kept off the lists for two years. If you request, complete, and return the CRA form provided for this purpose, you must be taken off the lists indefinitely.

- **You may seek damages from violators.** If a CRA, a user or (in some cases) a provider of CRA data, violates the FCRA, you may sue them in state or federal court.

FOR QUESTIONS OR CONCERNS PLEASE CONTACT

Federal Trade Commission
Consumer Response Center- FCRA
Washington, DC 20580 * 202-326-3761

How to Get Your Own Free Credit Report–*For Real!*

Beware of those unscrupulous companies that claim you can get a "free" copy of your credit report – *dozens of these companies swarmed the market deceptively using the phrase "FREE CREDIT REPORT"* to try and capitalize on the **FTC's FACT Act**, which required the three major credit bureaus (**Equifax**, **Experian** and **TransUnion**) to provide all consumers – upon request – a free copy of their credit report once a year. Well, **there is only one place you can get a free copy of your own personal credit report without also being coaxed into signing up for some membership or subscription that will cost you a fortune over time…**

Get your free copy today by visiting the *official website endorsed by the* FTC: **www.AnnualCreditReport.com – this is the *only* site that is operated by all three credit bureaus and where you can obtain your free copy without any strings attached**. If do not have Internet access, you may **call toll-free (877) 322-8228** to have your free copy mailed to you.

It's unfortunate that you may never see *this* advertised on television – instead, you see everything else with "FREE CREDIT REPORT" in its name or tag line that deceptively implies you get a free credit report without any obligation. **AmerUSA.net recommends** to all of its clients to *take advantage of this service at least once a year* **to monitor their credit reports for identity theft and creditor inaccuracies** – after all, it is **100% FREE** – *for real!*

Chapter 7

Tenant Screening, Part IV: Eviction Records

This Chapter Discusses:

★ **The Eviction Process**
★ **Eviction Record Sample**
★ **Where to Find Them**

The word, **"eviction,"** can be *a landlord's worst nightmare* – which is why multiple tenant screening chapters have been included in this book. **The more tools and knowledge you have at your fingertips** (and *actually use*), **the better your chances of not having to experience the eviction of a tenant.** *No one wants to go through an eviction; it can be very time-intensive, emotionally draining and financially devastating* for those who do not screen their applicants carefully – or simply don't bother to maintain good landlord-tenant relations throughout the term of the lease.

This chapter will introduce you to the **basics behind the eviction process**, its key attributes and **how to search and use eviction records as a companion to the credit report**. Since *each state has very specific legal requirements*, **evicting a tenant can be a complicated process.** If you require a *more detailed analysis of the mandatory steps and*

forms needed to initiate eviction proceedings for each state, you can read a more complete reference, *American Landlord Law*, which is *the ultimate companion guide for every landlord to easily understand his or her rights and responsibilities.*

The Eviction Process

Okay, so you ultimately decided to **take a chance on that applicant who was (admittedly) late a few times on his bills and had the credit rating to prove it, but vowed to pay you on time** – which panned out for the first couple of months until the **checks started bouncing**. Or perhaps this was the tenant that **didn't like cats or dogs**, but then Scooby and Scrappy happened to move in a few weeks later and decided to redecorate the property to *their* liking. Or possibly this was the **tenant that was here to stay (permanently) and just plain didn't want to leave after you told her that her lease expired and you weren't going to renew it.** Being the nice, reasonable person that you are, you may have **placed a friendly phone call** and **even mailed a letter reminding the tenant about the terms and conditions of the lease being violated** – *but no corrective action was taken and the problem still remains.*

Now the nice, reasonable person has to become *the smart, law-abiding landlord who has a valuable asset that needs to be protected from those who refuse to honor a legally-binding lease agreement.* It's unfortunate, but **you now have no choice but to enforce your rights**, put on your ten-gallon hat, the biggest, brassiest belt buckle you can muster and that **American Landlord "badge,"** so you can take that first step towards **regaining control of your property.**

The **eviction process essentially has three steps that are very similar**, regardless of where your property is located. *Even though the overall process has been outlined below, it is strongly recommended you read more about evictions in your individual state* in the *American Landlord Law* volume – and, of course, **it is prudent to always consult with your local legal counsel.**

The three steps to evicting a tenant are listed on the following pages:

★ Step 1: Terminating Tenancy

The *first step in the eviction process* is to – as the heading would suggest – *terminate tenancy*. There are *two types of termination*: **"With cause"** and **"Without cause."** A termination **with cause** *requires you to give the tenant a notice* (such as a notice to pay or to quit – see the **American Landlord Law** volume for eviction forms) *that basically spells out the problem* (such as past due rent or any other lease violations). The notice gives the tenant **a limited number of days to rectify the problem or the lease terminates and the tenant must vacate immediately**. *Many states will even allow you to terminate without giving the tenant the opportunity to correct the problem if it's a particularly severe situation* (such as drug dealing or other illegal activities taking place on the premises).

A termination **without cause** is just what it indicates – and is **usually enacted when a tenant refuses to vacate once the lease has expired** (or is about to expire) **and you don't want to renew the lease.** *This termination requires a notice to vacate, which is given a few days in advance.* Obviously, **you will need to provide proof that the tenant has been notified in either type of termination;** *each state will have its own requirements for the type of delivery method* (e.g., certified mail) that can be used *and the relevant supporting documentation required.*

★ Step 2: Filing an Unlawful Detainer Lawsuit

If the tenant does not move out or rectify the problem, you must then proceed with the second step in the eviction process, filing an **unlawful detainer lawsuit, which entitles you to go before a judge and petition the court for a judgment to take repossession of your property**. You might also want to **consider seeking a monetary judgment against the tenant for any outstanding unpaid rent.**

If you ever actually find yourself in this predicament, *be prepared!* This whole process *may not be as easy as it sounds, because the tenant (if they choose to) can easily delay and complicate matters by offering a defense*. While most tenants fail to ever actually appear in court, you still need to be prepared – by **clearly and thoroughly documenting *all* correspondence and evidentiary items you may have concerning these tenants**, so that you can better ensure yourself a swift and painless victory.

★ Step 3: Removing the Tenant

After the judge rules in your favor, the third, and final, step in having a tenant evicted is to receive a **writ of possession (*a court order stating that the landlord has the right to regain control of the property*)**. This **writ of possession must then be given to your local sheriff or police department so that a deputy or officer can visit the property and post a notice on the door**, informing the tenant to vacate by a certain date or else be physically removed. (***The tenant may be arrested if he or she chooses not to abide by the law*.**)

You, as the landlord, *cannot* lawfully take it upon yourself to forcibly remove the tenant – either directly or indirectly (e.g., coercing the tenant to leave by shutting off the water, electricity or gas) – *even if you have a writ of possession*. **The last thing you want to do is to give the tenant an opportunity to sue you – or worse, to have criminal charges filed against you!** So, *leave it to your local law enforcement professionals to get the job done legally and protect yourself at the same time!*

Eviction Record Sample

A sample of an eviction record has been provided on the next page. While credit reports may come across as intimidating and time-intensive, *an eviction record* (as you can plainly see) *is actually incredibly easy to read and understand.*

Eviction Record

AmerUSA Corporation
3665 East Bay Drive #204-183
Largo, Florida 33771
Ph 727.467.0908 Fx 727.467.0918

AMERUSA®

Eviction
An AmerUSA Tenancy Report

PREPARED EXCLUSIVELY FOR

LANDLORD: JANE JOE LANDLORD   FAX: 555-555-5555   DATE: 1/1/2008

APPLICANT

APPLICANT: JOHN DOE APPLICANT

EVICTION SEARCH

RESULT: **HIT**   JURISDICTION: NEW YORK

RECORD ABSTRACT

Name: JOHN Z DOE
Offender Record ID: 4379025

No Photo on Record

Home Address: 1300 MAKE BELIEVE DR S G-2043
ANYTOWN, NY 12345

Parties

Type: Plaintiff
Full Name: ACME PROPERTY MANAGEMENT LLC

Eviction

Case Number: 134473
Court:
State: NY

Filing Date: 1/1/2008
Rent Amount: 750
Case Type: LT
Hearing Result: WRIT

Page 1 of 1

SAMPLE

Where to Find Them

Now that you have a basic understanding of the eviction process, **you can see why you would want to avoid having to experience one.** Fortunately, *you can now search eviction records online to see if your applicant has ever been evicted before.* Chances are that **if a person has been evicted once, there is a** *reasonable* **chance that it may happen again –** *but not if you can find out beforehand.*

If you have the time – and you encounter mostly local applicants – **you can search for eviction records for free (or for at least a minimal clerk fee) by moseying on down to your local courthouse.** For those applicants that originate outside of your county (or local courthouse jurisdiction), **AmerUSA.net** offers an *exhaustive set of eviction records for most jurisdictions* in the United States – **and it costs only a few dollars to search an entire state –** *a worthy investment.* **For more information about the areas covered and the frequency in which data is updated,** check out: www.AmerUSA.net/eviction_records.

Eviction record searches are especially recommended when you encounter the following scenarios on an applicant's credit report:

☆ No Credit History (No Credit Score)

If an applicant *has no historical payment data on file and no credit score, you should always run an eviction search* as a secondary back-up measure.

☆ Insufficient Credit History with Derogatory Accounts

An *eviction search is highly recommended for those applicants that not only have insufficient credit, but bad credit as well.* A good prospect can still have an insufficient credit rating with no credit score because he or she has had no activity on file in the past six months due to all of the accounts being paid off and closed. It's true – even though the accounts were paid on time, if there is nothing left open and the file just sits there without any activity, no credit score will be generated after six months. Therefore, *an eviction search is not necessarily essential in this instance.*

☆ Credit Score of 649 or Less

If an applicant's credit score is 649 or less, that means the applicant is ranked lower than the average consumer and is in a higher rate of delinquency. You should *consider conducting an eviction search on anyone with a below-average score* that isn't directly attributed to medical debt, student loans or excessive credit inquires.

☆ Unpaid Civil Judgment

Since evidence of a possible eviction can be reported on a credit report (under public records) in the form of a civil judgment, *it is wise to specifically search eviction records should you encounter an unpaid civil judgment.* This is the *only way to rule out the possibility* that it may be attributed to an actual unlawful detainer lawsuit. **A paid civil judgment demonstrates the applicant's ability and willingness to satisfy outstanding obligations.** *Therefore, an eviction search is not necessarily required for such an occurrence*, but that depends on your own personal philosophy.

☆ Unpaid Utility Collection or "Charge-Off"

If an applicant doesn't pay a utility bill (and we're not talking about it just being a little late) *to the point of sending the account into collections* or a **"profit-and-loss write-off,"** there is **good reason to suspect that there may** *also* **have been a rent payment left behind with it.**

C. Michael
Ohio
Landlord

Eviction records are well worth the search. I had one person apply that had marginal credit. I think they scored right around 660, but there was something peculiar about the file. There were three different types of utilities reported under the collection accounts section that occurred within a few months of each other less than a year ago. I didn't see a judgment recorded, but the fact that the gas, electric and cable were not paid led me to believe something was up—and I was right. I did a search for eviction records and found that the last landlord filed against them, but never received a judgment—therefore, there was nothing reported on the credit report. I also later discovered the reason why the credit score was still in an acceptable range—most of the credit cards had low balances and were open for a very long time plus there were no credit inquiries on file for the past two years. Luckily, I trusted my intuition to investigate a little further.

Whether you can search records for free – or prefer to use an experienced service like **AmerUSA.net**, *it will be to your benefit either way to screen as best as you can…* and **to spend a few dollars (or a few moments of your time) in order to save thousands in the long run**. And remember, ***don't forget to charge an application fee*** (as detailed in **Chapter 4**) **to ease the burden of screening your applicants** – this is why most landlords collect a reasonable fee and offer to credit it toward a tenant's first month's rent contingent upon approval. ***Good will plus good screening equals good tenants!***

Tenant Screening, Part V:
Criminal Records

This Chapter Discusses:

★ **U.S. Department of Justice Statistics**

★ **Criminal Record Sample**

★ **Felonies and Misdemeanors**

★ **The Clerk of the Court**

★ **Government Websites**

★ **Professional Research**

As stated in **Chapter 4**, *a criminal record is nothing to take lightly*. While a criminal record search will not typically be used to evaluate an applicant's ability and willingness to satisfy his or her financial obligations, **it can be used to determine whether or not you will be housing a potential threat to yourself, your property *and* your community**.

As you can imagine, *landlords have unknowingly rented apartments and homes to convicted sex offenders, murderers, drug dealers, burglars, prostitutes, arsonists*… and the list goes on.

Everything U Need to Know...™

U.S. Department of Justice Statistics

TO PUT THINGS IN PERSPECTIVE: In case you think conducting a criminal background check on your tenant is not necessary (or is too expensive), here are some statistics from the **U.S. Department of Justice**. *[NOTE: Statistics concerning race and ethnicity have intentionally not been included to keep the focus on tenant screening and criminal convictions, not on racial or ethnic profiling.]*

☆ Prevalence of Imprisonment in the United States:

♦ **As of December 31, 2001, an estimated *5.6 million adults* had served some time in state or federal prison**, including 4.3 million former prisoners and 1.3 million adults currently housed in prisons.

♦ **Nearly *a third* of those former prisoners were *still under correctional supervision***, including 731,000 on parole, 437,000 on probation, and 166,000 in local jails.

♦ In 2001, an estimated *2.7% of adults in the U.S. had served time in prison*, **up from 1.8% in 1991 and 1.3% in 1974**.

♦ *Nearly two-thirds of the 3.8 million increase* **in the number of adults incarcerated between 1974 and 2001 occurred as a result of an increase in first-time incarceration rates**; only one-third occurred as a result of an increase in the number of individuals turning age 18 and older.

☆ Lifetime Likelihood of Going to State or Federal Prison:

♦ If recent incarceration rates remain unchanged, **an estimated *1 out of every 15 persons* (6.6%) will serve time in a prison during their lifetime**.

★ Recidivism Rates:

- Of the 272,111 persons released from prisons in 15 states in 1994, an estimated *67.5% were rearrested* **for a felony or serious misdemeanor** *within 3 years following their release*, *46.9% were reconvicted*, and *25.4% were sentenced to prison for a new crime altogether*.

- The **272,111 offenders** discharged in 1994 **accounted for** nearly *4,877,000 arrest charges* over their recorded careers.

- **Within 3 years of release, 2.5% of released rapists were rearrested for another rape**, and **1.2% of those who had served time for homicide were arrested for a** *new* **homicide.**

- **Sex offenders were** *less* **likely than non-sex offenders to be rearrested for any offense** — 43 percent of sex offenders versus 68 percent of non-sex offenders.

- However, **sex offenders were about four times** *more* **likely than non-sex offenders to be arrested for another sex crime after their discharge from prison** — 5.3 percent of sex offenders versus 1.3 percent of non-sex offenders.

★ Sex Offenders:

- In 1994, there were approximately **234,000 offenders convicted of rape or sexual assault** *while under* **the care, custody, or control of correctional agencies;** *nearly 60% of these sex offenders are under conditional supervision in the community*.

- *The median age of the victims of imprisoned sexual assaulters was less than 13 years old*; the **median age of rape victims was about 22 years.**

- An **estimated 24% of those serving time for rape and 19% of those serving time for sexual assault had been on probation or parole at the time of the offense** for which they were in state prisons in 1991.

- ♦ Of the **9,691 male sex offenders** released from prisons in 15 states in 1994, *5.3% were rearrested for a new sex crime within 3 years of release*.
- ♦ Of **released sex offenders who allegedly committed another sex crime**, *40% perpetrated the new offense within a year or less from their prison discharge*.

Fortunately, as an **American Landlord**, **you get to decide which offenses are** *acceptable* – **and which ones are not** – when it comes to housing someone who has been convicted of a crime. Sure, **many of those with a criminal record deserve a second chance after they settle their debt with society;** *it just takes some careful consideration and understanding to be able to determine whether or not to accept someone* with a tainted past that was commemorated with a celebratory mug-shot.

Criminal Record Sample

The image on the next page is an *actual* **criminal record abstract**, showing the typical details usually retrieved from a court search or state repository. The amount and type of information will change based upon the jurisdiction you are accessing, but **you can usually expect to see the subject's name and any significant identifiers, such as eye color, height, known aliases**, etc. You can also expect to see the **date and type of charge, along with the outcome – such as fines imposed, probation, jail time**, etc.

Criminal Record

AMERUSA®

AmerUSA Corporation
3665 East Bay Drive #204-183
Largo, Florida 33771
Ph 727.467.0908 Fx 727.467.0918

Criminal
An AmerUSA Tenancy Report

PREPARED EXCLUSIVELY FOR

LANDLORD: JOHN JOE LANDLORD   FAX: 555-555-5555   DATE: 1/1/2008

APPLICANT

APPLICANT: JANE DOE APPLICANT

CRIMINAL RECORD SEARCH

RESULT: **HIT**   JURISDICTION: CALIFORNIA

RECORD ABSTRACT

Name: JANE Z DOE
Offender Record ID: 10092887376

No Photo on Record

Home Address: 1300 MAKE BELIEVE DR S G-2043
ANYTOWN, NY 12345

Offenses

Description: ASSAULT
Type: M
Charge Date: 08/22/2007
Offense Disposition: CONVICTED
Date: 01/01/2008

Sentences

Fine: 100.00
Total Sentence Length: 90 DAYS

Page 1 of 1

SAMPLE

Felonies and Misdemeanors

You may be wondering which crimes to look for and how to rate them. Well, this is – of course – *very subjective*, but one thing is for sure: **You're going to ultimately have to bring your own personal experience to the table to gauge what is acceptable** *for you*.

Are you going to have an issue with the college graduate who was convicted five years ago for selling marijuana in high school as an 18-year-old adult? For some, maybe not, but others may have a serious issue with drug offenses, period. Or how about the applicant 30 years of age that was convicted of writing bad checks in a department store only two years ago, but has held a steady job since then? Would you cut him or her a break or be concerned the same checks may be issued to you?

There is obviously an *endless* **number of variables you'll encounter in conducting background checks** and – unfortunately – **there will never be just one cut-and-dry standard to apply**. But there are a few important suggestions that need to be shared with you.

The following is a list of just a few questions you should ask yourself:

➤ *Was it a violent offense?*

There are **varying degrees of these types of offenses**, ranging from a bar brawl to spousal abuse and, yes, even murder. This type of offense should obviously be *evaluated based on the severity of the crime*. It goes without saying that you should be *extra careful* – and **have a thorough understanding of the events that transpired** – and which you may well ultimately find to be too much effort for what it may be worth.

> ### *Were there drugs involved?*

Most landlords would agree that illegal drugs in general (*especially drug dealing*) will not be tolerated in their rental property. Illegal drugs are heavily frowned upon in most communities and **can easily give *you* an unfavorable reputation in the neighborhood**, *not to mention the impact on children, property values, crime*, etc.

> ### *Was it a sexual crime?*

This is probably **the most widely heard type of criminal conviction, due to the constant media attention, changes in legislation and the new government programs that have been instituted** such as **"Jessica's Law"** and the **"AMBER Alert."** *Expect this to be one of the most difficult types of applicants to consider.*

> ### *Did the crime involve banking or financial fraud?*

What you really want to know is if this was **merely a case of writing bad checks** – *or was there a more sinister plot involved such as assuming someone's identity.*

> ### *Was there prison or jail time?*

Sentencing imposed by a judge that involves **time spent behind bars** – *or the lack of it* – **can often be useful in weighing the severity of the crime.**

> ### *Is the applicant on parole or probation?*

Depending on the crime, **parole or probation periods can sometimes ensure a tenant is on their best behavior.** Sure, *this* *premise is in no way a guarantee*, **but it is nonetheless important to know, as it will likely be reflective of the original crime committed.**

> ➤ *How long ago was the offense?*

In general, **the longer amount of time that has elapsed since the date of the offense, the better.**

In addition to these basic questions, don't forget to include on the rental application (as mentioned in **Chapter 4**) **a question asking if your prospective tenant has ever been convicted of a crime and to please explain all offenses.** *Let the applicant have an opportunity to come clean about his or her past – Nothing says "Don't approve!" more than discovering that an applicant lied about having a criminal record.*

The Clerk of the Court

The **Clerk of the Court** is **an elected official, responsible for maintaining court records with the utmost care and security**. These **records are filed with the Clerk's Office** and *include criminal felony and misdemeanor cases, civil, family, probate and small claims proceedings, juvenile cases and traffic citations*. If your applicant has lived within the court's jurisdiction (which you can determine from the credit report you should have already pulled), **you can contact the Clerk's Office to inquire** *how* **to search criminal records.** Most of the records filed with the Clerk are available for public inspection during normal business hours, with the exception of those records specifically exempt by judicial order or statute. **You can pretty much count on each Clerk's Office around the country** (there are thousands – usually, one for each county) **to have its own individual policies and procedures.**

Don't worry! **Most public records are free searches** – after all, *you are the taxpayer* – and, if you're lucky, a portion of your tax dollars helped to pay for the development of an **official "Clerk of the Court" website**, so that **you can search online 24/7**. If not, you need to gallop on over to the Clerk's Office and stand in line like the rest of the cowpokes. **While the search itself is usually free,** *do* **expect to pay a fee per page or abstract, should you want an official copy to take home with you.**

Government Websites

You can't dispute the fact that *there is no greater investigative tool than the Internet* – almost *everyone* is online, *including most local, state and federal government offices.* And **while there is no publicly accessible website from the federal government for criminal record searches** per se, <u>there are two useful websites</u>:

> ⭐ **U.S. Department of the Treasury's Office of Foreign Assets Control**
>
> The **U.S. Department of the Treasury's Office of Foreign Assets Control** website – **(www.ustreas.gov/offices/enforcement/ofac/sdn)** – offers the **"Terrorist Watch List,"** which is usually **updated at least a couple of times a month**.

> ⭐ **Federal Bureau of Investigation**
>
> The **Federal Bureau of Investigation**'s website – **(www.fbi.gov/hq/cid/cac/states.htm)** – **offers a link to every states'** *sex offender registry* **website**.

As far as your **best source for free local resources,** *you should check your sheriff's or police department's website.* **Local law enforcement agencies often have a website that enables you to search for area sex offenders and often criminal records**. If not, you may want to consider using a **professional research service** as discussed on the next page.

Professional Research

While the Internet's reach is essentially limitless, **it still comes up a little short when trying to rely on free resources to adequately screen your applicants**. Companies like **AmerUSA.net** were **formed to provide professional research services that not only alleviate the landlord's time and effort, but also ensure you are getting the best and most reliable information** – *which might otherwise be unattainable to the average person.*

Every landlord agrees that *if there is a way to save money without sacrificing comfort or quality, then take advantage of as many free opportunities that come your way!* Therefore, **it is suggested** that you **exhaust your local resources first**; *if you still need further assistance* – or simply have applicants residing out of state – *you should consider having a third party conduct the search for you;* **this is usually done for a reasonable fee of $25 or less for most services**. Just make sure you never underestimate the likelihood of any applicant turning out to be Jesse James or Billy the Kid in sheep's clothing.

Chapter 9

Tenant Screening, Part VI:
Verifications and References

This Chapter Discusses:

★ **Employers**
★ **Landlords**
★ **Friends, Family and Others**

Verifying personal and business references is, for the most part, **still an antiquated process** – much as it used to be when the telegraph was invented back in the days of general stores and saloons. **Whether it's in writing or by phone, some landlords still prefer to continue to verify employment, prior tenancy and personal references.** The ironic aspect to this, of course, is that *it's unlikely for an applicant to openly disclose a contact that will not give them a favorable endorsement*.

The key to using references as a worthwhile tenant screening tool is, basically, to verify those who were listed as references. <u>**PONDER THIS!**</u>: **When was the last time you can recall** *any* **type of volunteered reference going against the grain and** *actually* **giving a negative recommendation?** References were far more useful back in the chuck wagon days, when a person's word used to be as good as gold (or at least as solid as oak). *Verifications and references may only be necessary when the unbiased official data (such as credit reports and criminal*

records) have blemishes that cause you to be concerned. Otherwise, **as long as the criminal record is clear and there is a strong payment history on file, you may forgo the needless games of phone tag and repetitive faxing.**

Employers

Don't be surprised if you sometimes feel that trying to verify someone's employment is like pulling teeth – *especially among the larger companies that have their toll-free or 900-H.R. number hotlines that require a ridiculous fee to simply verify your applicant's employment.* **Employers either don't want to be bothered** or are **too paranoid about the potential legal liability in rendering an opinion or offering information** about one of their employees. *You'll be lucky if you're able to verify how much money your prospective tenant earns.*

But enough of the banter – let's get down to business. First of all, *is it necessary for you to actually verify your applicant's employment?* After all, they could easily lose their job the next day. **The point is that – somewhere along the way – everyone has a lapse in employment (as a result of being laid off, resigning, being terminated).** There is *one theory* that says that if your applicant has been able to demonstrate over time the ability to satisfy their obligations regardless of the ups and down, does it really matter *at this particular point* whether or not he or she has a job?

Whether it's a tightening of the belt or friends and family that keep one going during the hard times, *a candidate who successfully gets through this type of predicament is a much better choice than someone who is gainfully employed but has been late on several personal accounts.* Odd, isn't it? But the fact of the matter is: **credit "worthiness" is *not* based upon your job** – if it were, then many people with high credit scores wouldn't be able to buy a home with no money down and without ever having to produce income or asset documentation (this is true of buying a car too). An applicant's income rarely ever matters – that's because credit reports have shown themselves to be a very reliable underwriting tool over the past 30 years.

It's up to you, but as long as the applicant's credit is good, there is very little need to verify income and employment status. You may still disagree, but keep in mind **this approach is only recommended for those applicants scoring at least 650 or above.**

If you do go ahead with contacting the employer to find out more information, then **the best way to proceed is with a standard form called** a "**Verification of Employment" (VOE).** The VOE, as mentioned earlier in **Chapter 5**, should be used to obtain as much information as the employer is willing to disclose – *a sample is shown on the next page*; you can also find one **on the enclosed CD-ROM.**

This form enables you to approach any employer – large or small – in a professional manner, *so you are given the attention you deserve.* You may still be at the bottom of the stack, but at least you're not in the shredding pile.

The **VOE** is **designed to be faxed to the personnel director** (whomever that may be; it may even be the owner of the company) **to solicit a written and signed response,** attesting to *the applicant's position within the company, their hire date, the likelihood of continued employment, etc.* While it's a great form, don't get your hopes up too high, as you will soon discover that *many employers don't like to provide some of the information requested.*

Everything U Need to Know...™

Verification of Employment (VOE)

AMERICAN LANDLORD
1234 Make Believe St
Anytown, USA 12345
Ph (555) 555-5555
Fx (555) 555-5555

Request for Verification of Employment

Part I - Request
Employer - Please complete either Part II or Part III as applicable. Complete Part IV and return directly to management listed above.

To: (Name and Address of Employer)

Attn:
Company:
Address:
City: State: ZIP Code:
Ph: Fax:

Applicant Information

Name:

Address:

City: State: ZIP Code:

Employee ID: Department: Badge #:

I have applied for residency and stated that I am now or was formerly employed by you. My signature below (*or accompanying Applicant Signature Authorization) authorizes verification of this information.

*Signature of applicant: Date:

Part II - Verification of Present Employment

Applicant's Present Position:

Probability of Continued Employment: Hire Date:

Gross Base Pay: $ Hourly   Weekly   Annually   (Please circle)   Bonus Income: $

For Military Personnel Only (Monthly Amounts)

Base Pay: $ Rations: $ Clothing: $

Quarters: $ Flight or Hazard: $ Variable Housing Allowance: $

Remarks:

Part III - Verification of Previous Employment

Position Held: Hire Date:

Reason for Leaving: Termination Date:

Gross Base Pay: $ Hourly   Weekly   Annually   (Please circle)   Bonus Income: $

Part IV - Authorized Signature

Name: Title: Phone:

Signature of employer: Date:

This form provided by USLandlord.com

SAMPLE

Verbal verifications over the phone are – for one – not documented. *It's always important to obtain and maintain a folder on your tenant, because you never know when you may need certain information.* While it may save you some time to place a quick phone call (that is, if you can actually get through to the appropriate person), **it's a good idea to get the company representative to use the VOE** *– so you will have the same response but sealed with the representative's name, title and signature.*

There is one final item of note about employers for you to keep in mind:

If you are taking the time to verify employment references, you might as well be comfortable with the fact that the employer even exists. So **take an additional five minutes to see if the company is listed either in directory assistance, with the Better Business Bureau or with the department that governs business registrations for your state** (usually, the **Secretary of State**). There have been **too many instances where people actually have been deceptive enough to get a friend, sibling or cousin to act on their behalf and give them rave reviews all the way around** *– the exact same situation applies with current and previous landlords.* Just **be sure you are comfortable with the impression that you receive** when speaking with the supposed "employer."

Landlords

Is my applicant going to be a good tenant? This chapter is not intended to be pessimistic; however, *let's seriously think about this question.* Let's assume that you are the current landlord and you have had a really bad time with a particular tenant of yours (late payments, suspicion of drug use, whatever). **If another landlord contacts you to verify tenancy** (as, apparently, this tenant has applied to go elsewhere – yeah!) – and you generously agreed to give them a right to renew clause in the lease agreement – *are you going to take a chance on being brutally honest about the tenant's problems and run the risk of having the tenant stick around your place for another term… or do you want to ensure they are able to move out with flying colors?*

This all goes back to the archaic nature of verifications and references. **You just don't know with whom or with what circumstances you are truly dealing when contacting someone like a current landlord.** *Previous landlords, on the other hand, can offer you invaluable insight, since they are fully detached from the tenant at this point and have nothing to lose by being honest.* In either case, **if you are uncomfortable with the applicant's credit report,** *you should not call the landlord.* Instead, *you need to take the same approach as with employers and document as much as you can in writing*.

There is a **form specifically for landlords** called a **"Verification of Rent" (VOR)** – a *sample of this form is provided on the following page* and can also be found *on the enclosed CD-ROM*. Similar to a **VOE**, this form is **intended to collect pertinent information in writing from the current landlord.** Once again, *you need to have records such as these for your files*… because you just never know what may happen.

Verification of Rent (VOR)

AMERICAN LANDLORD
1234 Make Believe St
Anytown, USA 12345
Ph (555) 555-5555
Fx (555) 555-5555

Request for Verification of Rent

Part I - Request

Landlord - Please complete either Part II or Part III as applicable. Complete Part IV and return directly to management listed above.

To: (Name and Address of Landlord)

Attn:
Company:
Address:
City: State: ZIP Code:
Ph: Fax:

Applicant Information

Name:

Address:

City: State: ZIP Code:

I have applied for residency and stated that I am now or was formerly your tenant. My signature below (*or accompanying Applicant Signature Authorization) authorizes verification of this information.

*Signature of applicant: Date:

Part II - Verification of Present Tenancy

Tenant has rented since (month/day/year):

Rent Amount: $ Weekly   Monthly   (Please circle)   Pets?:   Yes   No   (Please circle)

Number of times 30 days past due in last 12 months:

Remarks:

Part III - Verification of Previous Tenancy

Tenant has rented from (month/day/year):   to (month/day/year):

Rent Amount: $ Weekly   Monthly   (Please circle)   Pets?:   Yes   No   (Please circle)

Number of times 30 days past due in last 12 months (if applicable):

Remarks:

Part IV - Authorized Signature

Name: Title: Phone:

Signature of landlord: Date:

This form provided by USLandlord.com

SAMPLE

Landlords, just like employers, should also be checked out to the best of your ability. Search the local property tax records by going online to the **County Tax Collector**'s **website** and *see who actually owns the property* at the tenant's address. Hopefully, the rental is in the landlord's name – or perhaps a business entity that can be traced back to the landlord. If not, then **find out what's** *really* **going on!** Most honest people don't have any problem answering a few informational questions. *Ironically, it's actually common for parents and friends to pose as the current or previous landlord* – how would you know, right? Fortunately, **established apartment communities are easy to accept as factual information providers** – it's the **single family homes and condos that you just don't know** about – *eviction search, anyone?* Remember, it's **a mighty valuable backup tool**, if the applicant's credit is below par.

Friends, Family and Others

Getting references from those that know the applicant on a personal level is really only necessary if you are considering someone you discovered has been in trouble with the law *or* has serious financial problems. If it's a previous criminal conviction, you may want to consider *requesting permission to contact the probation officer* (if one was assigned); *otherwise, everyone listed on the application should be approached.*

Personal references, as you'd expect, **are going to be overly biased** and *should only be accepted if the reference is willing to write a formal letter of recommendation*. Although this may seem difficult to request, **if the reference is** *genuinely* **in favor of the applicant, they will help in any way possible to attest to the person's character, integrity and ability and willingness** to satisfy the terms of your lease.

When someone is willing to take the time to write a letter of recommendation, it speaks volumes over any verbal conversation. Sure, the **opinions are still going**

to be sugar-coated, but if you are insistent on accepting an applicant that needs references, *the only legitimate course of action is to ask for a letter to be mailed or faxed, explaining why this person is a good candidate for tenancy.*

> *I'll be the first one to admit that I am very skeptical about any applicant that wants to rent out my apartment above my convenient store. I just can't afford any problems because there is too much on the table for me to lose. There is one instance I can recall where this young kid (about 20 years old) needed a place to live but had very little credit, most of which was bad. He basically begged me and took it upon himself to have a couple of people (including a family friend who was a local fire fighter) write some letters on his behalf. This kid really showed a strong interest and was able to bring some character to the table which I thought was worth giving him a chance. He was late one time, but he was also a good tenant.*

K. Peterson
Kansas
Landlord

When discussing an applicant with any third party such as a personal reference, employer or landlord, *it is illegal to disclose or discuss any information contained on the applicant's consumer credit report - including account numbers, types of accounts, addresses, balances, etc.* **Always** remember to keep every bit of your applicant's personal information strictly confidential, as if it were your own personal information at stake.

CAUTION

The reality is that **you are bound to encounter those that** *truly do need a second chance and are desperate to redeem themselves in the best manner possible.* Some landlords have no tolerance for major mistakes – which is their prerogative; they can do what they want to do. But **if you are the type of landlord kind enough to give that chance, then letters from friends and family may actually help you to put your mind at ease**. *Just get it in writing for your records!*

Tenant Screening, Part VII: Wrangling Common Scenarios

This Chapter Discusses:

★ **Divorce**

★ **Medical Collections**

★ **Bankruptcy**

★ **Foreclosure**

★ **No Credit Score**

★ **No Credit History**

Not everyone is perfect – though you've probably discovered this many years ago. So **what do you do when your applicant's financial results come back and show a derogatory past?** You are probably wondering **when – or if – there are any exceptions**. After all, they *seemed* like such nice people – it's just that their credit file appears to be a lot worse than what was expected. Fortunately, *there are a few things you can look for that might help you sleep better at night knowing that you made the right decision* – one way or the other.

Sometimes, it's difficult to give the applicant the benefit of the doubt – especially if you've been burned before by previous tenants. This chapter focuses on **the most popular scenarios that are encountered regularly and discusses how to deal with the applicant's excuses or reasons that will often accompany each of them.**

Divorce

Without doubt – and 99% of those who have experienced it would agree! – **this definitely (and appropriately) tops the list.** *Divorce is the most commonly used reason why someone's credit report is poor* – **"I'm going (or went) through a bad divorce."**

True, divorce is rarely a pleasant experience to begin with, but *beware of those who use the misfortune as an excuse* – and are actually trying to tell you that, *even though they were aware of all of these accounts in their own name, their "ex" didn't pay the bills…* "so please blame my ex, not me." Great! So how do you now deal with this delicate matter, since you are now aware that **this reason is abused more than any other single excuse?**

Love is grand, they say – or, is it more aptly put: **love will** *cost you a grand* **one day?** **Before you challenge your applicant's explanation, you need to fish for a little more information.**

Here is what you need to find out and why:

➤ *When did the divorce occur?*

It is important to **understand the approximate time frame in which you would expect to see the derogatory information begin to appear** on the credit report. **If the majority of debt with negative remarks appears years before or after the supposed divorce,** *then you have a discrepancy on your hands that needs to be addressed.*

Someone who says they got divorced in 2003, but shows an unpaid utility in 1999, 2001 and 2005 or has an automobile repossession in 2001, an unpaid judgment in 2004 and credit card late payments in 2006 **evidences a pattern pointing to a *bad consumer***, not a bad divorce.

> ### ➤ *Did you guarantee (co-sign) any accounts?*

The **credit report will actually indicate if it's an individual or joint account**, but **you want to hear more about what caused the problems and whether or not the story checks out** – *so don't share your findings with the applicant until you've had a chance to review everything.* Just **let them feed you with as much information** as your ears can bear to hear.

Ultimately, *if you can see a direct correlation between the bad relationship and the bad debt, then the story is most likely valid.* However, **you must then decide if you want someone who is *possibly* not responsible enough to take charge of his or her personal finances.** What if they are planning on moving into your rental with a new partner and that relationship proceeds to go sour? *It's up to you to decide if the explanation behind the troubled finances is something you can personally accept.*

BY THE WAY: **Mortgage lenders, banks and other creditors don't hand out exceptions for bad divorces.** So, **this is your opportunity to humanize the situation if you choose** – *but make sure you are comfortable with* **all** *of the facts.*

I've encountered the divorce excuse so many times that I have a standard questionnaire I give those applicants that are quick to disclose they have credit problems for that reason. I simply want to know: how, what, where, when and why so I can see if it matches up (even a little) with what's on the credit report. I understand divorce, I've been through one, but I expect the person to be honest with me about their financial situation.

L. Harting
Maine
Landlord

Medical Collections

With the disarray in the U.S. healthcare system, you will see a lot of **medical collections** showing up on credit files. **Depending on your personal experiences, you may or may not dismiss them as easily as others.** It is safe to say that *medical debt has been considered by most credit grantors to be the lowest on the totem pole* as far as how much weight is given to this type of delinquency. People don't decide one day to take themselves or their child to visit a doctor or hospital emergency room without just cause. **These types of circumstances are usually beyond one's control –** *as opposed to other collection accounts, such as cell phones and credit cards,* which are initiated by consumers who simply change their mind midstream and decide to stop paying them altogether.

The prevalence of medical collections is widespread. **It is not uncommon to see a dozen or so medical collections for a single applicant** – many of which appear to be due to laboratory results or physicians' fees that are often related to emergency room visits. It is solely up to you to bring your own personal experience to the table – but **with escalating healthcare costs and insurance which is often unattainable, it's rare that an applicant is turned down based on medical collection accounts alone** – other factors usually prove to be the cause.

T. Jones
Oregon
Landlord

The problem with most tenants and medical collections that I've seen is that it is very difficult to regain a positive credit rating if you can't afford to pay a large hospital bill. Once you have a collection account on file, your credit rating becomes instantly poor and you can't apply for any good credit opportunities. Instead, you are forced to apply to those "loan shark" finance companies. I immediately dismiss all medical collections and look for more important accounts such as late payments on credit cards in the past year.

The truly unfortunate thing for those who cannot afford to pay for an impromptu visit to the ER is that it *will* **have a negative impact on their credit score**. *Since most credit decisions are score-driven, the chances of getting a favorable interest rate or financing program are limited,* which can diminish the quality of life and cause further financial stress that may have been manageable with a better program or rate.

Every **American Landlord** is encouraged to review the entire credit file on low-scoring applicants to determine where the problems lie – and **if medical collections happen to be discovered, you should see if any** *other* **accounts have late payments**, such as automobiles, credit cards, mortgages, etc. **If the prospective tenant's payments have been on time for the majority of their revolving and installment accounts, credit scoring is often thrown out the window, since the score is greatly affected by collection activity.** *As long as there are no other serious delinquencies, then it's okay to think about accepting someone whose credit report is bogged down by unforeseen circumstances.*

Bankruptcy

This is automatically a bad thing, right? Not necessarily. As you may already know, **bankruptcy is when people reach a point in their lives where they can no longer afford to satisfy their existing creditor obligations.** It's unfortunate, but *it happens all the time to those that had good intentions from the start, tried their best, but couldn't hang on any longer because the odds were stacked against them.*

There are *essentially two types of bankruptcy filings for individuals* that will commonly appear on a credit report – "**Chapter 7**" and "**Chapter 13.**" *Chapter 7* requires a person to *liquidate any property and assets that are not determined to be exempt*, in order to repay the creditors. *Chapter 13* allows the person to *keep his or her assets, but they must repay a portion of their obligations back to the original creditor* for the next several years. The amount and duration are determined by the size of the person's income, alongside current debt and assets. **To prevent abuse of the system,** *you can only file for bankruptcy protection once every eight years* according to the **Bankruptcy Abuse Prevention and Consumer Protection Act**, which became effective on October 17, 2005.

So **what does this all mean when you discover a bankruptcy** on file for one of your applicants? **For many, this may not mean anything as long as those accounts that were opened, or remained open, after the bankruptcy have been consistently reported as paid on time.** *The problem occurs when someone files for bankruptcy, but shows no signs of redemption on their credit file after the fact.*

Most people make at least one major financial blunder in the early stages of their lives and then learn from the experience. *It's okay to have made a mistake or two in the past, but when it becomes a recurring problem…* **well, there is** *very little* **a landlord can do to become comfortable.** This is when **you may ask for rent to be prepaid six to twelve months in advance.** Yes, this actually does happen, but don't count on seeing it too often – most people don't have that much cash saved. **Anytime you are going outside the normal parameters of what is deemed to be a good candidate,** *be sure to watch for the right red flags.*

Foreclosure

It's hard to reject someone who is facing foreclosure. After all, this is why the person *wants* to rent from you in the first place. It's a very depressing situation to be in – they are losing their home, have no place to go and their credit is shot due to several late payments.

Applicant's Current Mortgage Payment – 30% = Maximum Rent Amount

In order to consider a person going under foreclosure, you need to do some very basic math: *What you're looking for is to compare their monthly mortgage amount against what you are charging for rent.* If you don't see **your rent being at least 30% (preferably 40% or more) less than the mortgage payment they couldn't afford**, *then the rent probably won't arrive on time for too long.*

It's a basic money management issue that many just don't get – *and one which you see all the time.* A person can't afford to make a $3,500 mortgage payment (inclusive of principal, interest, taxes and insurance), so they lose the home and apply for a $3,000 rental – smooth move, right? *Chances are, if money was that tight to begin with and the person was willing to be that late on their mortgage, then what's the big deal being late on your rent?*

If the foreclosure occurred more than two years ago, comparison calculations aren't really necessary. You just need to *keep an eye out for those who continue making late payments on their other accounts years after being foreclosed upon.* If you are **willing to lower your standards once in a while,** *there are plenty of people out there who have demonstrated a good effort to bounce back and deserve another chance* to feel at home again.

It's been hard times for a lot of people and I have dealt with a number of applicants facing foreclosure. The ironic thing is that some of these people didn't seem to be saving any money to make sure the rent was going to be paid. Not only do I like to see the rent much lower than where their mortgage was, I also want to know what are they doing about getting control of the situation. If they are unable to come up with a basic strategy to help get them through this, then I'm sorry—I can't take the chance of renting to them—I have my own bills to pay on time.

J. Houston
Michigan
Landlord

No Credit Score

You pull the credit report and it comes back without a credit score. **Applicants without a credit score usually have insufficient credit or no account activity for the past six months**. The credit history can be either good or bad – it doesn't matter, because *if you have a dormant file, you don't generate a score.*

It's a **hurdle that can be overcome by simply jumping right into the report to review any collection activity and payment history** on any of the listed **tradelines** (accounts). Some may be a year old; others may be five or more years old. *If you can confirm that there were either no or minimal delinquencies reported* (such as one 30-day late payment), *the prospective tenant is probably okay*. **Just because there is no score doesn't mean the person is an automatic "no go"** – just **make sure *you* know how to read and understand credit report results** (see **Chapter 6**).

No Credit History

Commonly referred to as **"no hit"** or **"no record,"** *this is when the credit bureaus do not have any information on file for your applicant.* Don't be alarmed yet, because **a person can have no credit history for any of the following reasons:**

- **The person has never bothered to apply for credit** (no credit cards, car loans, mortgages, etc.); their money is basically kept under the mattress.
- **The applicant is a young adult**, perhaps fresh out of school.
- **The information that was inputted into the credit system to request a report was mistakenly entered – *either because of human error or because the handwritten application was genuinely indecipherable or unintentionally inaccurate*** (i.e., *"Lisa Petelle"* was actually typed in as *"Lisa Patel"*).
- **The applicant is intentionally trying to deceive you.**

With all these different types of possible scenarios, **you can see how you don't want to rush to judgment and accuse your applicant of doing something wrong**, when – in all likelihood – it's because either *the person honestly doesn't have credit* or there was an *innocent case of human error*. As stated in **Chapter 4**, *it's pretty easy to eliminate the last (and worst) possible reason merely by asking to see a driver's license and social security card.*

If the resulting record was eventually determined *not* **to be a human error and is a legitimate record of no credit history, then you should take the following steps**:

☆ **Step 1: Ask the applicant if they have a personal checking or savings account, so you can contact the bank for a reference.**
If you have used an appropriate rental application, *most banks will accept this as an authorization to verify* such things as the average daily collected balance, the current ledger balance and whether or not there were any bounced checks ("NSF"s) within the last six to twelve months. If the bank rejects your application, then you simply need to *go back to the applicant and have them sign a consent form that complies with the bank's requirements*.

☆ **Step 2: Ask for utility and any other reputable third-party statements that may show a positive payment history over the past 12 months.**

☆ **Step 3: As a last resort, you may want to consider asking the applicant if he or she knows someone (with a good credit rating) that would be willing to co-sign and guarantee the lease.**

It's certainly not an easy task to overcome a lack of credit history, but, *if you dig deep enough, you should be able to make a decision that you're ultimately comfortable with*, regardless of the outcome. **The burden of proof rests on the prospective tenant to bring forth evidence of their being a good credit risk**. This is not your responsibility – but if you want to appear accommodating, **the best way is to offer as many alternatives for supporting documentation as you are willing to accept.** Then **set a reasonable deadline**, hope for the best and *be sure never to turn down a back-up application from another interested party*.

Chapter 11

Tenant Screening, Part VIII: Turning Away the Herd

This Chapter Discusses:

★ **Making a Business Decision (including How to Deal with Denial Anxiety)**

★ **Notifying the Applicant**

★ **Protecting Yourself**

No good person ever really wants to reject or refuse service to anyone – whether it's a bank, employer, insurance company or whatever. **If the applicant doesn't meet your minimum requirements** *(those same requirements that have been applied to all other, potential tenants – regardless of race, color, creed or sexual orientation),* **then there is not much left for you to do, aside from turning that person down.** *After all, in the end, remember it's strictly business.*

Making a Business Decision

It's an odd thing to say, but **you *must* depersonalize the experience** – because **all you are doing when either accepting or rejecting an application** is *strictly making a business decision*. Too many individual landlords, in particular, dread **the "turndown."** Sure, **the applicant will be disappointed,** *but don't allow your emotions to get the best of you.* In fact, **the easiest way to avoid too much hardship is to preface the whole event with your own little caveat at the time you accept a tenant's application.**

For those that have **"denial anxiety,"** it's sometimes *much easier* to tell someone as they are applying that you are considering at least one other applicant that claims to have marginal credit. **You do not want to over-exaggerate by saying the other one has good credit, because this could easily deter anyone else from applying if they feel their own credit is less than perfect –** *after all, who wants to run the risk of paying a non-refundable application fee?* And unless you *really do* have another prospect lined up, you might find your property vacant again for yet another month! **If it makes you feel better not having to lie, then just be candid with them about the stringency of your individual guidelines.**

J. Miller
Hawaii
Landlord

I hated having to deny anyone, my stomach used to sink every time until I decided to approach the whole situation as an open casting call, just like American Idol. Every applicant that came my way, I told them that I had a few more people interested and would be reviewing all applications before making my decision. Not only did it help ease my discomfort, it also got me to actually consider multiple applications which enabled me to screen for the best of the bunch. In the past, I only processed one application as opposed to three or more.

In the end, as long **as you have given the applicant** *every possible courtesy* **when reviewing their application** – including *thoroughly and carefully considering* the person's credit report, eviction record, criminal record, employment, references and (for those with problems) even suggesting a list of acceptable alternative documents, **it's okay if the applicant doesn't pass muster – you've tried your best to be accommodating.** And, as cliché as it sounds, **you'll get used to it**. In fact, *you need to prepare yourself to review and turn down as many applications as it takes to find a decent tenant*. Otherwise, **you may be inclined to accept somebody who is just too much of a risk at a time when local market conditions don't justify lowering your standards** so substantially.

Notifying the Applicant

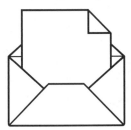 **It's up to you how you want to notify the applicant that their application was not approved.** If it's a local person, the **U.S. Postal Service** will *reach them within two business days* with your **Statement of Credit Denial** – or *if the applicant is anxiously waiting to hear from you, then simply pick up the phone and take care of business right away.*

<u>**DON'T FORGET, THOUGH**</u>: *Even if you choose to notify them by phone, you will still have to mail each rejected applicant* a **Statement of Credit Denial** (commonly known as a denial letter), detailed in **Chapter 7**.

REMEMBER: **It is always important to follow the law** and the **Fair Credit Reporting Act**, governed by the **Federal Trade Commission**, *which requires a denial letter to be issued.* Although verbal notifications are allowed under the **Act,** *it's standard practice to mail one, as no applicant wants to remain on the phone after being rejected* – just so you can save a stamp and envelope by reading the entire federal required notice. Once again, you can find a **Statement of Credit Denial** on the **enclosed CD-ROM**.

When it comes time to place the call, one thing is for certain: *you should never elaborate on the reason(s) behind your decision*. This can **expose you to a whole world of legal problems should the prospective tenant decide to challenge your decision**. So it's best – whether on the phone or in a denial letter – to **simplify your answer** to *one or more* of the following reasons:

- ☆ **Insufficient Credit**
- ☆ **Derogatory Credit**
- ☆ **No Credit History**
- ☆ **Insufficient Income**
- ☆ **Unable to Verify Employment**
- ☆ **Unable to Verify References**
- ☆ **Eviction Record**
- ☆ **Criminal Record**
- ☆ **Civil Judgment**

D. Young
Wisconsin
Landlord

When have you ever had a bank call you to tell you that your application for a new credit card was declined? I always try to avoid talking to the prospective tenant when its time to deliver my decision. I like to document everything I do with my rentals so I always mail my denial notice instead—this helps keep the rapport professional, not personal and if I'm asked questions, I basically regurgitate my written response.

You do not have to share with the person your entire list of requirements. **Every real estate attorney specializing in landlord-tenant law would likely agree to keep it simple** – *nothing more* than the following concept should be conveyed: "I'm sorry, but after carefully considering your application, I am unable to offer you a lease at this time." Of course, after telling this to the applicant, he or she is immediately going to ask, "Why?" **Your response should then be limited to**: "My decision was partially **based on information contained in your consumer credit file** *and you did not meet my current requirements because of* [for example] *insufficient credit*." As you would expect, **this conversation could drag on** – so be *very* matter of fact, *keep it short* and, at some point at the end of the conversation and *as diplomatically as possible*, **you always want to be sure to thank them for applying**.

Protecting Yourself

This is not intended to alarm you, but **you never know what types of applicants you may be dealing with from day to day**.

<u>REMEMBER</u>: **You don't know their background until you at least check them out** – *and that doesn't even guarantee a completely safe situation,* criminals have to start somewhere. There have been **plenty of media stories about violence toward landlords** – *not to mention the violence towards children* that often occurs by a tenant that was not screened at all and happened to live just a few doors down! So, as a precaution, **it is recommended that you do the following**:

> ★ **Set Up a Mailing Address**
> Whether it's at the post office, the UPS Store or local boxing and shipping store, it doesn't matter – *so long as it's not your home address*. **Getting a postal box that also serves as a valid physical address** (i.e., it's *not* a P.O. Box #) **is not only affordable, but can be very convenient for your own personal billing statements** – *especially if* you are the type of person that moves every 3-5 years just within your local area. ***The last thing you need is an irate***

applicant – or even tenant – knowing where you live. Sure, they can easily find out *if* they know where to search, but **why be open about it when the law does not require you to disclose your private residence** – plus how many people have the knowledge of available resources, let alone the time and energy, to actually go to the effort of tracking somebody down? **As long as you maintain a mailing address for lease notifications and rental payments, you are good to go**. *As far as a telephone number, it doesn't hurt to have an unlisted one*.

★ Never Bring an Applicant or Tenant to Your Home

Always meet people at the rental for showings, maintenance, repairs, etc. **This cannot be stressed enough:** *This is not a friendship, it's a business relationship!* **The more personal you get with a tenant** (although this relationship has worked for some), **the greater the risk for problems and increased expectations of "special treatment,"** such as requesting the rent be a little late this month… and then next month… and so on… and so on… and so on… It's kind of like working for a boss who is (or *was*) a friend – you just never know how the relationship will pan out.

It's important to note that, more often than not, the majority of prospective tenants are just like you – law-abiding citizens, trying to make the best for themselves and their family. It's unfortunate that there are a few people out there (landlords included) that have caused a great deal of emotional, financial and physical harm unjustly. *American Landlord* is **intended to help protect the landlord's interests**; for more on the tenant's perspective and options, reference this book's companion volume, *American Tenant*.

Chapter 12

Lease Agreement, Part I:
"Must-Have" Clauses

This Chapter Discusses:

- ★ Sample Lease Agreement
- ★ Subject of Lease
- ★ Term of Lease
- ★ Monthly Rental
- ★ Security Deposit
- ★ Number of Occupants
- ★ Assignment and Subletting
- ★ Showing Property for Rent
- ★ Entry for Inspection, Repairs and Alterations
- ★ Redecoration and Alterations
- ★ Taxes and Utilities
- ★ Maintenance and Repairs
- ★ Pets and Animals
- ★ Waste, Nuisance or Unlawful Use
- ★ Lessee's Holding Over
- ★ Redelivery of Premises
- ★ Default
- ★ Destruction of Premises and Eminent Domain
- ★ Delay in or Impossibility of Delivery of Possession
- ★ Binding Effect
- ★ Governing Law
- ★ Attorney Fees
- ★ Entire Agreement
- ★ Modification of Agreement
- ★ Paragraph Headings

Better known as *"the law of the land,"* **the lease agreement** is both your six-gun and your lever-action rifle, equipped with enough ammunition to stand your ground at the O.K. Corral. The problem is that *landlords often fail to recognize the importance of drafting a few pieces of paper*. **Instead, they use a generic form from a friend or some obscure website that comes with nothing more than a single page (***maybe*** two… if the signature lines spill over onto a second page), leaving you with very little ammunition – certainly not enough should there ever be a showdown.

Aside from getting a good tenant, **having an ironclad lease agreement is paramount for your protection** – and the ironic thing is that *many landlords don't even understand most of the lease agreement they have the tenant sign*. **Don't pass up an opportunity to control the language (within reason)** that says what a tenant *can* and *cannot* do while leasing your property. **For those that have the available finances, this is the time you should seek professional legal advice from an experienced real estate attorney**. *Otherwise, pay close attention to this chapter* to see exactly what is recommended for the **standard lease agreement**.

Sample Lease Agreement

Don't be intimidated now… the following four pages contain an entire *sample of a protective lease agreement*. The **main clauses** will be addressed, so you can easily understand the importance and reasoning behind *why you should consider incorporating them for your own use*. (Just in case you didn't know, the **landlord** is defined as the **"lessor"** and the **tenant** is the **"lessee."**) And as you've probably guessed, *a printer-friendly template of this very same lease agreement has also been included on the enclosed CD-ROM.*

Lease Agreement

Instructions:
1. Insert your IMAGE or LOGO (optional)
2. Highlight & complete LEASE AGREEMENT FIELDS
3. REPLACE ALL of this text with YOUR contact info
4. Click on 'PRINT FORM' when finished

Everything U Need to Know...

Click here to insert image/logo

Residential Lease Agreement

AGREEMENT TO LEASE

This agreement is entered into between _____, of
_____, _____County,
_____, referred to as "lessor," and _____, of
_____, _____County,
_____, referred to as "lessee."

RECITALS

A. Lessor is the owner and/or manager of real property that is available for lease.

B. Lessee desires to lease residential property to occupy and use as their residence.

C. The parties desire to establish an agreement to ensure a future lease of the residential property described in this agreement.

In consideration of the matters described above, and of the mutual benefits and obligations set forth in this agreement, the parties agree as follows:

SECTION I - SUBJECT OF LEASE

Lessor shall lease to prospective lessee the residential property owned by prospective lessor located at _____, _____, _____County, _____, for lessee and their family to occupy and use as their residence.

SECTION II - TERM OF LEASE

The premises shall be leased to lessee for a period of _____ starting from _____. Any option to renew, extend or modify this lease shall require the approval of both the lessee and lessor.

SECTION III - MONTHLY RENTAL

Lessee shall pay $ _____ per month as the monthly rental for the term of the lease with the first payment due on or before _____, and subsequent payments on the _____ day of each succeeding month. This rental payment shall be subject to renegotiation by the parties at any time either of the parties exercises the option to renew the lease under the provisions of any subsequent lease agreement. It is agreed that if the rental payment is not received by the _____ day of the month, then a late fee of _____ shall be assessed and due immediately. Additional terms: _____

SECTION IV - SECURITY DEPOSIT

On the execution of this lease, lessee deposits with lessor $ _____, receipt of which is acknowledged by lessor, as security for the faithful performance by lessee of the terms of this lease agreement, to be returned to lessee, without interest (unless required by law), on the full and faithful performance by lessee of the provisions of this residential lease agreement.

SAMPLE

Lease Agreement

SECTION V - NUMBER OF OCCUPANTS

Lessee agrees that the leased apartment shall be occupied by no more than _____ adults and _____ children under the age of 18 years without the prior, express, and written consent of lessor.

SECTION VI - ASSIGNMENT AND SUBLETTING

Without the prior, express, and written consent of lessor, lessee shall not assign this lease, or sublet the premises or any part of the premises. A consent by lessor to one assignment or subletting shall not be deemed to be a consent to any subsequent assignment or subletting.

SECTION VII - SHOWING PROPERTY FOR RENTAL

Lessee grants permission to lessor to show the property to new rental applicants with reasonable advance notice and during reasonable hours of the day, within 30 days of the expiration of the term of this lease.

SECTION VIII - ENTRY FOR INSPECTION, REPAIRS AND ALTERATIONS

Lessor shall have the right to enter the leased premises with reasonable advance notice for inspection and whenever necessary to make repairs and alterations of the property.

SECTION IX - REDECORATION AND ALTERATIONS

It is agreed that lessee will not make or permit to be made any alterations, additions, improvements, or changes in the leased property without in each case first obtaining the written consent of lessor. A consent to a particular alteration, addition, improvement, or change shall not be deemed a consent to or a waiver of restrictions against alterations, additions, improvements, or changes for the future. All alterations, changes, and improvements built, constructed, or placed in the leased property by lessee, with the exception of fixtures removable without damage to the apartment and movable personal property, shall, unless otherwise provided by written agreement between lessor and lessee, be the property of lessor and remain in the leased apartment at the expiration or earlier termination of this lease.

SECTION X - TAXES AND UTILITIES

A. Prospective lessor shall be liable for the payment of all real property taxes assessed against the residential premises as well as the following:

_____

B. Prospective lessee shall be liable for all personal property taxes as well as the following:

_____

SECTION XI - MAINTENANCE/REPAIRS

A. Prospective lessor shall be responsible for the following types of maintenance or repairs on the premises:

_____

B. Prospective lessee shall be responsible for the following types of maintenance or repairs on the premises:

_____

Lease Agreement

SECTION XII - ANIMALS

Lessee shall keep no domestic or other animals in or about the property or on the property premises without the prior, express, and written consent of lessor.

SECTION XIII - WASTE, NUISANCE OR UNLAWFUL USE

Lessee agrees that they will not commit waste on the premises, or maintain or permit to be maintained a nuisance on the premises, or use or permit the premises to be used in an unlawful manner.

SECTION XIV - LESSEE'S HOLDING OVER

The parties agree that any holding over by lessee under this lease, without lessor's written consent, shall be a tenancy at will which may be terminated by lessor on 30 days' notice in writing.

SECTION XV - REDELIVERY OF PREMISES

At the end of the term of this lease, lessee shall quit and deliver up the premises to lessor in as good condition as they are now, ordinary wear, decay, and damage by the elements excepted.

SECTION XVI - DEFAULT

If lessee defaults in the payment of rent or any part of the rent at the times specified above, or if lessee defaults in the performance of or compliance with any other term or condition of this lease agreement *[or of the regulations attached to and made a part of this lease agreement, which regulations shall be subject to occasional amendment or addition by lessor]*, the lease, at the option of lessor, shall terminate and be forfeited, and lessor may reenter the premises and retake possession and recover damages, including costs and attorney fees. Lessee shall be given 30 days *[written]* notice of any default or breach. Termination and forfeiture of the lease shall not result if, within 15 days of receipt of such notice, lessee has corrected the default or breach or has taken action reasonably likely to effect correction within a reasonable time.

SECTION XVII - DESTRUCTION OF PREMISES AND EMINENT DOMAIN

In the event the leased premises are destroyed or rendered untenantable by fire, storm, or earthquake, or other casualty not caused by the negligence of lessee, or if the leased premises are taken by eminent domain, this lease shall be at an end from such time except for the purpose of enforcing rights that may have then accrued under this lease agreement. The rental shall then be accounted for between lessor and lessee up to the time of such injury or destruction or taking of the premises, lessee paying up to such date and lessor refunding the rent collected beyond such date. Should a part only of the leased premises be destroyed or rendered untenantable by fire, storm, earthquake, or other casualty not caused by the negligence of lessee, the rental shall abate in the proportion that the injured part bears to the whole leased premises. The part so injured shall be restored by lessor as speedily as practicable, after which the full rent shall recommence and the lease continue according to its terms. Any condemnation award concerning the leased premises shall belong exclusively to lessor.

SECTION XVIII - DELAY IN OR IMPOSSIBILITY OF DELIVERY OF POSSESSION

In the event possession cannot be delivered to lessee on commencement of the lease term, through no fault of lessor or lessor's agents, there shall be no liability on lessor or lessor's agents, but the rental provided in this lease agreement shall abate until possession is given. Lessor or lessor's agents shall have 30 days in which to give possession, and if possession is tendered within that time, lessee agrees to accept the leased premises and this lease agreement. In the event possession cannot be delivered within that time, through no fault of lessor or lessor's agents, then this lease and all rights under this lease agreement shall be at an end.

SAMPLE

Everything U Need to Know...

Lease Agreement

SECTION XIX - BINDING EFFECT

The covenants and conditions contained in this lease agreement shall apply to and bind the heirs, legal representatives, and assigns of the parties to this lease agreement, and all covenants are to be construed as conditions of this lease.

SECTION XX - GOVERNING LAW

It is agreed that this agreement shall be governed by, construed, and enforced in accordance with the laws of the State of _____.

SECTION XXI - ATTORNEY FEES

In the event that any action is filed in relation to this agreement, the unsuccessful party in the action shall pay to the successful party, in addition to all the sums that either party may be called on to pay, a reasonable sum for the successful party's attorney fees.

SECTION XXII - ENTIRE AGREEMENT

This agreement shall constitute the entire agreement between the parties. Any prior understanding or representation of any kind preceding the date of this agreement shall not be binding upon either party except to the extent incorporated in this agreement.

SECTION XXIII - MODIFICATION OF AGREEMENT

Any modification of this agreement or additional obligation assumed by either party in connection with this agreement shall be binding only if evidenced in a writing signed by each party or an authorized representative of each party.

SECTION XXIV - PARAGRAPH HEADINGS

The titles to the paragraphs of this agreement are solely for the convenience of the parties and shall not be used to explain, modify, simplify, or aid in the interpretation of the provisions of this agreement.

In witness of the above, each party to this agreement has caused it to be executed on the date indicated below.

Signature of lessor: _____ Date: _____

Signature of lessee: _____ Date: _____

Signature of lessee: _____ Date: _____

This form provided by USLandlord.com

SAMPLE

Subject of Lease

This section specifies the *physical location* (street address, city, county and state) **of the property that is the subject of the lease** and *spells out the purpose for which it will be used*. **If your lease does not specify an intended use, then the tenant could (for example) use it for a business or exploit whatever zoning rights are available under the law**, of which you may not approve. **Hence, the need to include a** *specified purpose*.

SECTION I - SUBJECT OF LEASE

Lessor shall lease to prospective lessee the residential property owned by prospective lessor located at

_____, _____, _____County,

_____, for lessee and their family to occupy and use as their residence.

Term of Lease

As you would expect, **you must define** *the term of the lease* and *options*. **Most leases are for one year**, but **you can always rent month-to-month** – *or even for several years* if the tenant agrees. As far as the **right to renew, extend or modify**, *it's usually a good idea to leave this open-ended* – by *requiring both parties* to agree to **such changes. If you should guarantee the tenant the right to renew with a right of first refusal**, *you could be stuck with a bad tenant* – or perhaps somebody with whom you just didn't get along – for another year… or more.

SECTION II - TERM OF LEASE

The premises shall be leased to lessee for a period of _____ starting from

_____. Any option to renew, extend or modify this lease shall require the approval

of both the lessee and lessor.

Monthly Rental

Most lease agreements are paid monthly. This section spells out **how much the rent will be and when it is due.** The landlord **often collects the first month's rent in advance at the time of the lease signing** – *with all future payments due on a particular day of each month.* **This section is also a good place to spell out the late fees and returned check fees.** In most states, *it is customary to charge a flat fee or percentage of the month's rent, if the tenant fails to pay by a certain number of days* after the due date. If necessary, you can easily tailor your lease agreement to include additional terms required by your state.

You must always know and obey the law! *Most states have laws dictating how much (and when) you can charge a tenant for being late or bouncing a check.* Please see **Appendix C:** *Landlord-Tenant Laws* **at the back of this book** or the **enclosed CD-ROM** for a **summary of each state's requirements.**

SECTION III - MONTHLY RENTAL

Lessee shall pay $ _____ per month as the monthly rental for the term of the lease with the first payment due on or before _____ , and subsequent payments on the ____ day of each succeeding month. This rental payment shall be subject to renegotiation by the parties at any time either of the parties exercises the option to renew the lease under the provisions of any subsequent lease agreement. It is agreed that if the rental payment is not received by the ____ day of the month, then a late fee of ____ shall be assessed and due immediately. Additional terms: _____

_____

Security Deposit

This is an *essential* **part of any lease executed today.** **A security deposit** usually **protects against excessive wear and damage caused by the tenant,** *but can often include loss of rent.* **Some landlords also add a predetermined cleaning fee** (for example, $250) that is **automatically deducted upon moving out**, *regardless of whether or not there are any major problems.*

Another word of caution concerning the law: Most states **not only tell how much you can charge for a security deposit,** *but will also dictate* **how the money must be kept,** *whether interest must be paid* **and when and under what circumstances it must be returned.** For an **in-depth look at each state's requirements, please see the "Everything U Need to Know" companion volume,** *American Landlord Law.* In addition, a brief **summary of each state's requirements** has been *provided in Appendix C at the back of this book* and on the **enclosed CD-ROM.**

CAUTION

SECTION IV - SECURITY DEPOSIT

On the execution of this lease, lessee deposits with lessor $ _____ , receipt of which is acknowledged by lessor, as security for the faithful performance by lessee of the terms of this lease agreement, to be returned to lessee, without interest (unless required by law), on the full and faithful performance by lessee of the provisions of this residential lease agreement.

Number of Occupants

As you may recall, **this topic was discussed in detail** in **Chapter 4.** **There should be a** *limit on the number of occupants permitted for your property* **and** *additional occupants must be agreed to by you in writing*. Landlords are usually permitted to limit the number of occupants per unit as long as these limits are enforced equally. **Common exceptions protecting the tenant** under some housing laws (or rules) are **pregnancy** and **adoption.** So, unless there is a standard exception in place for pregnancy or adoption, **the only other way the tenant can** *legally* **add an additional occupant is with your written permission.**

SECTION V - NUMBER OF OCCUPANTS

Lessee agrees that the leased apartment shall be occupied by no more than ____ adults and ____ children under the age of 18 years without the prior, express, and written consent of lessor.

Assignment and Subletting

Unless you are more amenable to the idea of automatically giving the tenant the right to assign their lease or sublet to another party than most people tend to be, *it's strongly recommended that you include a clause that requires your approval*. This way, **you have the opportunity to check out the new potential tenant and determine what kind of additional subletting terms** (if any) might then be required.

SECTION VI - ASSIGNMENT AND SUBLETTING

Without the prior, express, and written consent of lessor, lessee shall not assign this lease, or sublet the premises or any part of the premises. A consent by lessor to one assignment or subletting shall not be deemed to be a consent to any subsequent assignment or subletting.

See **Chapter 13** for more information on **subletting** and **the sublease agreement**.

Showing Property for Rent

When your lease is about to expire or terminate, you will be glad you have this section included when it comes to re-renting the apartment – which basically *gives you the right to advertise the upcoming vacancy and show it to prospective tenants with a reasonable advance notice*. No landlord wants a vacant unit and getting a head start (**usually, 30 days**) can only help to reduce any loss.

SECTION VII - SHOWING PROPERTY FOR RENTAL

Lessee grants permission to lessor to show the property to new rental applicants with reasonable advance notice and during reasonable hours of the day, within 30 days of the expiration of the term of this lease.

Entry for Inspection, Repairs and Alterations

Every landlord needs to have the right to enter his or her property with a reasonable amount of notice (*usually, 24-48 hours*) – and it is *customary to set up a*

window of time when you expect to remain at the property, not just a time when you will show up. This is **not just for maintenance and repairs**, it's *also for inspecting the unit for potential lease violations*, such as unauthorized pets or occupants, hazardous materials… and the list goes on.

Most states regulate a landlord's access to his or her rental property when occupied by a tenant (e.g., showing property for rent, entry for inspection, repairs and alterations). **For a summary of each states' Notice of Entry Requirements,** *see* **Appendix C** in the back of this book or **the enclosed CD-ROM.**

CAUTION

SECTION VIII - ENTRY FOR INSPECTION, REPAIRS AND ALTERATIONS

Lessor shall have the right to enter the leased premises with reasonable advance notice for inspection and whenever necessary to make repairs and alterations of the property.

Redecoration and Alterations

The last thing you want is to walk back into a vacant unit that now has a built-in horse trough that was originally designed to be a bathtub – or maybe you discover that your outdoor patio is now a saloon. (Not that this may not be without its advantages…) In all seriousness, **the idea behind this *very important clause* is not only to prevent outrageous occurrences such as these, but also to protect the sanctity of your unit from even the simple stuff like migraine-inducing wallpaper and/or paint colors.** It is *recommended that you require any changes to be approved by you in writing*, except for fixtures that can be easily and safely removed and then *replaced* by the tenant prior to vacating. **It's rare – but every so often, a tenant will come along that will do wonders of improvement for your property and at no cost to you.** These tenants are usually contractors or do-it-yourself gurus that know how to lay tile, put in hardwood floors and perform other aesthetic feats which you may gladly welcome. But I wouldn't exactly hold your breath on that one, partner…

SECTION IX - REDECORATION AND ALTERATIONS

It is agreed that lessee will not make or permit to be made any alterations, additions, improvements, or changes in the leased property without in each case first obtaining the written consent of lessor. A consent to a particular alteration, addition, improvement, or change shall not be deemed a consent to or a waiver of restrictions against alterations, additions, improvements, or changes for the future. All alterations, changes, and improvements built, constructed, or placed in the leased property by lessee, with the exception of fixtures removable without damage to the apartment and movable personal property, shall, unless otherwise provided by written agreement between lessor and lessee, be the property of lessor and remain in the leased apartment at the expiration or earlier termination of this lease.

Taxes and Utilities

Property taxes are always taken care of by the landlord and *personal taxes are – of course – the tenant's responsibility.* However, **utilities are *always* open to negotiation** – so **this section of the lease is an** *absolute "must-have,"* so that there is no disagreement later as to who was supposed to have been paying for what…

SECTION X - TAXES AND UTILITIES

A. Prospective lessor shall be liable for the payment of all real property taxes assessed against the residential premises as well as the following:

_____

B. Prospective lessee shall be liable for all personal property taxes as well as the following:

_____

Maintenance and Repairs

In commercial leases, the tenant is usually responsible for interior repairs and maintenance – but **in residential lease agreements,** *the landlord will usually take care of everything,* **unless you define each person's respective responsibilities for maintaining and repairing the unit.** Most of the time, **the landlord is responsible for anything that would render the unit uninhabitable** like faulty appliances, plumbing, heating or air conditioning – but, ultimately, *you are entitled to draft your lease agreement anyway you choose, as long as the law permits.*

SECTION XI - MAINTENANCE/REPAIRS

A. Prospective lessor shall be responsible for the following types of maintenance or repairs on the premises:

_____

B. Prospective lessee shall be responsible for the following types of maintenance or repairs on the premises:

_____

Pets and Animals

This topic was **previously addressed** in **Chapter 4** – in regards to how to use a rental application to forewarn you about the Shetland pony that'll be moving into your unit next week. *It's up to you whether you want to accept pets*. According to the **American Pet Products Manufacturers Association (APPMA) 2005 – 2006 National Pet Owners Survey,** *39% of all U.S. households own at least one dog* and *34% own at least one cat*. After reading those statistics – if you hadn't given it much thought before – **you may now want to seriously consider accepting animals to better ensure keeping your vacancy filled**. *Just be sure you maintain the right to approve any and all occupants stemming from the animal kingdom* – **and the human one, for that matter!**

SECTION XII - ANIMALS

Lessee shall keep no domestic or other animals in or about the property or on the property premises without the prior, express, and written consent of lessor.

Waste, Nuisance or Unlawful Use

Simply put, **this has tenants agree not to collect extra mounds of nasty, smelly trash on the front lawn for their compost pile** or open up an auto restoration business with the backyard as the scrap yard/motor oil recycling center. **You may** want to elaborate on this clause to curtail commonly seen problems in your area – *kind of like imposing your own* "**Homeowners' Association (HOA)**" *regulations or deed restrictions.* If your property happens to be in a **deed-restricted area**, then *be sure to give the tenant a copy of the* **HOA bylaws (rules and regulations)** *– and also to add verbiage that the tenant acknowledges having received them and agrees to abide by them*.

SECTION XIII - WASTE, NUISANCE OR UNLAWFUL USE

Lessee agrees that they will not commit waste on the premises, or maintain or permit to be maintained a nuisance on the premises, or use or permit the premises to be used in an unlawful manner.

Lessee's Holding Over

When the lease expires, there should be no holding over – *(the tenant continues to stay)* **– unless both parties agree in writing**. This clause is added just in case you forget about the expiration date and the tenant happens to stay without authorization. *It allows the landlord to give a 30-day notice to terminate at any time* **– unless there is a problem with the tenants, you would probably want to keep them on until you find a replacement.** *Otherwise, you would normally give the tenant a 60-day courtesy notice telling them that the lease is expiring and whether or not you are willing to renew.*

SECTION XIV - LESSEE'S HOLDING OVER

The parties agree that any holding over by lessee under this lease, without lessor's written consent, shall be a tenancy at will which may be terminated by lessor on 30 days' notice in writing.

Redelivery of Premises

Very simply put, **this single sentence of a section has the tenants agree that they will give your property back in the same basic condition that it is was given to them** *– aside from minor wear and tear that is expected.*

If there is a specific part of your house or apartment that you feel warrants special attention, this section is the place to note it.

Prior to the tenant moving in, you just installed a brand-new screen enclosure for the patio – which can be very expensive to repair – and your tenant happens to have pets and small children. This could be *specifically addressed as a "brand-new item"* that you want to make sure is not left with a door that no longer closes and a screen that looks more like used chicken wire...!

SECTION XV - REDELIVERY OF PREMISES

At the end of the term of this lease, lessee shall quit and deliver up the premises to lessor in as good condition as they are now, ordinary wear, decay, and damage by the elements excepted.

Default

This section spells out **what happens should the tenant violate any term or condition of the lease agreement (past due rent, damage, nuisance, unauthorized pets or animals, etc.).** When a violation occurs, *usually the landlord will give the tenant an opportunity to correct whatever it may be or at least allow them to show that they have initiated the appropriate steps to correct the problem*.

SECTION XVI - DEFAULT

If lessee defaults in the payment of rent or any part of the rent at the times specified above, or if lessee defaults in the performance of or compliance with any other term or condition of this lease agreement *[or of the regulations attached to and made a part of this lease agreement, which regulations shall be subject to occasional amendment or addition by lessor]*, the lease, at the option of lessor, shall terminate and be forfeited, and lessor may reenter the premises and retake possession and recover damages, including costs and attorney fees. Lessee shall be given 30 days *[written]* notice of any default or breach. Termination and forfeiture of the lease shall not result if, within 15 days of receipt of such notice, lessee has corrected the default or breach or has taken action reasonably likely to effect correction within a reasonable time.

Destruction of Premises and Eminent Domain

Okay, you have a tenant in your unit located in the Midwest – and, all of a sudden, a tornado wipes out the building while no one is there. This part of the lease explains that **if the property is essentially destroyed, the lease agreement terminates immediately –** *unless the unit is only partially damaged (and still legally habitable); then, the tenant will pay* **only an agreed portion of the rent** *until it is fully restored*.

An example of "destruction of premises" is if one of the bathrooms should flood and it takes a month to repair – the tenant should have that month's rent reduced by a small reasonable percentage. An example of the other – albeit *extremely* rare – situation of "eminent domain" occurs if the government was to step in and take control of the property for some specified purpose (e.g., time of war, highway expansion plans, etc.), then the lease would automatically terminate.

SECTION XVII - DESTRUCTION OF PREMISES AND EMINENT DOMAIN

In the event the leased premises are destroyed or rendered untenantable by fire, storm, or earthquake, or other casualty not caused by the negligence of lessee, or if the leased premises are taken by eminent domain, this lease shall be at an end from such time except for the purpose of enforcing rights that may have then accrued under this lease agreement. The rental shall then be accounted for between lessor and lessee up to the time of such injury or destruction or taking of the premises, lessee paying up to such date and lessor refunding the rent collected beyond such date. Should a part only of the leased premises be destroyed or rendered untenantable by fire, storm, earthquake, or other casualty not caused by the negligence of lessee, the rental shall abate in the proportion that the injured part bears to the whole leased premises. The part so injured shall be restored by lessor as speedily as practicable, after which the full rent shall recommence and the lease continue according to its terms. Any condemnation award concerning the leased premises shall belong exclusively to lessor.

Delay in or Impossibility of Delivery of Possession

If, for some reason, **the property is** *not* **ready for the tenant to move in on the effective date** of the lease agreement, **this clause allows the landlord a certain amount of time to get the property ready or the lease shall terminate**. This is *particularly useful* if you are *in the process of making some repairs or improvements that run behind schedule* due to *unforeseen circumstances* (e.g., supply shortages, contractor issues, severe weather conditions).

SECTION XVIII - DELAY IN OR IMPOSSIBILITY OF DELIVERY OF POSSESSION

In the event possession cannot be delivered to lessee on commencement of the lease term, through no fault of lessor or lessor's agents, there shall be no liability on lessor or lessor's agents, but the rental provided in this lease agreement shall abate until possession is given. Lessor or lessor's agents shall have 30 days in which to give possession, and if possession is tendered within that time, lessee agrees to accept the leased premises and this lease agreement. In the event possession cannot be delivered within that time, through no fault of lessor or lessor's agents, then this lease and all rights under this lease agreement shall be at an end.

Binding Effect

This legal jargon basically says that **if the tenant dies, his or her estate is actually responsible for paying the remainder of the lease** *or* **if the lease is assigned to another person (upon approval of the landlord), all the terms and conditions of the lease agreement shall remain in full force**. By the same token, *if the landlord sells the rental property, the new owner (landlord) assumes control over the lease agreement for whatever time may be remaining*.

SECTION XIX - BINDING EFFECT

The covenants and conditions contained in this lease agreement shall apply to and bind the heirs, legal representatives, and assigns of the parties to this lease agreement, and all covenants are to be construed as conditions of this lease.

Governing Law

This aspect of the lease agreement ensures that **the landlord gets to fight any landlord-tenant legal entanglements on the landlord's home field**– which is, customarily, **the state in which the property is located**. *For those tenants coming from out of state, this will serve to remind them of which state's laws they now need to obey*. It is also common in this section to see a notation regarding **in which county any and all legal actions must be filed**.

SECTION XX - GOVERNING LAW

It is agreed that this agreement shall be governed by, construed, and enforced in accordance with the laws of the State of _____ .

Attorney Fees

This clause is **intended to deter the tenant from filing frivolous lawsuits**. It simply states that **if a lawsuit is filed, the losing party must pay the prevailing party reasonable attorney's fees** – *in addition to any monetary judgment that may be awarded by the court*.

SECTION XXI - ATTORNEY FEES

In the event that any action is filed in relation to this agreement, the unsuccessful party in the action shall pay to the successful party, in addition to all the sums that either party may be called on to pay, a reasonable sum for the successful party's attorney fees.

Entire Agreement

In case you have discussions with the tenant prior to – or even after – the execution of the lease that may be misconstrued by the tenant as a binding agreement, **this section clearly states that the only terms and conditions that are legally binding are the ones stated in the *written* lease agreement, *regardless* of what has been – *or will be* – discussed verbally**.

SECTION XXII - ENTIRE AGREEMENT

This agreement shall constitute the entire agreement between the parties. Any prior understanding or representation of any kind preceding the date of this agreement shall not be binding upon either party except to the extent incorporated in this agreement.

Modification of Agreement

This section appropriately supports the **"Entire Agreement"** clause, by stating that *any and all* changes to the lease must be *mutually agreed to in writing* by both the landlord and tenant.

SECTION XXIII - MODIFICATION OF AGREEMENT

Any modification of this agreement or additional obligation assumed by either party in connection with this agreement shall be binding only if evidenced in a writing signed by each party or an authorized representative of each party.

Paragraph Headings

Everyone has their own interpretation of agreements and *the simple statement contained within this clause* eliminates at least one element from having to be debated and misinterpreted: *"all* of the paragraph headings"!

SECTION XXIV - PARAGRAPH HEADINGS

The titles to the paragraphs of this agreement are solely for the convenience of the parties and shall not be used to explain, modify, simplify, or aid in the interpretation of the provisions of this agreement.

In witness of the above, each party to this agreement has caused it to be executed on the date indicated below.

Signature of lessor:_____ Date:_____

Signature of lessee:_____ Date:_____

Signature of lessee:_____ Date:_____

Chapter 13

Lease Agreement, Part II: Addendums

This Chapter Discusses:

★ **Pets and Animals**

★ **Option to Purchase**

★ **Sublease (Subletting)**

★ **Modification of Lease**

As we stated in **Chapter 12**, *any time* you want to add, delete or modify anything that pertains to a lease agreement, <u>**you must always do so in writing!**</u> **Handshakes and promises will not hold up in court should there be a disagreement between you and your tenant months down the road.**

While some of *American Landlord*'s chapters may appear to reiterate the need to carefully protect your legal rights, you may one day find this redundant prodding to prove itself indispensably invaluable, when you're unexpectedly served with that summons some Saturday afternoon. **When faced with unforeseen circumstances concerning a tenant whom** (let's face it: most of the time) **you hardly know *anything* about, you never know what can happen**. So, once again, be a good scout and *be prepared*.

Everything U Need to Know...™

Pets and Animals

Suppose an applicant or a current tenant approaches you to get permission to have Morris or Chewie – or, yes, *even* Wilbur – move in to your property ~ **[First off** – **Be sure to thank 'em for asking alone!** – *many tenants never bother to disclose their true intentions*] then if – after considering the type of animal (namely, its breed and size) – you decide to welcome the new addition to your rental, you should decidedly *add a written addendum to your lease agreement.*

This addendum should specifically identify and address each type of pet, specifying its breed, weight, offspring and should also stipulate the additional funds that must be added to the existing security deposit that are often paid as a onetime non-refundable fee – *approximately $250 per pet depending on what the rental is capable of commanding, based upon the quality of amenities and features.*

On the following two pages there is an example of a pet agreement, which can also be printed from the enclosed CD-ROM:

Pet Agreement

Instructions:
1. Insert your IMAGE or LOGO (optional)
2. Complete PET AGREEMENT FIELDS
3. REPLACE ALL of this text with YOUR contact info
4. Click on 'PRINT FORM' when finished

Everything U Need to Know...

Click here to insert image/logo

Pet Agreement

AMENDMENT TO LEASE

For valuable consideration, receipt of which is hereby acknowledged, _____, "Lessor" and _____, "Lessee", parties to the Lease Agreement made for property located at _____, _____, _____ County, _____ and dated on _____ agree to modify and amend said Lease Agreement in the following way(s):

Lessee desires to keep the following described pet in the dwelling referred to above:

Type: _____

Breed: _____

Weight: _____

TERMS AND CONDITIONS

1. Lessee agrees that they are solely responsible for the maintenance of the above described pet, and agree to keep their pet under control at all times.

2. Lessee agrees to keep their pet restrained, but not tethered, when it is outside their dwelling.

3. Lessee agrees to adhere to local ordinances, including leash and licensing requirements.

4. Lessee agrees not to leave their pet unattended for unreasonable periods.

5. Lessee agrees to clean up after their pet and to dispose of their pet's waste properly and quickly.

6. Lessee agrees not to leave food or water for their pet or any other animal outside their dwelling where it may attract other animals.

7. Lessee agrees to keep their pet from being unnecessarily noisy or aggressive and causing any annoyance or discomfort to others and will remedy immediately any complaints made.

8. Lessee agrees to provide their pet with an identification tag while on the premises.

9. Lessee agrees not to breed or allow the pet to reproduce. If this should occur, the pet's offspring must be placed within 10 weeks of birth.

10. Lessee agrees to immediately pay for any damage, loss, or expense caused by their pet, and in addition, they will add $ _____ to their security/cleaning deposit, which may be used for cleaning, repairs or delinquent rent when Lessee vacates. This added deposit, or what remains of it when pet damages have been assessed, will be returned to Lessee within 10 days after they have proved that they no longer keep this pet.

11. Lessee agrees that this Agreement applies only to the specific pet described above.

12. Lessee agrees that the Lessor reserves the right to revoke permission to keep the pet should the Lessee break this agreement. Lessee will be given 10 days to remove the pet from the premises.

Pet Agreement

TERMS AND CONDITIONS (Continued)

13. Any animals on the property not registered under this agreement will be presumed to be strays and will be removed according to law, at the option of the Lessor.

ORIGINAL LEASE AGREEMENT

All other terms and covenants of the original Lease Agreement shall remain in full force and effect.

In witness of the above, each party to this agreement has caused it to be executed on the date below.

Signature of lessor:_____   Date:_____

Signature of lessee:_____   Date:_____

Signature of lessee:_____   Date:_____

This form provided by USLandlord.com

Option to Purchase

If you ever have any intention of **selling your unit,** *this is an addendum you may want to consider.* **While this option is** *usually intended for the benefit of the tenant,* **it** *can also be favorable for the landlord* **if local market conditions make it difficult to find qualified buyers.**

There are two essential ideas behind the "purchase option:"

 Predetermine the Purchase Price

Usually done at the time of the original lease signing, this addendum *gives the tenant the right to purchase the property at a fixed price that was determined a year or more in advance* . This is great for the tenant if the property value increases – but **chances are you would consider this option only if you inflate the purchase price unless you'd be willing to settle for the current value because the local real estate market has been a little sluggish and you feel it will not improve anytime soon or may even get worse.**

 Build a Down Payment

"Purchase options" can state that **a portion of the rent is to be credited toward the tenant's down payment.** In this case, **rent payments are usually adjusted upward,** *with at least 100% or more of the adjustment credited toward the down payment.* **In such an instance, this down payment credit is usually required by law** ~ (Check with your state or reference the ***American Landlord Law*** volume!) ~ **to be kept in a separate escrow bank account,** *so the tenant's funds are not intermingled with your own personal funds* – thereby, clearly establishing the distinction of their intended use.

An example of how to build a down payment using an *option to purchase agreement* **appears on the next page.**

Let's say the monthly rent is normally $1,050 – and the option to purchase states that the tenant has the right to purchase your home at any time over the next 24 months, for a purchase price of $150,000. As the landlord, you require an *initial, non-refundable* "option payment" of $2,000 *in lieu of a security deposit* – and, *along with the monthly rent*, **there would be an additional option payment of $250 per month.** Therefore, the **total monthly payment for the tenant is $1,300** ~ *$1,050 rent + $250 option to buy.* **All of the option money paid is considered** *non-refundable*, so don't worry about the security deposit! If the tenant does not exercise his or her option to purchase, then you keep the money.

You can see the **advantage of this option**, where it **allows the tenant time** (with terms of up to 24 months available) **to save up for the down payment** (and time to improve their credit, if needed), **while** – in the meantime – **the purchase price remains fixed**.

☆ **A 24-month option on a home with a base rent of $1,050 per month and a $150,000 purchase price could be calculated like this:**

♦ **Option (in Lieu of a Security Deposit): $2,000**
♦ **Monthly Option Payment:** $250 @ 24 months = **$6,000**
♦ **Total Down Payment (Credit): $8,000** (non-refundable)

This **$8,000** collected by the landlord **can be applied to the purchase of the home** and *represents more than 5% of the purchase price of $150,000.* Depending on the tenant's credit, income and assets, **this amount is usually an acceptable down payment.** And, as far as the move-in expenses, **the cost is about the same for the tenant as moving into any other rental except for the monthly option payment.**

★ Move-in expenses for the tenant would be as follows:

- **First Month's Rent: $1,300** ($1,050 + $250 monthly option)
- **Initial Option Fee: $2,000** (in lieu of a security deposit)
- **Total Move-In Expenses: $3,300**

A sample of an **"Option to Purchase"** agreement has been provided on the next page – and **on the enclosed CD-ROM.** This agreement can be easily customized to allow for the accumulation of a down payment or any other creative maneuver that you and the tenant wish to use. However, it is *strongly suggested* that *both of you* **contact a licensed mortgage lender to find out exactly what the underwriting requirements are for such an agreement** – especially if you intend on allowing the tenant to build a down payment or a **"gift of equity."** The state of the mortgage industry has been in such turmoil of late that **lenders are continually modifying their loan product matrices, terms and conditions to reduce their foreclosure risk**, while – at the same time – trying to remain competitive enough to survive.

Everything U Need to Know...

Option to Purchase Agreement

Instructions:
1. Insert your IMAGE or LOGO (optional)
2. Highlight & complete AGREEMENT FIELDS
3. REPLACE ALL of this text with YOUR contact info
4. Click on 'PRINT FORM' when finished

Everything U Need to Know...

Click here to insert image/logo

Option to Purchase Leased Property

OPTION TO PURCHASE

This agreement is entered into between _____, of _____, _____ County, _____, referred to as "lessor," and _____, of _____, _____ County, _____, referred to as "lessee."

Lessor agrees to sell to lessee, at their option, the following property owned by lessor, namely: _____, _____, _____ County, _____, subject to the following terms and conditions:

1. This option to purchase will expire on _____.

2. Notice of election to purchase by lessee shall be in writing and given to lessor by _____.

3. The price to be paid for the property, if this option is exercised, is $ _____ dollars. After payment is made to lessor in full, lessor agrees to execute and deliver to lessee a deed conveying the property to lessee, and to deliver possession of property free of all liens and encumbrances.

4. _____

5. _____

ORIGINAL LEASE AGREEMENT

All other terms and covenants of the original Lease Agreement shall remain in full force and effect.

In witness of the above, each party to this agreement has caused it to be executed on the date below.

Signature of lessor: _____   Date: _____

Signature of lessee: _____   Date: _____

Signature of lessee: _____   Date: _____

This form provided by USLandlord.com

SAMPLE

Sublease (The Practice of Subletting)

It's **bound** to happen at some point or other: a tenant signs a lease and then – before you know it – they already want to move. **If this happens, you basically have three options**: (1) *let the tenant go without any repercussions*; (2) *ask (or sue, if necessary) for the total number of remaining months of the lease agreement*; or; (3) *tell them to find you a tenant to fill his or her place for the remaining term*.

> ☆ **Let the tenant go without any repercussions.**

> ☆ **Ask (or sue, if necessary) for the total number of remaining months of the lease agreement.**

> ☆ **Tell them to find you a tenant to fill his or her place for the remaining months.**

This last option is commonly referred to as **"subletting" – where someone else agrees to fulfill the remaining term of an existing lease agreement –** *and this is important!* – while *continuing to hold the original tenant responsible* **should the "sublessee"** (the new tenant) **fail to abide by the lease terms.** Subletting is a **great and reasonable** alternative to consider if a tenant needs to vacate early; *just be sure you don't forget to screen the sublessee as well.*

A **copy of a standard sublease agreement** appears on the following pages and *can also be printed* from the **enclosed CD-ROM**.

Sublease Agreement

Instructions:
1. Insert your IMAGE or LOGO (optional)
2. Highlight & complete LEASE AGREEMENT FIELDS
3. REPLACE ALL of this text with YOUR contact info
4. Click on 'PRINT FORM' when finished

Everything U Need to Know...

Click here to insert image/logo

Residential Sublease Agreement

AGREEMENT TO SUBLEASE

This agreement is entered into between _____, of
_____, _____, _____, County,
_____, referred to as "sublessor," and _____, of
_____, _____, _____, County,
_____, referred to as "sublessee."

RECITALS

A. Sublessor is the lessee of real property that is available for subleasing.

B. Sublessee desires to sublease residential property to occupy and use as their residence.

C. Lessor of the master lease agreement described in Section VI desires to permit the sublessor the right to sublease the residential property described in Section I.

In consideration of the matters described above, and of the mutual benefits and obligations set forth in this agreement, the parties agree as follows:

SECTION I - SUBJECT OF SUBLEASE

Sublessor shall sublease to prospective sublessee the residential property leased by sublessor located at
_____, _____, _____County,
_____, for sublessee and their family to occupy and use as their residence.

SECTION II - TERM OF LEASE

The premises shall be subleased to lessee for a period of _____ starting from
_____. Any option to renew, extend or modify this lease shall require the approval of the lessor.

SECTION III - MONTHLY RENTAL

Sublessee shall pay $ _____ per month as the monthly rental for the term of the sublease with the first payment due on or before _____, and subsequent payments on the ____ day of each succeeding month. This rental payment shall be subject to renegotiation by the sublessee and the lessor under the master lease agreement. It is agreed that if the rental payment is not received by the ____ day of the month, then a late fee of ____ shall be assessed and due immediately. Additional terms (optional):
_____
_____

SECTION IV - SECURITY DEPOSIT

On the execution of this sublease, sublessee deposits with sublessor $ _____, receipt of which is acknowledged by lessor, as security for the faithful performance by sublessee of the terms of this lease agreement, to be returned to sublessee, without interest (unless required by law), on the full and faithful performance by lessee of the provisions of the originial master lease agreement.

SECTION V - NUMBER OF OCCUPANTS

Sublessee agrees that the leased apartment shall be occupied by no more _____ adults and _____ children under the age of 18 years without the prior, express, and written consent of sublessor.

SECTION VI - MASTER LEASE AGREEMENT

The sublease agreement incorporates and is subject to the master lease agreement between the sublessor and lessor, a copy of which is attached hereto, and which is hereby referred to and incorporated as if it wereset out here at length. The sublessee agrees to assume all of the obligations and responsibilities of the sublessor under the master lease agreement for the duration of the sublease agreement.

SECTION VII - BINDING EFFECT

The covenants and conditions contained in this lease agreement shall apply to and bind the heirs, legal representatives, and assigns of the parties to this lease agreement, and all covenants are to be construed as conditions of this lease.

SECTION VIII - GOVERNING LAW

It is agreed that this agreement shall be governed by, construed, and enforced in accordance with the laws of the State of _____.

SECTION IX - ATTORNEY FEES

In the event that any action is filed in relation to this agreement, the unsuccessful party in the action shall pay to the successful party, in addition to all the sums that either party may be called on to pay, a reasonable sum for the successful party's attorney fees.

SECTION X - ENTIRE AGREEMENT

This agreement shall constitute the entire agreement between the parties. Any prior understanding or representation of any kind preceding the date of this agreement shall not be binding upon either party except to the extent incorporated in this agreement.

SECTION XI - MODIFICATION OF AGREEMENT

Any modification of this agreement or additional obligation assumed by either party in connection with this agreement shall be binding only if evidenced in a writing signed by each party or an authorized representative of each party.

In witness of the above, each party to this agreement has caused it to be executed on the date indicated below.

Signature of sublessor: _____ Date: _____

Signature of sublessee: _____ Date: _____

As lessor of the attached master lease agreement, I hereby give my consent to the above described provisions as set out in this sublease agreement.

Signature of lessor: _____ Date: _____

This form provided by USLandlord.com

Modification of Lease

This is the **universal form that is commonly used to renew or extend an existing lease agreement**, but can be **used to easily and legally modify, add or delete any of the original terms and conditions.** **By itself, it does nothing more than reference the existence of such a lease agreement.** It then *leaves it up to the parties involved to draft the modification verbiage* that will then be *permanently affixed to the original lease agreement.* A **sample of such a modification form** appears on the following page and is also available **on the enclosed CD-ROM**.

Modification of Lease Agreement

Instructions:
1. Insert your IMAGE or LOGO (optional)
2. Complete AMENDMENT FIELDS
3. REPLACE ALL of this text with YOUR contact info
4. Click on 'PRINT FORM' when finished

Everything U Need to Know...

Click here to insert image/logo

Modification of Lease Agreement

AMENDMENT TO LEASE

For valuable consideration, receipt of which is hereby acknowledged, _____,
"Lessor" and _____ , "Lessee", parties to the Lease Agreement made
for premises located at _____, _____,
_____ County, _____ and dated _____ agree
to modify and amend said Lease Agreement in the following way(s):

_____

_____

_____

_____

_____

ORIGINAL LEASE AGREEMENT

All other terms and covenants of the original Lease Agreement shall remain in full force and effect.

In witness of the above, each party to this agreement has caused it to be executed on the date indicated below.

Signature of lessor:_____   Date:_____

Signature of lessee:_____   Date:_____

Signature of lessee:_____   Date:_____

This form provided by USLandlord.com

SAMPLE

Chapter 14

Maintaining and Repairing Your Rental: The Key to Prosperity

This Chapter Discusses:

★ **Preventative Maintenance**

★ **Be Prepared – Something Inevitably Goes Wrong!**

★ **Do-It-Yourself**

★ **Contractor and Vendor Relations**

Therhe key to rental property prosperity and successful landlord-tenant relations is simply **performing routine maintenance and timely repairs on your property**. Tenants undoubtedly appreciate attentive landlords who make that extra effort as much as landlords appreciate tenants who are equally as attentive with their rent every month. That being said, *the task of maintaining a unit properly without cutting too many corners or accruing too much in expenditures is much easier said than done*.

It's not easy being green – or being a landlord, for that matter. **You want to accommodate every need to make the property not only habitable, but also comfortable**… and your pockets are only *so* deep. It is important, though, to curb this generosity because – just like in any other relationship – *a landlord who gives too much too soon may lead a tenant to*

develop expectations the landlord may not have intended to be ongoing "gifts." And a landlord who is neglectful or is a procrastinator may find that he or she has more problems than ever before – even including possible legal action to defend.

Preventative Maintenance

Basic logic will tell you that regular and routine maintenance far outweighs being forced to perform that *one major repair* **that could have been prevented** – or at least for which you could have been prepared for months ago. **Simple preventative maintenance is often mistakenly left up to the tenant.** *However, a little extra effort on your part may ensure that it is actually done and not neglected.* Even when it comes to the **small stuff**, it doesn't matter how much it's addressed in your lease agreement, **you may just want to take care of it yourself to avoid any unnecessary headaches**. After all, **spending a little now will usually save you a lot later!**

One of the best examples is the ***routine changing of air conditioning filters***. Air filters, as you already know, are usually found in the ceiling or high on the walls and filter out impurities in the air – thereby clogging up after so many months. **If the tenant should fail to replace the filters every three to six months, this could easily lead to major problems** *for you* **months or even years later, problems that may cost you thousands prematurely** – *and completely unnecessarily*.

Air filter replacement needs only to be performed four times a year *(at best!)* **and will cost you about $10 for each filter**. The best part is that the entire air conditioning system won't freeze up, saving you an unwanted, needless repair bill. Furthermore, the longevity of the air conditioning unit isn't further compromised because it isn't overworking – *and* – your tenant's electricity bill will even be significantly lower, to boot!

(Another benefit to performing such effortless maintenance is that this gives you an excuse to inspect the property for any potential lease violations in the process...)

In addition to performing routine inspection and maintenance yourself, there is always the option of **establishing a "service contract" with a local contractor or handyman service**. *However, be careful of these companies* – some have so many exceptions written into their agreements, there is no benefit in signing a long-term contract. In other words, *make sure you are protected from the big ticketed items – small problems are usually self-manageable, unless you reside out of town or simply have no desire to perform any maintenance work.*

In either case, here is a basic list of preventative maintenance issues you want to consider throughout the year:

☆ Spring/Summer

Exterior

- ♦ Examine and repair **caulking of the windows, stucco, and trim** (to prevent water, dust, dirt and insects from entering the dwelling which could lead to serious problems years from now).
- ♦ Examine **paint on siding, trim, and doors** (paint is essential for protection and appearance).
- ♦ Clean and **remove debris from gutters.**
- ♦ **Examine roof for loose, cracked, or missing shingles/tiles**. Repair and replace as necessary.
- ♦ **Trim trees and shrubs away from home, including roof** (to prevent rodents and insects from entering the dwelling and to reduce the risk of damage caused by falling branches during severe weather).

Interior

♦ Examine and **repair any caulking at the windows** –
for weatherization *and* insect control.

♦ **Close the chimney damper** to keep cool air-conditioning inside
the dwelling.

♦ Examine and repair/replace (if needed) **weather stripping on
exterior doors and windows** – to reduce energy costs.

♦ Examine and **repair bath tile grouting** (if needed) *to prevent
moisture damage*.

♦ Lubricate and adjust **locks, hinges and latches**.

♦ Examine **window locks** and repair as needed.

♦ Adjust **heating and cooling registers (balance flow)**.

♦ Lubricate **garage door roller shafts (not tracks)** and **tighten
bolts**.

♦ Examine **cabinets, drawers, and hinges** for proper alignment –
tighten and adjust as necessary.

♦ Clean **dryer vent duct and damper** to remove lint or debris.

♦ Have your **air conditioning, heat pump and/or evaporative
cooler cleaned and serviced by a qualified technician.**

♦ Replace **air conditioning** or **heat pump filters**.

♦ **Drain and flush out** hot water tank.

★  Fall/Winter

Exterior

♦ Clean and remove **debris from gutters**.

♦ Check **outside faucets** and **hoses for leaks**.

♦ **Reseed the lawn** for green grass all winter long.

♦ Inspect and repair **caulking of windows, siding, trim** and **other
exterior areas**, as needed.

♦ Rinse off **air-conditioning compressor/condensing unit coil** to
remove dirt and plant debris.

♦ **Drain and clean evaporative cooler** for the winter and make
ready for spring service.

Interior

- ◆ **Turn on the furnace** to make sure it is in proper working order. **Have it serviced by a qualified technician.**
- ◆ Inspect and repair (as needed) **caulking in sinks, tubs, showers, thresholds, walls, windows and other interior areas**, as needed.
- ◆ Check the **fireplace. Open the damper of the chimney before tenant's first use.**
- ◆ Replace **air conditioning** or **heat pump filters.**

Be Prepared – Something Inevitably Goes Wrong!

This section is *not meant to scare you* – **quite the opposite!** It is, instead, <u>to reassure you</u> that **even the most seasoned landlord cannot foresee** *everything*. Don't think that just because you finally closed on your new investment property that nothing can possibly go wrong during the first year – or that, since you have regularly performed scheduled maintenance, the hot water tank is therefore incapable of leaking in the middle of the night.

There are a lot of unpredictable circumstances that can take you by surprise. Just as you should be doing with your own primary residence, **establish an emergency repair fund so that you and your tenant are not unnecessarily stressed**. If possible, *it's a good habit to set a portion of the monthly proceeds aside in a separate bank account* – perhaps even a relatively conservative, **high-yield savings or money market fund with Citibank, Capital One, ING Direct, Schwab and the list goes on...** As the funds grow over time, you'll grow more confident about being able to handle anything that comes your way.

Of course, there's always **credit cards** and **lines of credit**, but *why finance something if you can afford to avoid paying someone else for using their money?* **The last thing you want to turn your investment property into is a burdening fifth wheel** – *especially* as a series of high-interest credit cards that just never seem to get paid off… The managing of your own personal finances is at your sole discretion.

Just remember, *"cash is king"* for more reasons than one – so save as much of it as possible for those rainy days… and, to stay on the safe side, *count on a storm to occur* on at least one of those days…

Do-It-Yourself

For those of you with a predilection for craftsmanship (or, at the least, for those of us that think we're skilled craftspeople!), the superstores (**Home Depot** and **Lowe's**) and the demographic-specific cable television networks (**DIY Network** and **HGTV**) have turned everyday homeowners into self-made contractors – **a recent trend that has been fueled by these corporations, enabling you to** *falsely* **believe you can do almost anything, so long as time permits.** *Some experts say to leave the larger jobs to the professionals and the small jobs to the landlord* – such as lighting and fixtures, landscaping and painting.

So **how do you determine if you should take the work on yourself** or hire an experienced professional? **Here is a list of things to consider before you go donning a yellow hard hat with a leather tool belt and matching gloves:**

⭐ **Find Out if a Building Permit is Required**

In the case of rental property where there is an increased risk of liability and legal action, **you should always contact your local building permit office and find out if the work you are about to perform requires a permit.** As much as people like to cut costs and evade their local government, *building permits were introduced to ensure all construction projects are completed in accordance with the latest safety standards.* **If a permit is required, then you may want to seriously consider some professional help** if you are still insistent on performing the work yourself.

★ Assess Your Skills

Okay, so you have the work ethic, drive and determination to get the job done – but **do you also possess the basic skills to complete the project correctly?** Now, before you go running off smugly answering, "Yes," *you should take the time to list all of the steps involved* and *evaluate your ability to complete each one accurately*. **The last thing you want is a tenant suing you** because something goes wrong with the work you performed and it turned out substandard.

★ Consider the Costs

Eliminating the labor expense by doing handiwork yourself **can save you upwards of 50% –** *but do you already own or have access to the required tools or will you have to rent or buy them?* **Tools are very expensive and professionals come already well-stocked.** In addition, **professionals can often use existing supplies left over from previous jobs** – and they are able to purchase new ones through their own contacts at a discount you wouldn't otherwise receive – so *it's always wise to get at least a couple of quotes from some local professionals*, so you can see whether or not you are *truly* saving in the end – especially considering the required effort on your part in addition to any financial costs incurred regardless.

By the way!: You can always consider hiring a professional to perform only the highly skilled tasks – or perhaps someone who is less expensive to perform the prep work, to free up some of your time so *you* can tackle the more important tasks.

In addition to saving money, **the nice thing about doing most of the work yourself is the extra attention you are inclined to give to the detail**. *No one will take greater pride in your rental property than you.* In the end, there is a lot of satisfaction that accompanies all of the work you do by yourself – and it only gets better as you continue to complete more **"Do-It-Yourself"** projects. **Just be sure you carefully consider all of your options – *and*** weigh the pros and cons – before you even think of beginning.

Contractor and Vendor Relations

For those of you who live out of town from your unit or who simply don't desire to get "down and dirty" with your rental, your only option is to **establish a solid database** (or Rolodex, if that's still your thing… and there's nothing wrong with that!) **of highly skilled and moderately priced local contractors and vendors whom you can rely on to be there for both you and your tenants**.

Unfortunately, it's not quite *that* easy, because even though there are plenty of housing professionals that make an honest day's living by performing quality work or services, the industry still has a few masked men and women that won't think twice about robbing you blind.

As expected, this "Rolodex" may take time to fill – usually accomplished by relying on good ol' **trial and error**, if you don't have the luxury of that **invaluable "word-of-mouth"** from a source you already trust. Fortunately, *there are some tips you can use to try and weed out the bandits.* Depending on the type of contractor or vendor, they can be applied accordingly.

Assess Their Skills

Asking friends, family and associates if they have ever had *similar* work performed before – or if they, in turn, know of someone who has – is a **very good way to begin your search**. You can even *ask fellow professionals in the industry* – such as architects, engineers, suppliers, etc. – *if they know of someone they trust* or about whom they may have heard good things.

Ask for References

Although we saw in **Chapter 10** that **you never know for certain whom you are contacting** (close friend, family member or other associate), **it's a good idea to ask for at least three references** and *require that one of them be from an established local company that knows of their reputation*.

Check Professional Licensing

You **need to make sure that the person you are dealing with has been appropriately licensed with the applicable licensing board for your state**. Each state will usually have a dedicated **department of business and professional regulations** that will tell you if the license is active and in good standing.

Ask for Evidence of Insurance

When it comes to hiring contractors, **you never want to just take the contractor's word regarding him or her having a liability and workmen's compensation policy**. *You should request the contractor to have the insurance company directly provide to you a certificate of insurance*. This is the *only* way to ensure you are protected in case of a mishap that occurs on your property.

☆ Check Consumer Protection Groups

In addition to **checking the contractor's or vendor's** *Better Business Bureau (BBB)* **file and the consumer review repository, Angie's List (www.AngiesList.com)**, there are *many local groups popping up online* that maintain customer satisfaction ratings. Contact your local **Chamber of Commerce** for more information about such resources available for prescreening a contractor.

☆ Ask for Professional Associations

Many times, **reputable contractors and vendors will spend the extra money to maintain a membership with an applicable and reputable professional organization**. While anyone can usually join such organizations, provided their license is in good standing, *it is a little more reassuring to know someone is interested in the presentation of their public image – and, usually by extension, their reputation.*

In the end, after you've compiled all your research, you're ultimately going to need to trust your gut instinct and hope for the best – word-of-mouth recommendation or none. If the contractor or vendor works out well for you, then quickly add that person into that Rolodex! **The advantages of establishing good contractor and vendor relations are invaluable**. **Just make sure you pay their bill on time,** *every time,* **to keep that goodwill vibe.**

<u>One thing is for sure</u>: *You'll sleep a whole lot better at night knowing that you have people whom you can trust to handle almost any problem.* Even if you're only renting a single unit at this time, **you can still reap the benefits of becoming a loyal customer,** by making sure you tell others about *your* trusted contractors and vendors – *and don't forget to have everyone mention that the referral came from you!*

Chapter 15

Landlord Insurance:
Protecting More Than Just Your Property

This Chapter Discusses:

- ★ Is Insurance Necessary?
- ★ Choosing Policy Coverage
- ★ Going Above and Beyond with an Umbrella Policy
- ★ How to Minimize Your Liability
- ★ Getting a Free Quote

Landlord insurance is *a little different from* the standard homeowner's policy you are accustomed to having protect your primary residence or second home. The difference is that *a landlord insurance policy covers those issues that are directly related to the landlord-tenant relationship.*

If a *hurricane* drifts into town and wipes out your rental property, **your standard homeowners policy wouldn't cover your loss of rent** – *nor* would it protect you if you had a tenant who maliciously caused damage to your property (e.g., punching holes in the walls, smashing doors, breaking windows, etc.). *A standard homeowners policy wouldn't even cover accidental damage that was caused by your tenant.*

Great – just another bill, right? Actually, **landlord insurance could very well be a blessing in disguise** – but, first, *you must weigh the pros and cons to determine its necessity in your individual case.* After all, if luck's on your side, insurance never has to pay for itself. So the question is… *"Do ya feel lucky, Landlord?"*

Is Insurance Necessary?

No one wants to have to pay another bill, but **this is one that may actually pay you back *100 times* over.** The *decision to have a standard homeowners or automobile policy is made for you by your lender or state's law*, so *you have no choice but to have both of them* (unless you're fortunate enough to own your home with no mortgage attached).

The general rule of thumb when determining if you need insurance coverage is to determine whether or not you have anything to lose. This is *most likely why many low-income drivers (against their state's law) answer this question by either canceling their vehicle's insurance policy once the car is paid off or simply paying for a car with cash and never even bothering to insure it.* In the end, what's the risk to them – a possible ticket or a suspended license? But – even then – *only if* they're caught? In their mind, they clearly have nothing to lose by not paying for insurance. However, *you do* **have something to lose**!

<u>**REMEMBER**</u>: *This is an investment property, not your primary residence*, for those of you living in a **homestead state**, where **your primary residence is protected from almost anything** – except for *mortgage liens*, *mechanics liens* (liens from those who have performed work on the house, but who never got paid) and, of course, *federal tax liens* (the **IRS** always gets its money, one way or another!).

If you are a small landlord, **you may not think you have more than one vulnerable asset, your rental property, but** *chances are you probably do*. So the question then becomes *how much* do you have to lose?

If you have considerable assets that are not **"creditor-proof"** (you'll want to consult with your financial planner or attorney on that matter), you need to realize that **a landlord can easily be liable for tenant (and visitor) injuries caused by dangerous or defective conditions on your rental property**, as well as *criminal activity* and *environmental hazards* – such as lead paint and asbestos.

The laws in many states are very **"tenant-friendly"** – *enabling almost anyone to be able to file a lawsuit against you* for medical bills, lost wages, pain and suffering, permanent physical disability or disfigurement, emotional distress – *or even an unlawful eviction*. So ask yourself, **do you – personally – have enough to lose to justify paying for the extra protection and piece of mind?** *Only you* can make this decision…

Choosing Policy Coverage

Not all insurance policies are the same – and so *expect coverage and methods of settling your claims to be different from one policy or carrier to another*. Therefore, it's important first to **determine what you want your policy to do for you in the event of a claim**. If you only want **minimal coverage** – to *protect the property from major causes of loss*, such as fire, wind or explosion – you should consider what's called a **"named peril policy"** (a policy that *specifically names the types of losses that would be covered*). If you want the best possible coverage for you and your property, then you need a **"comprehensive policy"** (a policy that *covers all types of accidental losses* – excepting those that are specifically excluded).

In addition to these two basic types of policies, there is **"optional coverage"** that can be purchased and then *added to the base coverage within your policy*. This will require careful consideration on your part, as far as getting **what you deem *truly* necessary**, as opposed to getting excessive coverage.

Everything U Need to Know...

<u>**Optional coverage can include – but is not limited to:**</u> personal liability, loss of rent, other structures on the premises, theft, personal property, vandalism or malicious mischief (which is sometimes included in a basic policy) – and, of course, earthquake coverage for those properties located near the West Coast.

> **If getting a policy that covers personal injury, be sure that it also covers libel, slander, discrimination, unlawful eviction and invasion of privacy. *You not only have to protect yourself from the tenant – but also from all of their guests and visitors too!***

TIP

Going Above and Beyond with an Umbrella Policy

As if all of the coverage we've already discussed isn't enough, **there is another option** to consider – and that is an **"umbrella policy,"** which *goes above and beyond the limits of your normal landlord insurance coverage.* **Fortunately, it's very inexpensive – usually a few hundred dollars a year for an extra million or two in coverage –** *as opposed to standard policy premiums which are thousands of dollars each year.* However, **umbrella policies don't take effect until your preceding coverage is exhausted;** *so don't think you can cancel you primary policy and still be covered under your umbrella.*

☆ How an Umbrella Policy Works

Say, for example, your liability limit is $1,000,000 with your primary landlord insurance policy, but you incur a loss that totals $1,500,000. *Your primary insurance carrier will reimburse you* for $1,000,000, minus the deductible of course, but now you are short $500,000. Fortunately, you also purchased a **separate umbrella policy** worth $1,000,000, which is *more than adequate to pay* for the remaining $500,000. So if you've ever had even a single dream about *catastrophic events* pertaining to your tenants or your rental property – it's *never* a bad idea to think about getting an "umbrella" *before* the storm hits and the sky starts falling...

How to Minimize Your Liability

Okay – now that you're completely and utterly paranoid about **all the many things that can go wrong which could drag you** into either a civil – or, heaven forbid – a **bankruptcy** court, its time to **ease your anxiety with some helpful advice for reducing your risk of being sued**. So, once again – sit back and *relax*, it'll all be okay...!

Focus your thoughts on these suggestions:

★ Develop a Written Inspection List

Similar to the **preventative maintenance** one discussed in **Chapter 14**, *a well-constructed list can help you eliminate any problems before the tenant moves in*. And for those of you who have been inclined in the past to casually sweep items under a rug, **when it pertains to the safety of others, you don't want to turn a blind eye even to the smallest of items** – *spending a few dollars now may save you a million or two later!*

★ Create a Safety Notice

This can **either be a letter that the tenant can acknowledge receipt of upon moving in or a displayable notice that can be posted** in the utility room, garage or common areas if it is a multiunit complex. **The safety notice *instructs the tenant to immediately notify you of any problems, repairs or concerns with regard to his or her personal safety*. A reminder notice can also be included** should you ever correspond with the tenant by mail for other reasons (i.e., the rent is past due, you need to schedule routine maintenance, you have a forwarding address for holiday rent checks).

★ Document Everything!

As stated before, **you need to maintain a file on each tenant and on the property as a whole**. *Every complaint that is made needs to be recorded in a logbook of some kind*, which should either be stored on your computer or kept in some type of physical form (for all of you Rolodex hold-outs!). *Each entry should be accompanied by a description of how it was resolved or handled and include copies of any applicable receipts*. The more you can show that you are *not* a neglectful landlord, the better you'll appear in the eyes of any judge.

★ Use a Tenant Checklist

Just in case your notices are ignored, another suggestion is to **create a checklist for the tenant to fill out quarterly or semi-annually** *concerning any problems of which they may be aware, either within or outside the property*. There should be a **spot on the checklist for the tenant to sign and date.** This is an *extremely good way to protect yourself from ever being accused by a tenant of neglecting a long-standing problem*.

★ Address Urgent Problems Urgently!

Okay, now this one is a no-brainer… If the tenant calls you up and says there is some exposed electrical wiring, **don't wait** for the lights to dim and the sun to set… **Take care of it right away** – *ideally, within 24 hours!* (**FYI:** This is *another* good reason why it's so important to have those great contractor and vendor relations that you've worked so hard to establish, just as suggested back in **Chapter 14**.)

★ Don't Discriminate

It's **sometimes too easy to** innocently and unintentionally **ask the wrong questions** – or perhaps say something that *may be considered discriminatory.* In order to **prevent yourself from being sued and prosecuted for violating civil rights**, you must always remember that the **Fair Housing Laws** *prohibit a landlord from being influenced by a person's race, color, religion, gender, familial status, disability, medical condition, sexual orientation, involvement in a government assistance program or age* (unless it is a designated senior citizen community).

It really doesn't take much to sue anyone today which is why I am fully insured now. I had a previous tenant accuse me of discriminating against her and her boyfriend who was of a different race. There were already five occupants in a two bedroom unit and she had him move in without asking me, so I decided to enforce my rights by telling them one person will have to move (not necessarily the person of a different race). She had an attorney pursue the matter and it became the biggest headache that fortunately was dismissed by the judge. It's scary, because you never know how these issues will end.

S. Goodman
New York
Landlord

So **there's absolutely no reason to get so stressed about reducing your liability**, to the point of developing an obsessive-compulsive disorder or high blood pressure. *Ironically, even attorneys often find themselves getting sued over the same common problems about which they regularly lecture their clients.* **Just do your best and be conscientious not to ignore legitimate complaints or problems.** *Even if a tenant seems to be overreacting, you need to at least address their concern and dignify it with a response explaining why a repair isn't necessary or why they may be partially or fully responsible.* If you've never worked in customer service before, this may be a good opportunity for you to take a part-time position at your local thrift shop for the experience – or, in all seriousness, to at least remember that *being an* **"American Landlord"** *is* largely *a customer service job.*

Getting a Free Quote

One good thing about landlord insurance is that *it doesn't cost anything to get a quote*. Being the responsible consumer you are, it's naturally your civic duty to **shop for the best coverage at the best price.** Now, there are many ways of going about this – *contact your current agent, flip through the yellow pages or go online and search for "landlord insurance"* using your search engine of choice. *You can also visit* **AmericanLandlord.com** *to utilize the same tools that* **AmerUSA's** *current roster of* "American Landlord" *clients receive on a day-to-day basis.*

It's never too late to start saving money – even on your life and auto policies. This is why **American Landlord** has made this process easier for you by *providing a direct link to a trusted insurance quote provider which has already helped thousands of landlords save on all types of insurance coverage.*

By visiting **AmericanLandlord.com**, all readers of this book, as well as current clients, are **invited to submit one form detailing your needs and** *you will receive* **up to three free quotes** *from the nation's top insurance providers* **within 48 hours.**

No fees, no risks, no worries – after all, this is why *your valuable time is being spent on learning the ropes* of being an **"American Landlord…"**

Chapter 16

Move 'Em In, Move 'Em Out:
What to Do Before Tenancy Begins and Ends

This Chapter Discusses:

★ A Picture Is Worth a Thousand Words and Dollars!

★ Assessment of Condition Checklist

★ Retaining or Returning a Security Deposit

Everything discussed in this chapter centers on **the single most important concern for any tenant**: *the prompt and full refund of their sacred security deposit*.

This is **such a sensitive issue** that it must be dealt with *long before the tenant actually moves into the property*. **Otherwise, an unnecessary battle may ensue** and you may have a difficult time prevailing.

A Picture Is Worth a Thousand Words and Dollars!

Every landlord should capture the condition of his or her rental property on film before a tenant takes possession. So, if you don't own a video camera – or even a still camera – it's 'round about time you get one. Visit your local "general store" (e.g., **Target, Wal-Mart, Best Buy, K-Mart**, etc.); it doesn't matter which; **with newer and inexpensive digital technology, you can get a good deal almost anywhere you shop – and a simple, uncomplicated camera will do just fine.** *As long as it can take pictures that are in focus so quality prints (or digital images) can be produced to be archived with your records.*

Having a clear visual record of the condition and contents will speak volumes should there ever be a dispute over excessive wear or damage! – *Just make sure you are organized and keep everything filed away securely so you know exactly where it is.* You never know when – or how quickly – you may suddenly need to piece it all together to support your position in a legal dispute.

By the way, **if you decide to become a videographer, keep the camera steady.** Home movies and bad wedding videos notoriously have that one thing in common – the camera jerks around so badly that viewers are more prone to epileptic seizures and severe migraines than to seeing your perspective. **Don't walk about – *stand still at designated points outside and inside* –** around the entire perimeter of the property – so that you can steadily capture 30 seconds of each angle. This way, if you ever need to watch the footage back, you'll be able to see everything without biting your tongue or having to offer some necessary audio commentary of your own to clarify what you were attempting to show.

For those items of great importance – perhaps newer appliances, fixtures, etc. – **close-ups should be taken,** just in case you need to provide evidence of excessive wear and tear that *occurred during the term of the lease.* Oh, and **don't forget about documenting all of the secondary rooms and surface areas** – such as *ceilings,*

switch plates, outlets, window treatments, doors, storage spaces, utility rooms, patios and even cabinets. Are you being too anal? Not in the slightest! **You should expose everything in its current state from head to toe** – *and it shouldn't take you more than 30 minutes of your time for about 1,500 square feet.*

Assessment of Condition Checklist

In addition to your film or video document, **both you and the tenant should perform a walk-through together – with an accompanying checklist**. This way, you can *both* assess the condition of the unit and (if necessary) *immediately address any "pre-move-in concerns"* – such as carpet stains, holes in the walls, faulty fixtures, etc. **The idea is that you obviously wish to have the unit returned to you in the same condition you left it, allowing (of course) for reasonable wear and tear that just occurs naturally over time.**

The basic principle behind **"normal wear and tear"** is *to expect to see some minor cosmetic blemishes that occur naturally over time when used in accordance with the manufacturer's recommendations.* Appliances, fixtures and hardware throughout the rental are expected to be left in working order, devoid of obvious abuse or neglect. An exception to this rule would be those items that are several years old and known to be on the way out.

Although it's better for you to be present at this time, **you can also have the tenant perform their own inspection alone upon moving in, then return a signed and dated checklist to you within a mandatory time-frame** *(usually within three business days).* After all, you should be well aware of the condition of your unit already – and **as long as their assessment is turned in right away, there shouldn't be any major discrepancies.**

A sample of an **"Assessment of Condition"** checklist form appears on the next several pages and, of course, one has also been provided **on the enclosed CD-ROM.**

Assessment of Condition

Assessment of Condition of Rental Property

This checklist will help you protect your security deposit. Using the key on the right, fill in the letter that best describes the condition of your unit. This checklist must be returned within 3 days after the start of your lease. Before you move out, request a copy of this checklist, fill in the "End of Lease" column, and then return it so we may corroborate your assessment using the "Landlord's end-of-lease assessment" column.

Key	
Missing	M
Good condition	G
Scratched	S
Damaged	D
Broken	B
Repair needed	R

Exterior	Beginning of lease	End of lease	Landlord's end-of-lease assessment	Comments
Front door				
Front screen door				
Back door				
Back screen door				
Screens and storm windows				
Windows and frames				
Mailbox				
Doorbell				
Apartment number				
Garbage container				
Recycling containers				
Security intercom				
Other				

SAMPLE

Assessment of Condition

Kitchen	Beginning of lease	End of lease	Landlord's end-of-lease assessment	Comments
Windows				
Blinds/curtains				
Floor				
Walls				
Ceiling				
Lights and switches				
Outlets				
Stove				
Refrigerator				
Dishwasher				
Garbage disposal				
Sink				
Cabinets and counter				
Baseboards				
Trim				
Other				

Dining room	Beginning of lease	End of lease	Landlord's end-of-lease assessment	Comments
Windows				
Blinds/curtains				
Carpet or floor				
Walls				
Ceiling				
Lights and switches				
Outlets				
Baseboards				
Trim				
Other				

Page 2 of 7

Assessment of Condition

SAMPLE

Living room	Beginning of lease	End of lease	Landlord's end-of-lease assessment	Comments
Windows				
Blinds/curtains				
Carpet or floor				
Walls				
Ceilings				
Outlets				
Lights and switches				
Baseboards				
Trim				
Cable outlet				
Other				

Hallway and stairwell	Beginning of lease	End of lease	Landlord's end-of-lease assessment	Comments
Carpet or floor				
Walls				
Ceiling				
Lights and switches				
Outlets				
Baseboards				
Trim				
Stair treads				
Landing and handrail				
Other				

Assessment of Condition

Bedroom #1	Beginning of lease	End of lease	Landlord's end-of-lease assessment	Comments
Door				
Windows				
Blinds/curtains				
Carpet or floor				
Walls				
Ceiling				
Lights and switches				
Outlets				
Closet				
Baseboards				
Trim				
Other				

Bedroom #2	Beginning of lease	End of lease	Landlord's end-of-lease assessment	Comments
Door				
Windows				
Blinds/curtains				
Carpet or floor				
Walls				
Ceiling				
Lights and switches				
Outlets				
Closet				
Baseboards				
Trim				
Other				

SAMPLE

Assessment of Condition

SAMPLE

Bedroom #3	Beginning of lease	End of lease	Landlord's end-of-lease assessment	Comments
Door				
Windows				
Blinds/curtains				
Carpet or floor				
Walls				
Ceiling				
Lights and switches				
Outlets				
Closet				
Baseboards				
Trim				
Other				

Bathroom #1	Beginning of lease	End of lease	Landlord's end-of-lease assessment	Comments
Door				
Window				
Blinds/curtains				
Floor				
Walls				
Ceiling				
Sink				
Tub and/or shower				
Toilet				
Cabinet, shelves, closet				
Towel bars				
Lights and switches				
Outlets				
Baseboards				
Trim				
Other				

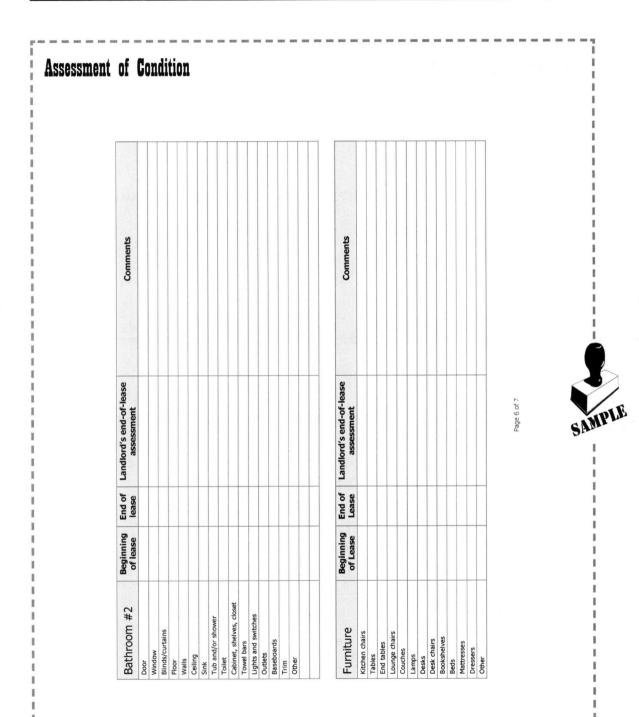

Assessment of Condition

Bathroom #2	Beginning of lease	End of lease	Landlord's end-of-lease assessment	Comments
Door				
Window				
Blinds/curtains				
Floor				
Walls				
Ceiling				
Sink				
Tub and/or shower				
Toilet				
Cabinet, shelves, closet				
Towel bars				
Lights and switches				
Outlets				
Baseboards				
Trim				
Other				

Furniture	Beginning of Lease	End of Lease	Landlord's end-of-lease assessment	Comments
Kitchen chairs				
Tables				
End tables				
Lounge chairs				
Couches				
Lamps				
Desks				
Desk chairs				
Bookshelves				
Beds				
Mattresses				
Dressers				
Other				

Page 6 of 7

SAMPLE

Assessment of Condition

SAMPLE

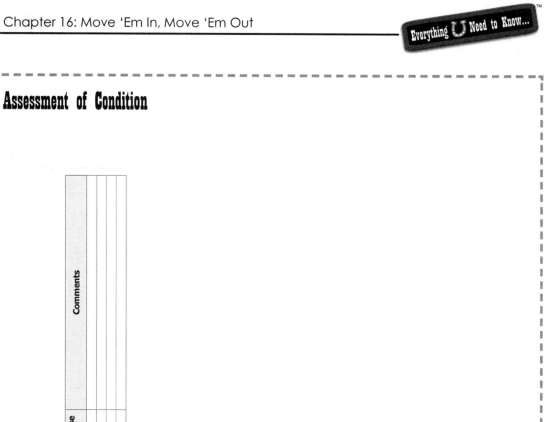

Furniture	Beginning of Lease	End of Lease	Landlord's end-of-lease assessment	Comments

Retaining or Returning a Security Deposit

As soon as your tenant moves, you need to immediately inspect your property! *Don't delay your inspection!* **Some states only give you so much time to notify the tenant if you determine it necessary to retain some or all of their security deposit.** Not to mention, there **may be some damage present that could actually** *get worse* as each day goes by, if not repaired. So get back into the unit as soon as possible after your tenant has vacated…

If you do indeed discover the tenant has left any part of the unit in disrepair, you have every right to retain all – or at least a portion of – his or her security deposit, *as was defined in the lease agreement.* **In order to exercise your right to retain, you need to prepare a letter that itemizes the damage(s) and the cost(s) to repair or replace.** *Be prepared to back up the damage(s) with pictures, estimates and/or receipts from contractors and vendors.* If you decide to perform the work yourself, then be sure to bill no more than an industry-accepted hourly wage for the labor portion – not what *you* think your time is worth.

When finalizing your letter, it's always recommended that you keep the language as cordial as possible. *You may even want to start off by thanking the tenant for their stay before you segue into the security deposit.* **There is no reason to "stick it to them"** – *just maintain an amiable (but still professional) approach*, so they feel as if there was *an effort made* to return all of their funds, but – unfortunately – there was some new damage that was not present at the time of the initial "assessment." **Any reasonable tenant should understand the discrepancy because they personally assessed the condition of the property and were encouraged to notate anything out of the ordinary.** Of course, if the tenant is unreasonable, don't expect them to agree with anything you say – *just have everything documented and leave it at that.*

If your calculations reveal that there is money left over, a check for the remaining funds plus any applicable interest should be enclosed with the letter.

Here are two important notes regarding the law: (1) If you happened to receive *any interest from the security deposit*, **some states require that you share some of the interest received (if not all of it) with the tenant.** (2) There are other states that have a **mandatory interest requirement** where *even if you do not benefit from the security deposit by keeping it in an interest bearing account, you must still credit the tenant with a certain percentage of interest* (e.g, 3%, 4%, 5%). While we would like to fit as much information as possible into this **American Landlord** volume, these types of legal issues require a more detailed assessment of the many landlord-tenant laws and statutes which can be found in the *American Landlord Law* volume (available at www.EverythingUNeedToKnow.com).

When you finally finish your letter, *make a copy of it and put it in the mail right away and be sure to use some type of service that includes delivery confirmation* (e.g., priority mail, certified mail, express mail) – there is no reason to hold on to it, even if you are unable to have a professional assess the condition of the property due to supply shortages, strikes, natural disasters or any other reason. Many states' laws require **you to at least notify the tenant that you intend on making a claim against the security deposit within a specific number of days** (with or without a formal estimate of the repairs in your hand).

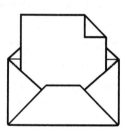

If the contractor or vendor you are used to dealing with is unable to provide a timely quote, *consider finding a different one or approximating the damage yourself in case you need to maintain your compliance with your state's law* – there may be a substantial penalty for delaying the returning of a tenant's security deposit.

In either case, **both types of letters (retaining or returning) need to be mailed to the tenant as soon as possible** - *as a general rule, notifying the tenant within 14 days after the end of the lease will keep you compliant in most states.*

If there is no damage to the property – and the tenant did their part by patching any nail holes, cleaning the carpet, bathrooms, kitchen, etc. – then **it is *strongly* recommended that you reciprocate by returning the entire security deposit, *along with a thank you letter*. These kinds of tenants are a true treasure and need to be reminded how much their efforts are greatly appreciated.** As you would expect, **each state does have its own required time frame within which security deposits *must* be returned.**

On the following page, a reference chart has been provided showing the deadlines for returning security deposits for all 50 states and the District of Columbia. For your convenience, this chart can also be printed from the enclosed CD-ROM.

Please Note: "No statute" appearing next to a state means that at the time this volume was published, there was no comment made within the state's landlord-tenant laws pertaining to this subject matter. Therefore, *one could possibly infer that there is no required timeframe.* However, we would suggest **a maximum of 14 days.**

An important note about this book's references to state laws and statutes: While this information is deemed to be accurate, *you are always encouraged to consult an expert in the area of landlord-tenant law or (at the very least) contact your state's equivalent to a "department of real estate"* to make sure the information provided in this book is still current at the time you are referencing it.

CAUTION

Deadlines for Returning Security Deposits

Alabama	35 days
Alaska	14 days if proper termination notice given, 30 days if not
Arizona	14 days
Arkansas	30 days
California	3 weeks
Colorado	1 month unless lease provides for longer period up to 60 days, 72 weekday non-holiday hours if emergency termination due to gas equipment hazard
Connecticut	30 days or within 15 days of receipt of forwarding address from tenant, whichever is later
Delaware	20 days
District of Columbia	45 days
Florida	15 days if no deductions, 30 days to give notice of what deductions will be made then tenant has 15 days to dispute any deduction and remaining deposit must be returned within 30 days of initial deduction notification
Georgia	1 month
Hawaii	14 days
Idaho	21 days unless both parties agree, then up to 30 days
Illinois	45 days if no deductions, 30 days to itemize deductions
Indiana	45 days
Iowa	30 days
Kansas	30 days
Kentucky	No statute
Louisiana	1 month
Maine	21 days if tenancy at will, 30 days if written lease
Maryland	45 days, 10 days to itemize deductions if tenant utilizes a surety bond
Massachusetts	30 days
Michigan	30 days
Minnesota	3 weeks, 5 days if termination due to condemnation

Mississippi	45 days
Missouri	30 days
Montana	10 days if no deductions, 30 days if deductions
Nebraska	14 days
Nevada	30 days
New Hampshire	30 days, if shared facilities and deposit is more than 30 days' rent then 20 days unless written agreement otherwise
New Jersey	30 days, 5 days if termination due to fire, flood, condemnation, evacuation
New Mexico	30 days
New York	Reasonable time
North Carolina	30 days
North Dakota	30 days
Ohio	30 days
Oklahoma	30 days
Oregon	31 days
Pennsylvania	30 days
Rhode Island	20 days
South Carolina	30 days
South Dakota	2 weeks
Tennessee	No statute, 10 days to itemize deductions
Texas	30 days
Utah	30 days or within 15 days of receipt of forwarding address from tenant, whichever is later
Vermont	14 days
Virginia	45 days
Washington	14 days
West Virginia	No statute
Wisconsin	21 days
Wyoming	30 days or within 15 days of receipt of forwarding address from tenant, whichever is later, 60 days if unit has damage

Chapter 17

Non-Owner Occupied Financing:
Making Dollars and Sense Out of Mortgages

This Chapter Discusses:

- ★ Why the Title (Deed) Should Be in Your Name
- ★ Your Personal Credit
- ★ Income and Asset Requirements
- ★ Mortgage Programs
- ★ Getting a Free Quote

There is nothing more confusing than the ever-changing mortgage industry. While this chapter cannot cite specific interest rates and underwriting guidelines (*due to the current mortgage and foreclosure crisis* that has caused lenders to either close their doors or drastically change their lending habits), it can *prepare you for industry accepted standards that have stood the test of time regardless of the current state of the economy or the real estate market*.

Why the Title (Deed) Should Be in Your Name

Your attorney and accountant may disagree with this section, but if you ever need to **refinance or get an equity line on an investment property** (better known in the mortgage industry as **"non-owner occupied property"**), the *only way to qualify for the best term and rate from a traditional lender is to have it titled under your name*.

If it's titled in the name of an LLC, partnership, corporation or whatever else your attorney can muster up, *almost every lender will restrict your loan-to-value ratio to 70-80% and your interest rate will be hiked*. The **"loan-to-value" (LTV)** ratio is basically the **amount of money you can borrow against the property's value**. If the property is valued at $100,000, lenders will allow you to finance only up to $70,000 – $80,000, while many other lenders may allow you to go to the full value of $100,000 (100%), *so long as the property is in your name*.

> ➢ *What about using a "quit-claim deed" to transfer title from my business into my name before I need financing?*

> A **"quit-claim deed"** is a simple, no-frills, one- or two-page legal document that **transfers one's interest in a property without any expressed warranty or guarantee to another person**. The problem is that *it has to be formally recorded in the public record and your county will most likely require you to pay recording and document stamp fees – which could cost you thousands*. However, the biggest difficulty with this tactic is that **lenders require the title of the property to have been in your name for at least six months – some even twelve months**.

> ➢ *Okay, but I thought lenders limited the number of properties you can finance under your own name, right?*

> This is **true of conforming** or **prime lenders,** such as the major banks, where the cap is usually five – but if things are really going

well for you, there are **nonprime lenders that will allow many more properties** *as long as you have enough income*.

If you, your attorney and your accountant are *that* adamant about titling the property under a different legal entity, you **may want to try approaching a local credit union or small-town bank** that you have built a relationship with over several years – and **have the balance to back up this banking relationship.** *That way, you may be able to get a personal exception.*

<u>In case you are in disbelief</u>: Contact any established bank or lender and ask them about their requirements for financing and refinancing non-owner occupied property – and even if you don't doubt our claims, *it's always a good idea to shop around as far in advance as possible to learn of any new requirements or restrictions*.

I tried to refinance my investment property to pay for a desperately needed a/c system a few years ago. About six months before that, my husband decided to put the title to our property under an LLC for asset protection. Sounded like a good idea at the time, but as it turns out, every lender I later contacted said they could not give me the amount of cash I needed. Even though it's a residential property, the lenders looked at the mortgage as if it was a commercial loan which naturally comes with more restrictions and a higher rate.

J. Edwards
Arkansas
Landlord

Your Personal Credit

Nothing will have a greater impact on your ability to refinance or buy more investment property more so than your personal credit. *You can finance almost anything today with a high credit score – regardless of your income.* There are even **ways to buy non-owner occupied property** *without putting any money down and without even having to prove your income.* **Don't get too excited, though**, because the **interest rate is usually a good 2-3% higher than the average** – and you **must be able to show adequate cash** sitting in a bank account (six to twelve months' worth).

Before you apply for a mortgage – or any type of financing for that matter – you need to be prepared by doing the following at least three months in advance:

⭐ **Pull your credit report from all three major credit bureaus.**

If there is a problem with your credit that needs to be disputed (such as an account that is not yours or an inaccurate account status), *it will take 30 days simply to dispute it.* If the problem then still remains, *you will need at least an additional 30 days to contact the creditor* and hopefully resolve the problem.

⭐ **Pay off as many revolving accounts as possible.**

The *more revolving accounts that you have with a zero balance, the higher your credit score will climb* – which means you get the **best of the best** in mortgage programs, terms and rates. Once you pay off an account, it may take the creditor 30-60 days to update their records with those of the credit bureaus.

⭐ **Stop applying for credit.**

The more times you apply (for a car, credit card, furniture, etc.), the lower your score goes. So – unless it is absolutely necessary – stop as far in advance as you can. **Remember:** Credit inquires stay on file for two years, but it's the ones that occur within the most recent year that have the greatest impact.

⭐ **Stop spending.**

Lenders love to see as much cash sitting in the bank as possible – *this makes you look heavy* (i.e., the more cash, the more weight you have to swing credit decisions in your favor) – that's a good thing. However, **you can't wait until the last minute to deposit money because it looks suspicious** – *get it in there as early as you can!*

⭐ **Contact your mortgage broker or lender to find out what they need.**
Do not let them coax you into pulling your credit. It's unnecessary
and potentially harmful – it *only takes one point* to knock you out of
one program and into another, less favorable one. **Just give them
the scenario, your credit scores from all three bureaus and ask
them what you will need to have in place three months from now**.
If they ask any questions, be as honest as possible – *this should be a
very candid conversation*. **Remember, you are not applying just
yet** – *so this would be an ideal time to lay everything on the table.*
Your goal is to get as much information as possible so you are fully
prepared to apply when the time comes.

The world of credit and mortgage lending is a game that can easily go on for as long
as you are prepared. **Gather as much information as possible in advance**, *so you
can be sure of getting exactly what you want.* If you can't get the program you most
want, then go for the next best thing. **Getting approved can be a challenge for
anyone** – *even millionaires!* – **if accounts and credit files are even** *just a little* **out
of line, your application may be denied.**

Income and Asset Requirements

Your lenders will be able to more accurately describe what is
needed for their particular programs. However, **you do need
to be made aware of some important things as far in
advance as possible**. *If two out of your three credit scores
is 720 or above, you do not need to be concerned with having
to document your income, but if you score just one point
lower, you may have to prove how much money you make* –
of course, this refers to getting the highest **LTVs**, like 100%
financing. The more money you have to put down, the lower
the score needed – and the more lax the lender's requirements become.

For the sake of discussion – **If you are required to prove your income, here is a list of the most common forms of documentation accepted by mortgage lenders:**

⭐ **Last Two Years' W-2s/1099s and Last 30 Days of Pay Stubs**

⭐ **6-12 months of Personal Bank Statements**
If you are unable to produce W-2s/1099s and pay stubs, this is often an acceptable alternative. 100*% of the deposits are tallied* to determine your *average monthly income*.

⭐ **12 months of Business Bank Statements**
If you are self-employed and cannot show your tax returns because of excessive deductions, many lenders will accept your business bank statements. However, *lenders will count only 75% of the total amount of deposits* made.

⭐ **Rental Income**
In addition to your standard income, you are *allowed to count 75% of your annual rental income in addition to your other income*. Lenders count on a mandatory vacancy rate of 25%, regardless of how many years your tenants have been there. Landlord, beware! – *Lenders may require copies of your lease agreements*.

⭐ **Child Support and Alimony**
You can claim *100% of child support and alimony income* – as long as you can demonstrate you will continue to receive these payments *for the next three years*.

⭐ **Disability and Social Security**
Government issued checks are actually calculated at 125%.
For example: If you get $10,000 a year in Social Security, lenders will count it as $12,500 because it is not taxed like payroll checks.

There are two types of **standard asset requirements** that are an *inherent part* of an average mortgage loan:

 ## Asset Requirement Type I: Closing Costs

The first type requires you to **show that you have had enough funds sitting in a bank account for at least two months to cover your closing costs (e.g., down payment, lender/broker fees, taxes, title insurance, interest, etc.).** <u>**For example**</u>: If your down payment is $10,000 and your closing costs are about $6,000, you would need to source a total of $16,000 from one or more of your accounts (that has had an average collected balance of *at least* this amount – or higher – for the past two months).

Asset Requirement Type II: Reserves

The second asset requirement is what is known as **reserves.** Reserves are **the amount of money necessary to continue paying the proposed mortgage payment (including principal, interest, taxes and insurance) for a specific amount of time, should you become unemployed.** The amount of time required by lenders *ranges from two to twelve months* and *must also be sourced from one or more of your accounts for the past two months*.

If your total proposed mortgage payment is $2,000 and the lender requires reserves of six months, you would have to show that you've had at least $12,000 or higher as an account balance for the past two months – this is in addition to the $16,000 you would need to show for the closing costs mentioned above.

EXAMPLE

One of the reasons lenders require both types of assets to be sourced from accounts with an average balance equal to or greater than the required amount is to prevent the laundering of money obtained from illegal sources (e.g., drugs, weapon sales, theft, etc.) from being washed into real estate – which then makes it difficult to trace.

Mortgage Programs

Depending on your **credit**, the **type of documentation** you are willing to provide and the proposed **LTV** of the property, there are bound to be programs to accommodate your needs through a broad spectrum of different types of lenders.

<u>In the end</u>: The lower your credit score, the fewer income and asset documents you are able to provide, and the higher your LTV (above 80%), *the higher your interest rate is going to climb because you are considered more of a risk* in lenders' eyes.

To assist you in your search for future financing, **here is a list of how lenders are classified and what type of programs are available, with regards to income and asset documentation requirements**:

★ Conforming

These are **mortgage lenders** *that conform to the strict guidelines of* **Fannie Mae** *and* **Freddie Mac**. They **have the strictest requirements** – but *offer the lowest rates*.

★ Prime

These lenders **model the strict guidelines of conforming lenders, but offer higher loan amounts.** *Minimum credit scores are usually 620 and above with no more than one late payment allowed* on an existing mortgage.

★ Alt-A

These alternative lenders **cater to borrowers who have excellent credit (680+), but who do not fit exactly into either the prime or conforming lenders guidelines.** This may be because they need a higher LTV ratio, lack traditional employment or have nontraditional assets that are difficult to verify.

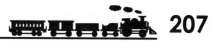

★ Nonprime

Also known as **"subprime lenders,"** these *allow credit scores to start as low as 500* and *will permit several mortgage late payments*. However, the lower the credit score (*usually dropping below 580*), the more the **LTV** ratios requirements decrease – and programs consequently come with significantly higher interest rates.

★ Hard Money

These types of lenders **usually don't bother to require or verify income or assets** – and they *usually require LTVs of 75% or less*. Needless to say, **this is the bottom of the barrel for hard-to-fund borrowers.** Interest rates from these lenders have commonly been seen up in the double digits.

If you decide to **search around online for mortgage lenders and quotes**, chances are you are going to run into *some commonly used terms and acronyms* that may need further explanation.

★ Full Documentation (Full Doc)

This is the **classic mortgage requiring two years of W-2s/1099s, 30 days' worth of pay stubs and two years of tax returns.** If you are self-employed, you will need the last two years of your personal tax returns and two years of your business tax returns. **For both cases,** *you will also need to verify your assets such as bank accounts, mutual funds, stocks, retirement accounts, etc.*

★ Stated Income Verified Assets (SIVA)

If you are unable to prove your income for the past two years, but can **verify your assets**, you can use this program to state your income on your mortgage application without providing further proof of it.

★ Stated Income Stated Assets (SISA)

The same as a "**SIVA**" – except that you are *unable to also verify your assets, so they are simply stated as well*.

★ No Documentation (No Doc)

This type of mortgage **does not require that any income or assets be disclosed even on the mortgage application** – zip, zilch, nothing, nada, none.

★ Limited Documentation (Lite Doc)

Instead of providing W-2's and pay stubs as in the case with full documentation, this program **allows six to twelve months' worth of bank statements, where all of the recorded deposits are averaged to determine your gross monthly income**.

Getting a Free Quote

Never give out your social security number! How's that for a start? **Any lender can quote you a program, term and rate** *without pulling your credit*. And **if they tell you otherwise, move on to the next lender.** Traditionally, *it's the mortgage broker that will give you a hard time, but don't let this discourage you from using a mortgage broker*. When it comes to finding a loan for a difficult scenario, *then* **the mortgage broker is usually your best source.**

You just need to find someone that will take the time to *get you a quote without pulling your credit*. Traditional banks – and conventional mortgage lenders – will usually be more than glad to talk with you right over the phone. If you want to appear helpful, **check your credit yourself through all three major credit bureaus and tell the loan officer or mortgage broker your scores.**

A word of caution regarding loan officers and mortgage brokers: Unless you clearly stress the following, **"I am interested in financing a *non-owner* occupied property,"** *you will be misquoted most of the time*. Loan officers and mortgage brokers are so accustomed to giving quotes for **"owner-occupied homes,"** they **tend to forget to check their other underwriting matrices** – *all of which have completely different requirements and rates.*

CAUTION

If you are trying to put less than 10% down on an investment property and two out of your three credit scores are not close to 700, *don't bother wasting your time contacting conforming and prime lenders*. **This means**: Avoid the major banks and conservative mortgage lenders – unless they have alternative loan divisions.

You would be **far better served** by contacting a **local mortgage broker** or **going online to search for an Alt-A or nonprime lender who offers non-owner occupied (NOO) loans**. Of course, you can always visit **AmericanLandlord.com** to receive a free quote from affiliated lenders and brokers, a great number of whom offer **"non-owner occupied financing"** at very competitive rates.

Conclusion

The overall purpose of this book, as well as that of all the forthcoming volumes in this series, is to give you "**Everything U Need to Know…**" *so you can become successful with the bare essentials!*

There will always be other issues left unaddressed – including suddenly-deceased tenants, income tax preparation, rent control, and so on – but information about handling these issues is readily available when you need them.

Why haven't we addressed questions such as...

 What do you do when a tenant unexpectedly dies?

For one thing, problems like this are rarely encountered and since the solutions are matters of common sense, they have not been directly addressed in *American Landlord*. But seeing as we just posed this particular question, we'll answer it in case we piqued your curiosity.

If this should ever happen to you, **call the emergency contact listed on the rental application and coordinate the removal of their belongings and be sure to give the family your sincerest condolences.** Sure, you would have every right to pursue the tenant's estate for the remainder of the lease term, but **why aggravate the family during such a terrible time?** *Just get their permission to move on about your business and post a vacancy sign…* (And so you know, there are many attorneys out there right now disagreeing with the simplicity of this advice – and you are more than welcome to break out your checkbook for any one of them should you find yourself with a dead tenant.)

Rather than focusing your attentions on unlikelihoods – such as what to do with dead tenants – here is something more practical and useful that can never be stressed enough:

☆ Manage your money well!

Throughout this volume of **American Landlord**, the phrase *"less expensive"* is used instead of *"cheap"* for a specific reason: *to keep your overhead low, without compromising the comfort and safety of your tenants*. It's important to be known within your community as an **"American Landlord"** – not an **"American Slumlord."** If you give your tenants the respect they deserve by providing a comfortable and safe place to live, you should find their tenancy – and your professional relationship – to be an enjoyable and rewarding experience for both of you.

Headaches will always come and go, that's why there is always some type of pain reliever when you need one. *Don't ever get discouraged* – problems are an inherent part of everyday life and, despite what you may think, finding the appropriate remedy can be a worthwhile experience that you can draw upon for many years to come.

Whatever your concern, the **"Everything U Need to Know" series guidebooks** are intended to address those issues at a level that is both comprehensive for the industry professional, yet laid out step-by-step for the complete novice. And, if by chance, you cannot find the answers to your questions by reading one of our guidebooks, **EverythingUNeedToKnow.com** is only *a quick click away…*

In the end, it all comes down to one key piece of advice: *Take advantage of your available resources as much as possible*… and you'll find yourself a most prosperous **"American Landlord."**

Section 8:
Government Assisted Tenant-Based Housing

This Appendix Includes:

★ **A Brief History of Public Housing Assistance**

★ **Housing Choice Voucher Program**

★ **Responsibilities of Everyone Involved**

★ **How to Get Started**

★ **Housing Quality Standards Inspection**

★ **Tenancy Addendum for Lease Agreement**

★ **Housing Assistance Payments (HAP) Contract**

★ **Screening Housing Assisted Tenants**

As **government subsidized programs** (e.g., **Section 8**) are not utilized by most people who choose to become an **American Landlord**, this subject has not been specifically addressed within the main body of this volume.

However, *should you wish to explore the intricate ins and outs of tenant-based housing programs*, **this appendix is an** *invaluable treasure trove* **of information** that will provide you with **"Everything U Need to Know…"** about **"Section 8"** (now known as the **Housing Choice Voucher Program**), along with its countless rules and regulations. This way, *you* **will be able to** *personally* **assess the many benefits and obligations that are stringently involved.**

But… just so you can't say that you weren't warned: **The majority of this appendix is derived directly from United States federal government documents**… so, as you can imagine, some of this material is going to be dryer than James Bond's signature martini… [You needn't worry, though! *We* won't leave you either shaken *or* stirred!]

That being said, **since government sponsored programs** *are* **so heavily regulated and painstakingly detailed**, *it would take an entire volume* (if not a whole series) *to thoroughly explain the intricacies of the tenant-based housing programs.* Instead, **this appendix will provide you with "Everything U Need to Know…" to assess the latest requirements and benefits so** *you can decide if you want to participate in this federally subsidized program.*

A Brief History of Public Housing Assistance

It all began back toward the end of the Great Depression era, when the **federal government passed** the **U.S. Housing Act of 1937** *to provide affordable housing to low-income families.* This was **designed as a cooperative measure between the federal and state governments whereby** *each individual state would administer the program through its own* **Public Housing Authorities (PHAs).** For more than 25 years, this program exclusively used government housing, not privately owned real estate.

Private landlords were not integrated into the federal housing programs until 1965 when **Section 23** amended the **U.S. Housing Act of 1937.** Ironically, *this amendment did not allow the private landlord to interact with the tenant or even execute a lease.* Instead, **the Public Housing Authority** *required the landlord to lease* his or her **property to the PHA,** thereby **allowing the PHA to then sublease the property to the tenant** *and retain management control.*

It wasn't until **1974** when the **Section 8 program** (also known as the **"Rental Certificate Program"**) was introduced to **permit the individual landlord to perform his or her own duties** *(i.e., screening the tenant, collecting the rent and* *maintaining the property).* Under the **Rental Certificate Program**, *tenants generally paid 25% of their adjusted income* toward the rent; in 1983, each tenant's share *increased to 30%* of his or her adjusted income.

The **main restriction under Section 8** is that **HUD** (the **U.S. Department of Housing and Urban Development**) **established a maximum amount of gross rent** that a unit could be leased for under the program (known as **"Fair Market Rent"**). So, **in 1984, yet another program was introduced** called the **"Rental Voucher Program,"** which was *designed to give tenants a little more flexibility in choosing where they wanted to live* by allowing them to **rent a little more or less than the Fair Market Rent payment standard.** It was these two programs (**Section 8** and the **Rental Voucher Program**) that the **federal government ultimately decided to merge by October, 2001,** which *leads us to where we currently are in the area of tenant-based housing assistance* – the **"Housing Choice Voucher Program."**

Housing Choice Voucher Program

This **present day, tenant-based housing program** – backed by the federal government – **enables very low-income families, the elderly and the disabled to afford decent, safe, and sanitary housing by private landlords,** which may include single-family homes, townhouses and apartments. Basically, *the tenant is free to choose any housing that meets the requirements of the program.*

The **Housing Choice Vouchers are** *administered locally* **by Public Housing Authorities.** In turn, **the PHAs** *receive federal funding* **from HUD to administer the voucher program.**

A tenant that is issued a **Housing Voucher** is **responsible for finding a suitable housing unit of his or her choice where the landlord agrees to rent under the program.** *The rental property must meet minimum standards of health and safety, as determined by the* **PHA.**

A **housing subsidy is paid to the landlord** *directly by the* **PHA** on behalf of the participating tenant. *The tenant then pays the difference between the actual rent charged by the landlord and the amount subsidized by the program.* Under certain circumstances, if authorized by the PHA, a tenant may use their voucher to purchase a modest home.

Responsibilities of Everyone Involved

There are **four parties involved in the Housing Choice Program**: HUD, the **PHA**, the **landlord** and the **tenant** – *each of whom must perform his or her own respective mandatory obligations to comply with the program guidelines*. A list of these responsibilities has been provided below:

☆ HUD Responsibilities

- Developing policy, regulations, handbooks, notices and guidance to implement housing legislation;
- Allocating housing assistance funds;
- Providing technical assistance and training to **PHA**s; and;
- Monitoring **PHA** compliance with program requirements and performance goals.

☆ PHA Responsibilities

- Establishing local policies;
- Determining tenant eligibility and re-examination of tenant income;
- Maintaining a waiting list and selecting tenants for admission;
- Calculating the amount of the tenant's share of the rent, as well as the housing assistance payment;
- Establishing of utility allowances;
- Conducting outreach to owners – with special attention to those with units outside of areas of poverty or minority concentration;

♦ Assisting persons with disabilities in finding satisfactory housing;

♦ Approving units – including assuring compliance with **HUD's** housing quality standards – and determining the reasonableness of the rent;

♦ Making housing assistance payments to owners;

♦ Conducting informal reviews and hearings at the request of applicants and participants who challenge **PHA** administrative decisions; and;

♦ Complying with **Fair Housing** and equal opportunity requirements, **HUD** regulations and requirements (including **HUD**-approved applications for program funding), the **PHA**'s own administrative plan, as well as federal, state and local laws.

★ Landlord Responsibilities

♦ Screening, selecting and entering into leases with tenants;

♦ Complying with the **HAP (Housing Assistance Payment)** contract, lease, and tenancy addendum;

♦ Carrying out normal owner functions during the term of the lease, such as enforcing the contract, performing maintenance, collecting the tenant's share of rent and charging tenants for any damage to the unit;

♦ Maintaining unit compliance with the Housing Quality Standards;

♦ Complying with Fair Housing and equal opportunity requirements; and;

♦ Paying for utilities, maintenance and other related services (unless specified under the lease as being the responsibility of the tenant).

★ Tenant Responsibilities

♦ Supplying true and complete required information including:

- *Any information that the* **PHA** *or* **HUD** *determines necessary for the administering of the program* – including evidence of citizenship or eligible immigration status;

  - Information as requested for *regular or interim re-examinations of household income*; and;
  - **Social Security Numbers** and *signed consent forms for obtaining and verifying information*;

♦ Fixing any breach of housing quality standards *caused by the tenant*;

♦ Allowing the **PHA** *to inspect the unit* at reasonable times and with reasonable notice;

♦ Not committing any violation of the lease;

♦ Not engaging in criminal activity;

♦ **Notifying the PHA and the owner** *before* **moving or terminating the lease** with the landlord;

♦ Promptly **providing the PHA a copy of any eviction notice** from the landlord;

♦ **Using the assisted unit as a** *residence only* **and as the** *only residence of the tenant*. Members of the household may engage in legal profit-making activities within the unit, but *only if those activities are incidental* to the primary use of the unit as a residence. The members of the family also *may not receive another housing subsidy* in the same unit *or* a different unit;

♦ Promptly **informing the PHA of any change** in household composition and *obtaining* **PHA** *approval* to add a family member *by any means other* than birth, adoption, or court-awarded custody of a child;

♦ **Notifying the PHA of any extended absence** from the unit and then complying with PHA policies governing such an absence from the unit;

♦ *Not subletting* the unit, assigning the lease, or *having any financial interest in the unit;* and;

♦ *Not committing fraud, bribery, or any other corrupt or criminal act in connection with any assisted housing programs.*

How to Get Started

There are a few steps required to participate in the Section 8: Housing Choice Voucher Program. The first one would be **contacting your local PHA to begin the process** (you can visit **www.hud.gov/offices/pih/pha/contacts** to search for your local agency). *Each* **PHA** *should have the appropriate forms and be able to answer all of your questions concerning enrollment*.

To better understand the overall flow of events, **the next page shows a diagram that outlines the entire process for both the tenant and the landlord (the process begins with the tenant applying for eligibility):**

An Overview of the Section 8 Process

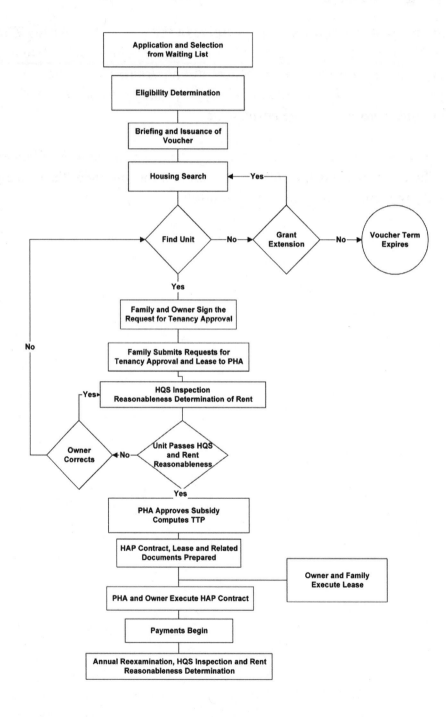

But *before* you place your phone call, **there are three important sets of documents** (each one a different step) **required of *all landlords* who wish to participate**. **You should *review these carefully*** so you have a very clear understanding of what is expected.

These are: the **Housing Standards Quality** inspection, a **Tenancy Addendum** for your Lease Agreement and the **Housing Assistance Payments (HAP)** contract.

Each of these is thoroughly discussed in the following sections of this appendix – and you can also review the *actual* HUD *documents required in these steps* under **Appendix B:** *Section 8 Forms and Agreements* or print them from the **enclosed CD-ROM**. *Any further questions should be directed to your local* **PHA.**

Housing Quality Standards Inspection

Every year, the local PHA is required to perform an inspection of the rental property to ensure the unit is a *"decent, safe and sanitary"* place to live. In addition to charging a reasonable monthly rent, there are *essentially 13 requirements that must be satisfied in order for your rental property to pass an inspection*.

<u>**These are outlined as follows:**</u>

☆ Sanitary Facilities

- The dwelling *must* include sanitary facilities within the unit.
- The sanitary facilities *must be in proper operating condition* and adequate for personal cleanliness and disposal of human waste.
- The sanitary facilities must be *usable in privacy*.
- The *bathroom must be located in a separate room* and have a flush toilet in proper operating condition.
- The unit *must have a fixed basin* (lavatory) with a sink trap and hot and cold running water in proper operating condition.
- The unit *must have a shower or tub* with hot and cold running water in proper operating condition.

♦ The facilities *must utilize an approved public or private disposal system*, including a locally approved septic system.

★ Food Preparation and Refuse Disposal

♦ The dwelling unit *must have suitable space and equipment to store, prepare, and serve food in a sanitary manner*.

♦ The dwelling unit *must have an oven and a stove or range*. A microwave oven may be substituted for a tenant-supplied oven and stove or range. A microwave may be substituted for an owner-supplied oven and stove or range *if* the tenant agrees and microwave ovens are furnished to both subsidized and unsubsidized tenants in the same building or premises.

♦ The dwelling unit *must have a refrigerator of appropriate size* for the family.

♦ *All required equipment must be in proper operating condition*. According to the lease, equipment may be supplied either by the owner or the family.

♦ The dwelling unit *must have a kitchen sink* in proper operating condition, with a sink trap and hot and cold running water. The sink must drain into an approved public or private system.

♦ The dwelling unit *must have space for storage, preparation, and serving of food.*

♦ Facilities and services for the *sanitary disposal of food waste and refuse*, including temporary storage facilities where necessary, are required.

★ Space and Security

♦ The dwelling unit must provide *adequate space and security for the family*.

♦ At a minimum, the dwelling unit *must have a* **living room**, a **kitchen** and a **bathroom**.

- The dwelling unit *must have at least one bedroom* or living/sleeping room *for every two occupants.* Other than very young children, **children of opposite sexes may not be forced to occupy the same bedroom** or living/sleeping room.
- Dwelling unit *windows that are accessible* from the outside *must be lockable*.
- *Exterior doors* to the unit *must be lockable*.

★ Thermal Environment

- The dwelling unit must be able to *provide a thermal environment that is healthy for the human body.*
- There must be a *safe system for heating the dwelling unit*, such as electric baseboard, radiator, or forced air systems. In order to ensure a *healthy living environment appropriate for the climate,* the system must be able to provide adequate heat either directly or indirectly to *each room* in the unit.
- If present, an air-conditioning system or evaporative cooler must *safely* provide adequate cooling to each room.
- The heating and/or air-conditioning system *must be in proper operating condition*.
- The dwelling unit *must not contain non-vented room heaters that burn gas, oil, or kerosene.* Electric heaters *are* acceptable.

★ Illumination and Electricity

- Each room *must have adequate natural or artificial illumination* to permit normal indoor activities and to support the health and safety of occupants.
- The dwelling unit *must have sufficient electrical sources* such that occupants can use essential electrical appliances.
- Electrical fixtures and wiring **must not pose a fire hazard**.
- There must be *at least one window* in the *living room* and *each sleeping room*.

- The *kitchen area and* the *bathroom must have a permanent ceiling or wall-mounted fixture* in proper operating condition.
- The *kitchen must have at least one electrical outlet* in proper operating condition.
- The *living room* and *each sleeping space must have at least two electrical outlets* in proper operating condition. Permanent overhead or wall-mounted light fixtures may count as one of the required electrical outlets.

★ Structure and Materials

- The dwelling unit *must be structurally sound.*
- The structure *must not present any threat to the health and safety of the occupants* and *must protect the occupants from the environment*.
- *Ceilings, walls and floors must not have any serious defects* – such as severe bulging or large leaning holes, loose surface materials, severe buckling, missing parts or other serious damage.
- The *roof must be structurally sound and weather-proofed*.
- The *foundation and exterior wall structure and surface must not have any serious defects* – such as serious leaning, buckling, sagging, large holes or defects that *may result in air infiltration or vermin infestation*.
- The *condition and equipment* of interior and exterior stairs, halls, porches, and walkways *must not present the danger of tripping and falling*.
- *Elevators must be working safely*.

★ Interior Air Quality

- The dwelling unit *must be free of air pollutant levels that threaten* the occupants' health including carbon monoxide, sewer gas, fuel gas, dust, and other harmful pollutants.
- There *must be adequate air circulation* in the dwelling unit.

- *Bathroom areas must have one window that can open* or other adequate ventilation.
- *Any sleeping room must have at least one window.*

☆ Water Supply

- The *water supply must be free of contamination*.
- The dwelling unit *must be served by an approved public or private water supply* that is *sanitary and free from pollutants*.

☆ Lead-Based Paint

- The **Lead-Based Paint Poisoning Prevention Act** as amended (42 U.S.C. 4821 - 4846) and the **Residential Lead-Based Paint Hazard Reduction Act** of 1992 and *implementing* **Regulation 24 CFR, Part 35, Subparts A, B, M** and **R** *apply to the Housing Choice Voucher Program.*
- The **requirements apply to dwelling units built prior to 1978** *that can be occupied by families with children under six years of age,* excluding zero bedroom dwellings.
- During initial and annual inspections of **pre-1978 units** that can be occupied by families with children under six years of age, the *inspector must conduct a visual assessment for deteriorated paint surfaces* and the *owner must stabilize deteriorated surfaces.* **Applicable areas include** *painted surfaces* within the dwelling unit, *exterior painted surfaces* associated with the dwelling unit, *common areas of the building* through which residents must pass to gain access to the unit and *areas frequented by resident children under six years of age* – especially play areas and child care facilities.

- For units occupied by **"environmental intervention blood lead level" (lead-poisoned) children under the age of six,** *a risk assessment must be conducted* (paid for by the PHA), *and the owner must complete hazard reduction activities* if lead hazards are identified during the risk assessment.

☆ Access

- Use and maintenance of the unit must be possible *without unauthorized use of other private properties.*
- The unit *must have private access.*
- *In case of fire, the building must contain an alternate means of exit,* such as fire stairs or windows – including use of a ladder for windows above the second floor.

☆ Site and Neighborhood

- The *site and neighborhood must be reasonably free from* disturbing noises and reverberations or other *dangers to the health, safety, and general welfare of the occupants.*
- The *site and neighborhood may not be subject to serious adverse natural or manmade environmental conditions* – such as dangerous walks or steps, instability, flooding, poor drainage, septic tank back-ups or sewer hazards, mudslides, abnormal air pollution, smoke or dust, excessive noise, vibration, or vehicular traffic, excessive accumulations of trash, vermin or rodent infestation or potential fire hazards.

☆ Sanitary Condition

- The dwelling unit and its equipment must be in sanitary condition.
- The dwelling unit and its equipment must be free of vermin and rodent infestation.

☆ Smoke Detectors

- ◆ *On each level of the dwelling unit* – including basements, but excluding spaces and unfinished attics – *at least one battery-operated or hard-wired smoke detector in proper operating condition must be present.*
- ◆ Smoke detectors *must be installed in accordance with and meet the requirements* of the **National Fire Protection Association Standards (www.nfpa.org).**
- ◆ *If a hearing-impaired person* is occupying the unit, *the smoke detectors must have an alarm system designed for hearing-impaired persons as specified* by the **National Fire Protection Association Standards.**

Tenancy Addendum for Lease Agreement

The **"tenancy addendum"** is *required by* **HUD** *to be attached to your existing lease agreement*. This addendum **sets forth the tenancy requirements for the program and the composition of the household,** *as approved by the* **PHA.**

The landlord must sign the HUD tenancy addendum along with the prospective tenant. NOTE: The **tenant has the right to enforce** the tenancy addendum *against the landlord* (should the landlord fail to perform his or her responsibilities) and **the tenancy addendum will prevail over** *any* **other provisions of the lease!**

Be sure to read this addendum very carefully – it can either be found in **Appendix B: *Section 8 Forms and Agreements*** or printed directly from the **enclosed CD-ROM**.

The **tenancy addendum** is outlined in the following manner:

- Voucher Program
- Lease
- Use of Contract Unit
- Rent to Owner (Landlord)
- Tenant Payment to Owner (Landlord)
- Other Fees and Charges
- Maintenance, Utilities and Other Services
- Termination of Tenancy Lease: Relation to HAP Contract
- PHA Termination of Assistance
- Tenant(s) Move Out
- Security Deposit
- Prohibition of Discrimination
- Conflict with Other Provisions of Lease
- Notices
- Definitions by Owner (Landlord)

Housing Assistance Payments (HAP) Contract

The **Housing Assistance Payments (HAP) contract** *is a written agreement between the* **PHA** *and the landlord.* The **HAP contract** *must be* **in the form prescribed by HUD** (a sample of which can be found under **Appendix B:** *Section 8 Forms and Agreements* and on the **enclosed CD-ROM**).

Under the **HAP contract, the PHA** *agrees to make housing assistance payments to the landlord on behalf of the tenant.* <u>**FOR EXAMPLE**</u>: The **PHA** may pay 70% of a given tenant's monthly rent, making that *tenant responsible for paying* the remaining 30%.

NOTE: Respective contributions *will vary depending* on the tenant's needs, *as determined by the* **PHA**. That being said, the same rules still apply: **If the tenant doesn't pay his or her share, you may evict them just like any other tenant.**

Prior to getting the **PHA**'s approval to execute a **HAP contract**, the **PHA** *is required by* HUD to *ensure the following program requirements* have been met:

- ◆ Owner is eligible;
- ◆ Unit is eligible;
- ◆ Unit has been inspected by the **PHA** and meets **Housing Quality Standards**;
- ◆ Lease includes the tenancy addendum; and;
- ◆ The rent charged by the landlord is reasonable.

Upon approval, the landlord and the **PHA** can execute the **HAP** contract. **Housing Assistance Payments are due to the landlord** *on the first day of each month.* **The landlord's right to receive Housing Assistance Payments** *depends on compliance with all the provisions of the* **HAP contract.** When the landlord endorses and deposits the **HAP** check, the landlord has reaffirmed his or her compliance with the terms of the **HAP** contract. **No payments may be made to the landlord after the tenant moves out of the rental property or when the lease term ends.**

Screening Housing Assisted Tenants

This observation is *NOT* true of everyone, but – more often than not – you will probably find that *those applicants who need housing assistance will have lower credit scores than those who do not.*

Obviously, the situation of low-income earners does not make it easy to satisfy creditor obligations – let alone a family's hunger – so **how do you appropriately evaluate their applications for tenancy?** Well, *you use the same exact screening steps as outlined in the various tenant screening chapters of this book*, starting with **Chapter 4. The only difference is that you can add the federal government's portion into the income equation as it will usually be paying the majority of the rent, but this does not mean you change your standard guidelines** – *that would be discriminatory!*

First of all, *not all assisted tenants will have bad credit, evictions and criminal records.* You may encounter frequent credit blemishes, but **if you have already predetermined that you are willing to consider any applicant with credit problems, it shouldn't matter if they are assisted or not;** *a normal, thorough screening will reveal the same criteria for you to yield a "yes" or "no."*

And... as if you haven't read *enough* about tenant-based housing assistance to know by now whether you have any interest in engaging in the process as an **American Landlord**, an excerpt from **HUD** *regarding tenant screening for the* **Section 8: Housing Choice Voucher Program** has been provided on the next page, for your reading pleasure:

An Excerpt from HUD Regarding Section 8 Tenant Screening

Office of the Assistant Secretary, HUD

(f) For purposes of this section, "owner" includes a principal or other interested party.

[60 FR 34695, July 3, 1995, as amended at 63 FR 27437, May 18, 1998; 64 FR 26644, May 14, 1999; 64 FR 56913, Oct. 21, 1999; 65 FR 16821, Mar. 30, 2000]

§ 982.307   Tenant screening.

(a) *PHA option and owner responsibility.* (1) The PHA has no liability or responsibility to the owner or other persons for the family's behavior or suitability for tenancy. However, the PHA may opt to screen applicants for family behavior or suitability for tenancy. The PHA must conduct any such screening of applicants in accordance with policies stated in the PHA administrative plan.

(2) The owner is responsible for screening and selection of the family to occupy the owner's unit. At or before PHA approval of the tenancy, the PHA must inform the owner that screening and selection for tenancy is the responsibility of the owner.

(3) The owner is responsible for screening of families on the basis of their tenancy histories. An owner may consider a family's background with respect to such factors as:

(i) Payment of rent and utility bills;

(ii) Caring for a unit and premises;

(iii) Respecting the rights of other residents to the peaceful enjoyment of their housing;

(iv) Drug-related criminal activity or other criminal activity that is a threat to the health, safety or property of others; and

(v) Compliance with other essential conditions of tenancy.

(b) *PHA information about tenant.* (1) The PHA must give the owner:

(i) The family's current and prior address (as shown in the PHA records); and

(ii) The name and address (if known to the PHA) of the landlord at the family's current and prior address.

(2) When a family wants to lease a dwelling unit, the PHA may offer the owner other information in the PHA possession, about the family, including information about the tenancy history of family members, or about drug-trafficking by family members.

§ 982.308

(3) The PHA must give the family a statement of the PHA policy on providing information to owners. The statement must be included in the information packet that is given to a family selected to participate in the program. The PHA policy must provide that the PHA will give the same types of information to all families and to all owners.

(Approved by the Office of Management and Budget under control number 2577–0169)

[60 FR 34695, July 3, 1995, as amended at 60 FR 45661, Sept. 1, 1995; 61 FR 27163, May 30, 1996; 64 FR 26645, May 14, 1999; 64 FR 49658, Sept. 14, 1999]

§ 982.308   Lease and tenancy.

(a) *Tenant's legal capacity.* The tenant must have legal capacity to enter a lease under State and local law. "Legal capacity" means that the tenant is bound by the terms of the lease and may enforce the terms of the lease against the owner.

(b) *Form of lease.* (1) The tenant and the owner must enter a written lease for the unit. The lease must be executed by the owner and the tenant.

(2) If the owner uses a standard lease form for rental to unassisted tenants in the locality or the premises, the lease must be in such standard form (plus the HUD-prescribed tenancy addendum). If the owner does not use a standard lease form for rental to unassisted tenants, the owner may use another form of lease, such as a PHA model lease (including the HUD-prescribed tenancy addendum). The HAP contract prescribed by HUD will contain the owner's certification that if the owner uses a standard lease form for rental to unassisted tenants, the lease is in such standard form.

(c) *State and local law.* The PHA may review the lease to determine if the lease complies with State and local law. The PHA may decline to approve the tenancy if the PHA determines that the lease does not comply with State or local law.

(d) *Required information.* The lease must specify all of the following:

(1) The names of the owner and the tenant;

Section 8 Forms and Agreements: Housing Choice Voucher Program

This Appendix Includes:

★ Request for Tenancy Approval

★ Housing Quality Standards Inspection

★ Tenancy Addendum for Lease Agreement

★ Tenancy Addendum for Lease Agreement (Manufactured Homes)

★ Housing Assistance Payments (HAP) Contract

★ Housing Assistance Payments (HAP) Contract (Manufactured Homes)

The forms and agreements provided in this section were obtained directly from the **U.S. Department of Housing and Urban Development** at the time that this edition of *American Landlord* was **first published in December 2007**. While these forms were the most up-to-date versions available at the time, it is strongly recommended that you visit the **HUD website (www.hud.gov/offices/pih/programs/hcv/forms)** if you are serious about participating in the **Section 8: Housing Choice Voucher Program**. This way, you can be absolutely certain that you have read *the latest information* available to the general public.

Request for Tenancy Approval

Request for Tenancy Approval
Housing Choice Voucher Program

U.S. Department of Housing and Urban Development
Office of Public and Indian Housing

OMB Approval No. 2577-0169
(exp. 07/31/2007)

Public reporting burden for this collection of information is estimated to average .08 hours per response, including the time for reviewing instructions, searching existing data sources, gathering and maintaining the data needed, and completing and reviewing the collection of information. This agency may not conduct or sponsor, and a person is not required to respond to, a collection of information unless that collection displays a valid OMB control number.

Eligible families submit this information to the Public Housing Authority (PHA) when applying for housing assistance under Section 8 of the U.S. Housing Act of l937 (42 U.S.C. 1437f). The PHA uses the information to determine if the family is eligible, if the unit is eligible, and if the lease complies with program and statutory requirements. Responses are required to obtain a benefit from the Federal Government. The information requested does not lend itself to confidentiality.

1. Name of Public Housing Agency (PHA)	2. Address of Unit (street address, apartment number, city, State & zip code)

3. Requested Beginning Date of Lease	4. Number of Bedrooms	5. Year Constructed	6. Proposed Rent	7. Security Deposit Amt.	8. Date Unit Available for Inspection

9. Type of House/Apartment

☐ Single Family Detached ☐ Semi-Detached / Row House ☐ Manufactured Home ☐ Garden / Walkup ☐ Elevator / High-Rise

10. If this unit is subsidized, indicate type of subsidy:

☐ Section 202 ☐ Section 221(d)(3)(BMIR) ☐ Section 236 (Insured or noninsured) ☐ Section 515 Rural Development

☐ Home ☐ Tax Credit

☐ Other (Describe Other Subsidy, Including Any State or Local Subsidy) _____

_____

11. Utilities and Appliances

The owner shall provide or pay for the utilities and appliances indicated below by an "O". The tenant shall provide or pay for the utilities and appliances indicated below by a "T". Unless otherwise specified below, the owner shall pay for all utilities and appliances provided by the owner.

Item	Specify fuel type					Provided by	Paid by
Heating	☐ Natural gas	☐ Bottle gas	☐ Oil	☐ Electric	☐ Coal or Other		
Cooking	☐ Natural gas	☐ Bottle gas	☐ Oil	☐ Electric	☐ Coal or Other		
Water Heating	☐ Natural gas	☐ Bottle gas	☐ Oil	☐ Electric	☐ Coal or Other		
Other Electric							
Water							
Sewer							
Trash Collection							
Air Conditioning							
Refrigerator							
Range/Microwave							
Other (specify)							

12.   Owner's Certifications.
a.   The program regulation requires the PHA to certify that the rent charged to the housing choice voucher tenant is not more than the rent charged for other unassisted comparable units. **Owners of projects with more than 4 units must complete the following section for most recently leased comparable unassisted units within the premises.**

	Address and unit number	Date Rented	Rental Amount
1.			
2.			
3.			

b.   The owner (including a principal or other interested party) is not the parent, child, grandparent, grandchild, sister or brother of any member of the family, unless the PHA has determined (and has notified the owner and the family of such determination) that approving leasing of the unit, notwithstanding such relationship, would provide reasonable accommodation for a family member who is a person with disabilities.

c. Check one of the following:

_____ Lead-based paint disclosure requirements do not apply because this property was built on or after January 1, 1978.

_____ The unit, common areas servicing the unit, and exterior painted surfaces associated with such unit or common areas have been found to be lead-based paint free by a lead-based paint inspector certified under the Federal certification program or under a federally accredited State certification program.

_____ A completed statement is attached containing disclosure of known information on lead-based paint and/or lead-based paint hazards in the unit, common areas or exterior painted surfaces, including a statement that the owner has provided the lead hazard information pamphlet to the family.

13.   **The PHA has not screened the family's behavior or suitability for tenancy. Such screening is the owner's own responsibility.**

14.   The owner's lease must include word-for-word all provisions of the HUD tenancy addendum.

15.   The PHA will arrange for inspection of the unit and will notify the owner and family as to whether or not the unit will be approved.

Print or Type Name of Owner/Owner Representative	Print or Type Name of Household Head
Signature	Signature (Household Head)
Business Address	Present Address of Family (street address, apartment no., city, State, & zip code)
Telephone Number Date (mm/dd/yyyy)	Telephone Number Date (mm/dd/yyyy)

Housing Quality Standards Inspection

Inspection Form
Housing Choice Voucher Program

**U.S. Department of Housing
and Urban Development**
Office of Public and Indian Housing

OMB Approval No. 2577-0169
(exp. 07/31/2007)

Public reporting burden for this collection of information is estimated to average 0.25 hours per response, including the time for reviewing instructions, searching existing data sources, gathering and maintaining the data needed, and completing and reviewing the collection of information. This agency may not conduct or sponsor, and a person is not required to respond to, a collection of information unless that collection displays a valid OMB control number.

This collection of information is authorized under Section 8 of the U.S. Housing Act of l937 (42 U.S.C. 1437f). The information is used to determine if a unit meets the housing quality standards of the section 8 rental assistance program.

PHA	Tenant ID Number	Date of Request (mm/dd/yyyy)
Inspector	Date Last Inspection (mm/dd/yyyy)	Date of Inspection (mm/dd/yyyy)
Neighborhood/Census Tract	Type of Inspection ☐ Initial ☐ Special ☐ Reinspection	Project Number

A. General Information
Street Address of Inspected Unit

City	County	State	Zip

Name of Family | Current Telephone of Family

Current Street Address of Family

City	County	State	Zip

Number of Children in Family Under 6

Name of Owner or Agent Authorized to Lease Unit Inspected | Telephone of Owner or Agent

Address of Owner or Agent

Housing Type (check as appropriate)
- ☐ Single Family Detached
- ☐ Duplex or Two Family
- ☐ Row House or Town House
- ☐ Low Rise: 3,4 Stories, Including Garden Apartment
- ☐ High Rise; 5 or More Stories
- ☐ Manufactured Home
- ☐ Congregate
- ☐ Cooperative
- ☐ Independent Group Residence
- ☐ Single Room Occupancy
- ☐ Shared Housing
- ☐ Other:(Specify)

B. Summary Decision on the Unit
(to be completed after the form has been filled in)

Housing Quality Standard Pass or Fail

☐ **1. Fail** If there are any checks under the column headed "Fail" the **unit** fails the minimum housing quality standards. Discuss with the owner the repairs noted that would be necessary to bring the unit up to the standard.

☐ **2. Inconclusive** If there are no checks under the column headed "Fail" and there are checks under the column headed "Inconclusive," obtain additional information necessary for a decision (question owner or tenant as indicated in the item instructions given in this checklist). Once additional information is obtained, change the rating for the item and record the date of verification at the far right of the form.

☐ **3. Pass** If neither (1) nor (2) above is checked, the unit passes the minimum housing quality standards. Any additional conditions described in the right hand column of the form should serve to (a) establish the precondition of the unit, (b) indicate possible additional areas to negotiate with the owner, (c) aid in assessing the reasonableness of the rent of the unit, and (d) aid the tenant in deciding among possible units to be rented. The tenant is responsible for deciding whether he or she finds these conditions acceptable.

☐ **Unit Size:** Count the number of bedrooms for purposes of the FMR or Payment Standard. Record in the box provided.

☐ **Year Constructed:** Enter from Line 5 of the Request for Tenancy Approval form. Record in the box provided.

☐ **Number of Sleeping Rooms**: Count the number of rooms which could be used for sleeping, as identified on the checklist. Record in the box provided.

C. How to Fill Out This Checklist
Complete the checklist on the unit to be occupied (or currently occupied) by the tenant. Proceeed through the inspection as follows:

Area	Checklist Category
room by room	1. Living Room
	2. Kitchen
	3. Bathroom
	4. All Other Rooms Used for Living
	5. All Secondary Rooms Not Used for Living
basement or utility room	6. Heating & Plumbing
outside	7. Building Exterior
overall	8. General Health & Safety

Each part of the checklist will be accompanied by an explanation of the item to be inspected.

Important: For each item numbered on the checklist, **check one box only** (e.g., check one box only for item 1.4 "Security,"in the Living Room.)

In the space to the right of the description of the item, if the decision on the item is: "Fail" write what repairs are necessary; If "Inconclusive" write in details.

Also, if "Pass" but there are some conditions present that need to be brought to the attention of the owner or the tenant, write these in the space to the right.

If it is an annual inspection, record to the right of the form any repairs made since the last inspection. If possible, record reason for repair (e.g., ordinary maintenance, tenant damage).

If it is a complaint inspection, fill out only those checklist items for which complaint is lodged. Determine, if possible, tenant or owner cause.

Once the checklist has been completed, return to Part B (Summary Decision on the Unit).

1. Living Room

1.1 Living Room Present

Note: If the unit is an efficiency apartment, consider the living room present.

1.2 Electricity

In order to qualify, the outlets must be present and properly installed in the baseboard, wall or floor of the unit. Do not count a single duplex receptacle as two outlets, i.e., there must be **two** of these in the room, or **one** of these **plus a permanently installed ceiling or wall light fixture**.

Both the outlets and/or the light must be working. Usually, a room will have sufficient lights or electrical appliances plugged into outlets to determine workability. Be sure light fixture does not fail just because the bulb is burned out.

Do not count any of the following items or fixtures as outlets/fixtures: Table or floor lamps (these are **not** permanent light fixtures); ceiling lamps plugged into socket; extension cords.

If the electric service to the unit has been temporarily turned off check "Inconclusive." Contact owner or manager after inspection to verify that electricity functions properly when service is turned on. Record this information on the checklist.

1.3 Electrical Hazards

Examples of what this means: broken wiring; noninsulated wiring; frayed wiring; improper types of wiring, connections or insulation; wires lying in or located near standing water or other unsafe places; light fixture hanging from electric wiring without other firm support or fixture; missing cover plates on switches or outlets; badly cracked outlets; exposed fuse box connections; overloaded circuits evidenced by frequently "blown" fuses (ask the tenant).

Check "Inconclusive" if you are uncertain about severity of the problem and seek expert advice.

1. 4 Security

"Accessible to outside" means: doors open to the outside or to a common public hall; windows accessible from the outside (e.g. basement and first floor); windows or doors leading onto a fire escape, porch or other outside place that can be reached from the ground.

"Lockable" means: the window or door has a properly working lock, or is nailed shut, or the window is not designed to be opened. A storm window lock that is working properly is acceptable. Windows that are nailed shut are acceptable only if these windows are not needed for ventilation or as an alternate exit in case of fire.

1.5 Window Condition

Rate the windows in the room (including windows in doors).

"Severe deterioration" means that the window no longer has the capacity to keep out the wind and the rain or is a cutting hazard. Examples are: missing or broken-out panes; dangerously loose cracked panes; windows that will not close; windows that, when closed, do not form a reasonably tight seal.

If more than one window in the room is in this condition, give details in the space provided on the right of the form.

If there is only "moderate deterioration" of the windows the item should "Pass." "Moderate deterioration" means windows which are reasonably weather-tight, but show evidence of some aging, abuse, or lack of repair. Signs of deterioration are: minor crack in window pane; splintered sill; signs of some minor rotting in the window frame or the window sill; window panes loose because of missing window putty. Also for deteriorated and peeling paint see 1.9. If more than one window is in this condition, give details in the space provided on the right of the form.

1.6 Ceiling Condition

"Unsound or hazardous" means the presence of such serious defects that either a potential exists for structural collapse or that large cracks or holes allow significant drafts to enter the unit. The condition includes: severe bulging or buckling; large holes; missing parts; falling or in danger of falling loose surface materials (other than paper or paint).

Pass ceilings that are basically sound but have some nonhazardous defects, including: small holes or cracks; missing or broken ceiling tiles; water stains; soiled surfaces; unpainted surfaces; peeling paint (for peeling paint see item 1.9).

1.7 Wall Condition

"Unsound or hazardous" includes: serious defects such that the structural safety of the building is threatened, such as severe buckling, bulging or leaning; damaged or loose structural members; large holes; air infiltration.

Pass walls that are basically sound but have some nonhazardous defects, including: small or shallow holes; cracks; loose or missing parts; unpainted surfaces; peeling paint (for peeling paint see item 1.9).

1.8 Floor Condition

"Unsound or hazardous" means the presence of such serious defects that a potential exists for structural collapse or other threats to safety (e.g., tripping) or large cracks or holes allow substantial drafts from below the floor. The condition includes: severe buckling or major movements under walking stress; damaged or missing parts.

Pass floors that are basically sound but have some nonhazardous defects, including: heavily worn or damaged floor surface (for example, scratches or gouges in surface, missing portions of tile or linoleum, previous water damage). If there is a floor covering, also note the condition, especially if badly worn or soiled. If there is a floor covering, including paint or sealant, also note the conditions, especially if badly worn, soiled or peeling (for peeling paint, see 1.9).

1.9 Lead-Based Paint

Housing Choice Voucher Units If the unit was built January 1, 1978, or after, no child under age six will occupy or currently occupies it, is a 0-BR, elderly or handicapped unit with no children under age six on the lease or expected, has been certified lead-based paint free by a certified lead-based paint inspector (no lead-based paint present or no lead-based paint present after removal of lead-based paint.), check NA and do not inspect painted surfaces.

This requirement applies to all painted surfaces (building components) within the unit. (Do not include tenant belongings). Surfaces to receive a visual assessment for deteriorated paint include walls, floors, ceilings, built in cabinets (sink bases), baseboards, doors, door frames, windows systems including mullions, sills, or frames and any other painted building component within the unit. Deteriorated paint includes any painted surface that is peeling, chipping, chalking, cracking, damaged or otherwise separated from the substrate.

All deteriorated paint surfaces **more than 2 sq. ft. in any one interior room or space, or more than 10% of the total surface area of an interior type of component with a small surface area (i.e., window sills, baseboards, and trim)** must be stabilized (corrected) in accordance with all safe work practice requirements and clearance is required. **If the deteriorated painted surface is less than 2 sq. ft. or less than 10% of the component, only stabilization is required. Clearance testing is not required.** Stabilization means removal of deteriorated paint, repair of the substrate, and application of a new protective coating or paint. Lead-Based Paint Owner Certification is required following stabilization activities, except for *de minimis level* repairs.

1. Living Room

For each numbered item, check one box only.

Item No. Description	Yes, Pass	No, Fail	Inconclusive	If Fail, what repairs are necessary? If Inconclusive, give details. If Pass with comments, give details.	If Fail or Inconclusive, date (mm/dd/yyyy) of final approval
1.1 Living Room Present Is there a living room?	☐	☐			
1.2 Electricity Are there at least two working outlets or one working outlet and one working light fixture?	☐	☐	☐		
1.3 Electrical Hazards Is the room free from electrical hazards?	☐	☐	☐		
1.4 Security Are all windows and doors that are accessible from the outside lockable?	☐	☐			
1.5 Window Condition Is there at least one window, and are all windows free of signs of severe deterioration or missing or broken out panes?	☐	☐			
1.6 Ceiling Condition Is the ceiling sound and free from hazardous defects?	☐	☐			
1.7 Wall Condition Are the walls sound and free from hazardous defects?	☐	☐			
1.8 Floor Condition Is the floor sound and free from hazardous defects?	☐	☐			
1.9 Lead-Based Paint Are all painted surfaces free of deteriorated paint?	☐	☐			
If no, does deteriorated surfaces exceed two square feet and/or more than 10% of a component?	☐	☐	☐ Not Applicable		

Additional Comments: (Give Item Number)

Comments continued on a separate page   Yes ☐   No ☐

2. Kitchen

2.1 Kitchen Area Present

Note: A kitchen is an area used for preparation of meals. It may be either a separate room or an area of a larger room (for example, a kitchen area in an efficiency apartment).

2.2 - 2.9 Explanation for these items is the same as that provided for "Living Room" with the following modifications:

2.2 Electricity

Note: The requirement is that at least one outlet and one permanent light fixture are present and working.

2.5 Window Condition

Note: The absence of a window does not fail this item in the kitchen. If there is no window, check "Pass."

2.10 Stove or Range with Oven

Both an oven and a stove (or range) with top burners must be present and working. If either Is missing and you know that the owner is responsible for supplying these appliances, check "Fail." Put check in "Inconclusive" column if the tenant is responsible for supplying the appliances and he or she has not yet moved in. Contact tenant or prospective tenant to gain verification that facility will be supplied and is in working condition. Hot plates are not acceptable substitutes for these facilities.

An oven is not working if it will not heat up. To be working a stove or range must have all burners working and knobs to turn them off and on. Under "working condition," also look for hazardous gas hook-ups evidenced by strong gas smells; these should fail. (Be sure that this condition is not confused with an unlit pilot light -a condition that should be noted, but does not fail.)

If both an oven and a stove or range are present, but the gas or electricity are turned off, check "Inconclusive." Contact owner or manager to get verification that facility works when gas is turned on. If both an oven and a stove or range are present and working, but defects exist, check "Pass" and note these to the right of the form. Possible defects are marked, dented, or scratched surfaces; cracked burner ring; limited size relative to family needs.

A microwave oven may be substituted for a tenant-supplied oven and stove (or range).

A microwave oven may be substituted for an owner-supplied oven and stove (or range) if the tenant agrees and microwave ovens are furnished instead of ovens and stoves (or ranges) to both subsidized and unsubsidized tenants in the building or premises.

2.11 Refrigerator

If no refrigerator is present, use the same criteria for marking either "Fail" or "Inconclusive" as were used for the oven and stove or range.

A refrigerator is not working if it will not maintain a temperature low enough to keep food from spoiling over a reasonable period of time. If the electricity is turned off, mark "Inconclusive." Contact owner (or tenant if unit is occupied) to get verification of working condition.

If the refrigerator is present and working but defects exist, note these to the right of the form. Possible minor defects include: broken or missing interior shelving; dented or scratched interior or exterior surfaces; minor deterioration of door seal; loose door handle.

2.12 Sink

If a permanently attached kitchen sink is not present in the kitchen or kitchen area, mark "Fail." A sink in a bathroom or a portable basin will not satisfy this requirement. A sink is not working unless it has running hot and cold water from the faucets and a properly connected and properly working drain (with a "gas trap"). In a vacant apartment, the hot water may have been turned off and there will be no hot water. Mark this "Inconclusive." Check with owner or manager to verify that hot water is available when service is turned on.

If a working sink has defects, note this to the right of the item. Possible minor defects include: dripping faucet; marked, dented, or scratched surface; slow drain; missing or broken drain stopper.

2.13 Space for Storage, Preparation, and Serving of Food

Some space must be available for the storage, preparation, and serving of food. If there is no built-in space for food storage and preparation, a table used for food preparation and a portable storage cabinet will satisfy the requirement. If there is no built-in space, and no room for a table and portable cabinet, check "Inconclusive" and discuss with the tenant. The tenant makes the final determination as to whether or not this space is acceptable.

If there are some minor defects, check "Pass" and make notes to the right. Possible defects include: marked, dented, or scratched surfaces; broken shelving or cabinet doors; broken drawers or cabinet hardware; limited size relative to family needs.

2. Kitchen

For each numbered item, check one box only.

Item No. Description	Yes, Pass	No, Fail	Inconclusive	If Fail, what repairs are necessary? If Inconclusive, give details. If Pass with comments, give details.	If Fail or Inconclusive, date (mm/dd/yyyy) of final approval
2.1 Kitchen Area Present Is there a kitchen?	☐	☐			
2.2 Electricity Are there at least one working outlet and one working, permanently installed light fixture?	☐	☐	☐		
2.3 Electrical Hazards Is the kitchen free from electrical hazards?	☐	☐	☐		
2.4 Security Are all windows and doors that are accessible from the outside lockable?	☐	☐			
2.5 Window Condition Are all windows free of signs of deterioration or missing or broken out panes?	☐	☐			
2.6 Ceiling Condition Is the ceiling sound and free from hazardous defects?	☐	☐			
2.7 Wall Condition Are the walls sound and free from hazardous defects?	☐	☐			
2.8 Floor Condition Is the floor sound and free from hazardous defects?	☐	☐			
2.9 Lead-Based Paint Are all painted surfaces free of deteriorated paint?	☐	☐			
If no, does deteriorated surfaces exceed two square feet and/or less than 10% of a component?	☐	☐		☐ Not Applicable	
2.10 Stove or Range with Oven Is there a working oven, and a stove (or range) with top burners that work?	☐	☐	☐		
If no oven and stove (or range) are present, is there a microwave oven and, if microwave is owner-supplied, do other tenants have microwaves instead of an oven and stove (or range)?	☐	☐	☐		
2.11 Refrigerator Is there a refrigerator that works and maintains a temperature low enough so that food does not spoil over a reasonable period of time?	☐	☐	☐		
2.12 Sink Is there a kitchen sink that works with hot and cold running water?	☐	☐	☐		
2.13 Space for Storage, Preparation, and Serving of Food Is there space to store, prepare, and serve food?	☐	☐	☐		

Additional Comments: (Give Item Number)(Use an additional page if necessary)

Comments continued on a separate page   Yes ☐   No ☐

3. Bathroom

3.1 Bathroom Present

Most units have easily identifiable bathrooms (i.e., a separate room with toilet, washbasin and tub or shower). In some cases, however, you will encounter units with scattered bathroom facilities (i.e., toilet. washbasin and tub or shower located in separate parts of the unit). At a minimum, there must be an enclosure around the toilet. In this case, count the enclosure around the toilet as the bathroom and proceed with 3.2-3.9 below, with respect to this enclosure. If there is more than one bathroom that is normally used, rate the one that is in best condition for Part 3. If there is a second bathroom that is also used, complete Part 4 of the checklist for this room. (See Inspection Manual for additional notes on rating the second bathroom.)

3.2 - 3.9 Explanation for these items is the same as that provided for "Living Room" with the following modifications:

3.2 Electricity

Note: The requirement is that at least one permanent light fixture is present and working

3.3 Electrical Hazards

Note: In addition to the previously mentioned hazards, outlets that are located where water might splash or collect are considered an electrical hazard.

3.5 Window Condition

Note: The absence of a window does not fail this item in the bathroom (see item 3.13, Ventilation, for relevance of window with respect to ventilation). If there is no window, but a working vent system is present, check "Pass."

3.7 Wall Condition

Note: Include under nonhazardous defects (that would pass, but should be noted) the following: broken or loose tile; deteriorated grouting at tub/wall and tub/floor joints, or tiled surfaces; water stains.

3.8 Floor Condition

Note: Include under nonhazardous defects (that would pass, but should be noted) the following: missing floor tiles; water stains.

3.10 Flush Toilet in Enclosed Room in Unit

The toilet must be contained within the unit, be in proper operating condition, and be available for the exclusive use of the occupants of the unit (i.e., outhouses or facilities shared by occupants of other units are not acceptable). It must allow for privacy.

Not working means: the toilet is not connected to a water supply; it is not connected to a sewer drain; it is clogged; it does not have a trap; the connections, vents or traps are faulty to the extent that severe leakage of water or escape of gases occurs; the flushing mechanism does not function properly. If the water to the unit has been turned off, check "Inconclusive." Obtain verification from owner or manager that facility works properly when water is turned on.

Comment to the right of the form if the toilet is "present, exclusive, and working," but has the following types of defects: constant running; chipped or broken porcelain; slow draining.

If drain blockage is more serious and occurs further in the sewer line, causing backup, check item 7.6, "Fail," under the plumbing and heating part of the checklist. A sign of serious sewer blockage is the presence of numerous backed-up drains.

3.11 Fixed Wash Basin or Lavatory in Unit

The wash basin must be permanently installed (i.e., a portable wash basin does not satisfy the requirement). Also, a kitchen sink used to pass the requirements under Part 2 of the checklist (kitchen facilities) cannot also serve as the bathroom wash basin. The wash basin may be located separate from the other bathroom facilities (e.g., in a hallway).

Not working means: the wash basin is not connected to a system that will deliver hot and cold running water; it is not connected to a properly operating drain; the connectors (or vents or traps) are faulty to the extent that severe leakage of water or escape of sewer gases occurs. If the water to the unit or the hot water system has been turned off, check "Inconclusive." Obtain verification from owner or manager that the system is in working condition.

Comment to the right of the form if the wash basin is "present and working," but has the following types of minor defects: insufficient water pressure; dripping faucets; minor leaks; cracked or chipped porcelain; slow drain (see discussion above under 3.10).

3.12 Tub or Shower in Unit

Not present means that neither a tub nor shower is present in the unit. Again, these facilities need not be in the same room with the rest of the bathroom facilities. They must, however, be private.

Not working covers the same requirements detailed above for wash basin (3.11).

Comment to the right of the form if the tub or shower is present and working, but has the following types of defects: dripping faucet; minor leaks; cracked porcelain; slow drain (see discussion under 3.10); absent or broken support rod for shower curtain.

3.13 Ventilation

Working vent systems include: ventilation shafts (non-mechanical vents) and electric fans. Electric vent fans must function when switch is turned on. (Make sure that any malfunctions are not due to the fan not being plugged in.) If electric current to the unit has not been turned on (and there is no openable window), check "Inconclusive." Obtain verification from owner or manager that system works. Note: exhaust vents must be vented to the outside, attic, or crawlspace.

3. Bathroom

For each numbered item, check one box only.

Item No. Description	Yes, Pass	No, Fail	Inconclusive	If Fail, what repairs are necessary? If Inconclusive, give details. If Pass with comments, give details.	If Fail or Inconclusive, date (mm/dd/yyyy) of final approval
3.1 Bathroom Present (See description) Is there a bathroom?	☐	☐			
3.2 Electricity Is there at least one permanently installed light fixture?	☐	☐	☐		
3.3 Electrical Hazards Is the bathroom free from electrical hazards?	☐	☐	☐		
3.4 Security Are all windows and doors that are accessible from the outside lockable?	☐	☐			
3.5 Window Condition Are all windows free of signs of deterioration or missing or broken out panes?	☐	☐			
3.6 Ceiling Condition Is the ceiling sound and free from hazardous defects?	☐	☐			
3.7 Wall Condition Are the walls sound and free from hazardous defects?	☐	☐			
3.8 Floor Condition Is the floor sound and free from hazardous defects?	☐	☐			
3.9 Lead-Based Paint Are all painted surfaces free of deteriorated paint?	☐	☐			
If no, does deteriorated surfaces exceed two square feet and/or more than 10% of a component?	☐	☐		☐ Not Applicable	
3.10 Flush Toilet in Enclosed Room in Unit Is there a working toilet in the unit for the exclusive private use of the tenant?	☐	☐	☐		
3.11 Fixed Wash Basin or Lavatory in Unit Is there a working, permanently installed wash basin with hot and cold running water in the unit?	☐	☐	☐		
3.12 Tub or Shower Is there a working tub or shower with hot and cold running water in the unit?	☐	☐	☐		
3.13 Ventilation Are there openable windows or a working vent system?	☐	☐	☐		

Additional Comments: (Give Item Number)(Use an additional page if necessary)

Comments continued on a separate page   Yes ☐   No ☐

4. Other Room Used for Living and Halls

Complete an "Other Room" checklist for as many "other rooms used for living" as are present in the unit and not already noted in Parts I, 2, and 3 of the checklist. See the discussion below for definition of "used for living." Also complete an "Other Room" checklist for all entrance halls, corridors, and staircases that are located within the unit and are part of the area used for living. If a hall, entry and/or stairway are contiguous, rate them as a whole (i.e., as part of one space).

Additional forms for rating "Other Rooms" are provided in the checklist.

Definition of "used for living." Rooms "used for living" are areas of the unit that are walked through or lived in on a regular basis. Do not include rooms or other areas that have been permanently, or near permanently, closed off or areas that are infrequently entered. For example, do not include a utility room, attached shed, attached closed-in porch, basement, or garage if they are closed off from the main living area or are infrequently entered. Do include any of these areas if they are frequently used (e.g., a finished basement/play-room, a closed-in porch that is used as a bedroom during summer months). Occasional use of a washer or dryer in an otherwise unused room does not constitute regular use.

If the unit is vacant and you do not know the eventual use of a particular room, complete an "Other Room" checklist if there is any chance that the room will be used on a regular basis. If there is no chance that the room will be used on a regular basis, do not include it (e.g., an unfinished basement) since it will be checked under Part 5, All Secondary Rooms (Rooms not used for living).

4.1 Room Code and Room Location

Enter the appropriate room code given below:

Room Codes:

1 = Bedroom or any other room used for sleeping (regardless of type of room)

2 = Dining Room or Dining Area

3 = Second Living Room, Family Room, Den, Playroom, TV Room

4 = Entrance Halls, Corridors, Halls, Staircases

5 = Additional Bathroom (also check presence of sink trap and clogged toilet)

6 = Other

Room Location: Write on the line provided the location of the room with respect to the unit's width, length and floor level as if you were standing outside the unit facing the entrance to the unit:

right/left/center: record whether the room is situated to the right, left, or center of the unit.

front/rear/center: record whether the room is situated to the back, front or center of the unit.

floor level: identify the floor level on which the room is located.

If the unit is vacant, you may have some difficulty predicting the eventual use of a room. Before giving any room a code of 1 (bedroom), the room must meet all of the requirements for a "room used for sleeping" (see items 4. 2 and 4.5).

4.2 - 4.9 Explanations of these items are the same as those provided for "Living Room" with the following modifications:

4.2 Electricity/Illumination

If the room code is not a "1," the room must have a means of natural or artificial illumination such as a permanent light fixture, wall outlet present, or light from a window in the room or near the room. If any required item is missing, check "Fail." If the electricity is turned off, check "Inconclusive."

4.5 Window Condition

Any room used for sleeping must have at least one window. If the windows in sleeping rooms are designed to be opened, at least one window must be openable. The minimum standards do not require a window in "other rooms." Therefore, if there is no window in another room not used for sleeping, check "Pass," and note "no window" in the area for comments.

4.6 Smoke Detectors

At least one battery-operated or hard-wired smoke detector must be present and working on each level of the unit, including the basement, but not the crawl spaces and unfinished attic.

Smoke detectors must be installed in accordance with and meet the requirements of the National Fire Protection Association Standard (NFPA) 74 (or its successor standards).

If the dwelling unit is occupied by any hearing-impaired person, smoke detectors must have an alarm system designed for hearing-impaired persons as specified in NFPA 74 (or successor standards).

If the unit was under HAP contract prior to April 24, 1993, owners who installed battery-operated or hard-wired smoke detectors in compliance with HUD's smoke detector requirements, including the regulations published on July 30, 1992 (57 FR 33846), will not be required subsequently to comply with any additional requirements mandated by NFPA 74 (i.e. the owner would not be required to install a smoke detector in a basement not used for living purposes, nor would the owner be required to change the location of the smoke detectors that have already been installed on the other floors of the unit). In this case, check "Pass" and note under comments.

Additional Notes

For staircases, the adequacy of light and condition of the stair rails and railings is covered under Part 8 of the checklist (General Health and Safety)

4. Other Rooms Used for Living and Halls For each numbered item, check one box only.

4.1 Room Location

_____ right/left/center: the room is situated to the right, left, or center of the unit.

_____ front/rear/center: the room is situated to the back, front or center of the unit.

_____ floor level: the floor level on which the room is located.

Room Code ☐

1 = Bedroom or Any Other Room Used for Sleeping (regardless of type of room)
2 = Dining Room or Dining Area
3 = Second Living Room, Family Room, Den, Playroom, TV Room
4 = Entrance Halls, Corridors, Halls, Staircases
5 = Additional Bathroom (also check presence of sink trap and clogged toilet)
6 = Other:

Item No.	Description	Decision			If Fail, what repairs are necessary? If Inconclusive, give details. If Pass with comments, give details.	If Fail or Inconclusive, date (mm/dd/yyyy) of final approval
		Yes, Pass	No, Fail	Inconclusive		
4.2	**Electricity/Illumination**					
	If Room Code is a 1, are there at least two working outlets or one working outlet and one working, permanently installed light fixture?	☐	☐	☐		
	If Room Code is not a 1, is there a means of illumination?	☐	☐	☐		
4.3	**Electrical Hazards**					
	Is the room free from electrical hazards?	☐	☐	☐		
4.4	**Security**					
	Are all windows and doors that are accessible from the outside lockable?	☐	☐			
4.5	**Window Condition**					
	If Room Code is a 1, is there at least one window?	☐	☐			
	And, regardless of Room Code, are all windows free of signs of severe deterioration or missing or broken-out panes?	☐	☐			
4.6	**Ceiling Condition**					
	Is the ceiling sound and free from hazardous defects?	☐	☐			
4.7	**Wall Condition**					
	Are the walls sound and free from hazardous defects?	☐	☐			
4.8	**Floor Condition**					
	Is the floor sound and free from hazardous defects?	☐	☐			
4.9	**Lead-Based Paint**					
	Are all painted surfaces free of deteriorated paint?	☐	☐			
	If no, does deteriorated surfaces exceed two square feet and/or more than 10% of a component?	☐	☐		☐ Not Applicable	
4.10	**Smoke Detectors**					
	Is there a working smoke detector on each level?	☐	☐			
	Do the smoke detectors meet the requirements of NFPA 74?	☐	☐			
	In units occupied by the hearing impaired, is there an alarm system connected to the smoke detector?	☐	☐			

Additional Comments: (Give Item Number)(Use an additional page if necessary)

Comments continued on a separate page Yes ☐ No ☐

4. Supplemental for Other Rooms Used for Living and Halls   For each numbered item, check one box only.

4.1   Room Location

_____ right/left/center: the room is situated to the right, left, or center of the unit.

_____ front/rear/center: the room is situated to the back, front or center of the unit.

_____ floor level: the floor level on which the room is located.

Room Code [   ]

1 = Bedroom or Any Other Room Used for Sleeping (regardless of type of room)
2 = Dining Room or Dining Area
3 = Second Living Room, Family Room, Den, Playroom, TV Room
4 = Entrance Halls, Corridors, Halls, Staircases
5 = Additional Bathroom (also check presence of sink trap and clogged toilet)
6 = Other:

Item No. / Description	Decision — Yes, Pass	Decision — No, Fail	Decision — Inconclusive	If Fail, what repairs are necessary? / If Inconclusive, give details. / If Pass with comments, give details.	If Fail or Inconclusive, date of final approval
4.2 Electricity/Illumination If Room Code is a 1, are there at least two working outlets or one working outlet and one working, permanently installed light fixture?	☐	☐	☐		
If Room Code is not a 1, is there a means of illumination?	☐	☐	☐		
4.3 Electrical Hazards Is the room free from electrical hazards?	☐	☐	☐		
4.4 Security Are all windows and doors that are accessible from the outside lockable?	☐	☐			
4.5 Window Condition If Room Code is a 1, is there at least one window?	☐	☐			
And, regardless of Room Code, are all windows free of signs of severe deterioration or missing or broken-out panes?	☐	☐			
4.6 Ceiling Condition Is the ceiling sound and free from hazardous defects?	☐	☐			
4.7 Wall Condition Are the walls sound and free from hazardous defects?	☐	☐			
4.8 Floor Condition Is the floor sound and free from hazardous defects?	☐	☐			
4.9 Lead-Based Paint Are all painted surfaces free of deteriorated paint?	☐	☐			
If no, does deteriorated surfaces exceed two square feet and/or more than 10% of a component?	☐	☐		Not Applicable	
4.10 Smoke Detectors Is there a working smoke detector on each level?	☐	☐			
Do the smoke detectors meet the requirements of NFPA 74?	☐	☐			
In units occupied by the hearing impaired, is there an alarm system connected to the smoke detector?	☐	☐			

Additional Comments: (Give Item Number)(Use an additional page if necessary)

Comments continued on a separate page   Yes ☐   No ☐

4. Supplemental for Other Rooms Used for Living and Halls　For each numbered item, check one box only.

4.1　Room Location

_____　right/left/center:　the room is situated to the right, left, or center of the unit.

_____　front/rear/center:　the room is situated to the back, front or center of the unit.

_____　floor level:　the floor level on which the room is located.

Room Code [　]

1 = Bedroom or Any Other Room Used for Sleeping (regardless of type of room)
2 = Dining Room or Dining Area
3 = Second Living Room, Family Room, Den, Playroom, TV Room
4 = Entrance Halls, Corridors, Halls, Staircases
5 = Additional Bathroom (also check presence of sink trap and clogged toilet)
6 = Other: _____

Item No.　Description	Decision			If Fail, what repairs are necessary? If Inconclusive, give details. If Pass with comments, give details.	If Fail or Inconclusive, date (mm/dd/yyyy) of final approval
	Yes, Pass	No, Fail	Inconclusive		
4.2　Electricity/Illumination If Room Code is a 1, are there at least two working outlets or one working outlet and one working, permanently installed light fixture?	☐	☐	☐		
If Room Code is not a 1, is there a means of illumination?	☐	☐	☐		
4.3　Electrical Hazards Is the room free from electrical hazards?	☐	☐	☐		
4.4　Security Are all windows and doors that are accessible from the outside lockable?	☐	☐			
4.5　Window Condition If Room Code is a 1, is there at least one window?	☐	☐			
And, regardless of Room Code, are all windows free of signs of severe deterioration or missing or broken-out panes?	☐	☐			
4.6　Ceiling Condition Is the ceiling sound and free from hazardous defects?	☐	☐			
4.7　Wall Condition Are the walls sound and free from hazardous defects?	☐	☐			
4.8　Floor Condition Is the floor sound and free from hazardous defects?	☐	☐			
4.9　Lead-Based Paint Are all painted surfaces free of deteriorated paint?	☐	☐			
If no, does deteriorated surfaces exceed two square feet and/or more than 10% of a component?	☐	☐		☐ Not Applicable	
4.10 Smoke Detectors Is there a working smoke detector on each level?	☐	☐			
Do the smoke detectors meet the requirements of NFPA 74?	☐	☐			
In units occupied by the hearing impaired, is there an alarm system connected to the smoke detector?	☐	☐			

Additional Comments: (Give Item Number)(Use an additional page if necessary)

Comments continued on a separate page　Yes ☐　No ☐

Everything U Need to Know...

4. Supplemental for Other Rooms Used for Living and Halls   For each numbered item, check one box only.

4.1   Room Location

_____   right/left/center: the room is situated to the right, left, or center of the unit.

_____   front/rear/center: the room is situated to the back, front or center of the unit.

_____   floor level: the floor level on which the room is located.

Room Code ☐

1 = Bedroom or Any Other Room Used for Sleeping (regardless of type of room)
2 = Dining Room or Dining Area
3 = Second Living Room, Family Room, Den, Playroom, TV Room
4 = Entrance Halls, Corridors, Halls, Staircases
5 = Additional Bathroom (also check presence of sink trap and clogged toilet)
6 = Other:

Item No. Description	Decision			If Fail, what repairs are necessary? If Inconclusive, give details. If Pass with comments, give details.	If Fail or Inconclusive, date (mm/dd/yyyy) of final approval
	Yes, Pass	No, Fail	Inconclusive		
4.2 Electricity/Illumination If Room Code is a 1, are there at least two working outlets or one working outlet and one working, permanently installed light fixture?	☐	☐	☐		
If Room Code is not a 1, is there a means of illumination?	☐	☐	☐		
4.3 Electrical Hazards Is the room free from electrical hazards?	☐	☐	☐		
4.4 Security Are all windows and doors that are accessible from the outside lockable?	☐	☐			
4.5 Window Condition If Room Code is a 1, is there at least one window?	☐	☐			
And, regardless of Room Code, are all windows free of signs of severe deterioration or missing or broken-out panes?	☐	☐			
4.6 Ceiling Condition Is the ceiling sound and free from hazardous defects?	☐	☐			
4.7 Wall Condition Are the walls sound and free from hazardous defects?	☐	☐			
4.8 Floor Condition Is the floor sound and free from hazardous defects?	☐	☐			
4.9 Lead-Based Paint Are all painted surfaces free of deteriorated paint?	☐	☐			
If no, does deteriorated surfaces exceed two square feet and/or more than 10% of a component?	☐	☐		☐ Not Applicable	
4.10 Smoke Detectors Is there a working smoke detector on each level?	☐	☐			
Do the smoke detectors meet the requirements of NFPA 74?	☐	☐			
In units occupied by the hearing impaired, is there an alarm system connected to the smoke detector?	☐	☐			

Additional Comments: (Give Item Number)(Use an additional page if necessary)

Comments continued on a separate page   Yes ☐   No ☐

5. All Secondary Rooms (Rooms not used for living)

5. Secondary Rooms (Rooms not used for living)

If any room in the unit did not meet the requirements for "other room used for living" in Part 4, it is to be considered a "secondary room (not used for living)," Rate all of these rooms together (i.e., a single Part 5 checklist for all secondary rooms in the unit).

Inspection is required of the following two items since hazardous defects under these items could jeopardize the rest of the unit, even if present in rooms not used for living: 5.2 Security, 5.3 Electrical Hazards. Also, be observant of any other potentially hazardous features in these rooms and record under 5.4

5.1 None

If there are no "Secondary Rooms (rooms not used for living)," check "None" and go on to Part 6.

5.2 - 5.4 Explanations of these items is the same as those provided for "Living Room"

Additional Note

In recording "other potentially hazardous features," note (in the space provided) the means of access to the room with the hazard and check the box under "Inconclusive." Discuss the hazard with the HA inspection supervisor to determine "Pass" or "Fail." Include defects like: large holes in floor, walls or ceilings; evidence of structural collapse; windows in condition of severe deterioration; and deteriorated paint surfaces.

6. Building Exterior

6.1 Condition of Foundation

"Unsound or hazardous" means foundations with severe structural defects indicating the potential for structural collapse; or foundations that allow significant entry of ground water (for example, evidenced by flooding of basement).

6.2 Condition of Stairs, Rails, and Porches

"Unsound or hazardous" means: stairs, porches, balconies, or decks with severe structural defects; broken, rotting, or missing steps; absence of a handrail when there are extended lengths of steps (generally four or more consecutive steps); absence of or insecure railings around a porch or balcony which is approximately 30 inches or more above the ground.

6.3 Condition of Roof and Gutters

"Unsound and hazardous" means: The roof has serious defects such as serious buckling or sagging, indicating the potential of structural collapse; large holes or other defects that would result in significant air or water infiltration (in most cases severe exterior defects will be reflected in equally serious surface defects within the unit, e.g., buckling, water damage). The gutters, downspouts and soffits (area under the eaves) show serious decay and have allowed the entry of significant air or water into the interior of the structure. Gutters and downspouts are, however, not required to pass. If the roof is not observable and there is no sign of interior water damage, check "Pass."

6.4 Condition of Exterior Surfaces

See definition above for roof, item 6.3.

6.5 Condition of Chimney

The chimney should not be seriously leaning or showing evidence of significant disintegration (i.e., many missing bricks).

6.6 Lead-Based Paint: Exterior Surfaces

Housing Choice Voucher Units If the unit was built January 1, 1978 or after, no child under age six will occupy or currently occupies, is a 0-BR, elderly or handicapped unit with no children under age six on the lease or expected, has been certified lead-based paint free by a certified lead-based paint inspector (no lead-based paint present or no lead-based paint present after removal of lead), check NA and do not inspect painted surfaces . Visual assessment for deteriorated paint applies to all exterior painted surfaces (building components) associated with the assisted unit including windows, window sills, exterior walls, floors, porches, railings, doors, decks, stairs, play areas, garages, fences or other areas if frequented by children under age six. All deteriorated paint surfaces **more than 20 sq. ft. on exterior surfaces** must be stabilized (corrected) in accordance with all safe work practice requirements. **If the painted surface is less than 20 sq. ft., only stabilization is required. Clearance testing is not required.** Stabilization means removal of deteriorated paint, repair of the substrate, and application of a new protective coating or paint. Lead-Based Paint Owner Certification is required following stabilization activities except for *de minimis level* repairs.

6.7 Manufactured Homes: Tie Downs

Manufactured homes must be placed on a site in a stable manner and be free from hazards such as sliding and wind damage. Manufactured homes must be securely anchored by a tiedown device which distributes and transfers the loads imposed by the unit to appropriate ground anchors so as to resist wind overturning and sliding, unless a variation has been approved by the HUD Field Office.

5. All Secondary Rooms (Rooms not used for living) For each numbered item, check one box only.

Item No. / Description	Decision Yes, Pass	No, Fail	Inconclusive	If Fail, what repairs are necessary? If Inconclusive, give details. If Pass with comments, give details.	If Fail or Inconclusive, date (mm/dd/yyyy) of final approval
5.1 None ☐ Go to Part 6					
5.2 Security Are all windows and doors that are accessible from the outside lockable?	☐	☐			
5.3 Electrical Hazards Are all these rooms free from electrical hazards?	☐	☐	☐		
5.4 Other Potentially Hazardous Features Are all of these rooms free of any other potentially hazardous features? For each room with an "other potentially hazardous feature," explain the hazard and the means of control of interior access to the room.	☐	☐	☐		
6.0 Building Exterior					
6.1 Condition of Foundation Is the foundation sound and free from hazards?	☐	☐			
6.2 Condition of Stairs, Rails, and Porches Are all the exterior stairs, rails, and porches sound and free from hazards?	☐	☐			
6.3 Condition of Roof and Gutters Are the roof, gutters, and downspouts sound and free from hazards?	☐	☐			
6.4 Condition of Exterior Surfaces Are exterior surfaces sound and free from hazards?	☐	☐			
6.5 Condition of Chimney Is the chimney sound and free from hazards?	☐	☐			
6.6 Lead-Based Paint: Exterior Surfaces Are all painted surfaces free of deteriorated paint?	☐	☐			
If no, does deteriorated surfaces exceed 20 sq. ft. of total exterior surface area?	☐	☐		☐ Not Applicable	
6.7 Manufactured Homes: Tie Downs If the unit is a manufactured home, is it properly placed and tied down? If not a manufactured home, check "Not Applicable."	☐	☐			
	☐	☐		☐ Not Applicable	

Additional Comments: (Give Item Number)(Use an additional page if necessary)

Comments continued on a separate page   Yes ☐   No ☐

7. Heating and Plumbing

7.1 Adequacy of Heating Equipment

"Adequate heat" means that the heating system is capable of delivering enough heat to assure a healthy environment in the unit (appropriate to the climate). The HA is responsible for defining what constitutes a healthy living environment in the area of the country in which it operates. Local codes (city or state codes) should be instructive in arriving at a reasonable local definition. For example, for heat adequacy, local codes often require that the unit's heating facility be capable of maintaining a given temperature level during a designated time period. Portable electric room heaters or kitchen stoves or ranges with a built-in heat unit are not acceptable as a primary source of heat for units located in areas where climate conditions require regular heating.

"Directly or indirectly to all rooms used for living" means:

"directly" means that each room used for living has a heat source (e.g., working radiator; working hot air register; baseboard heat)

"indirectly" means that, if there is no heat source present in the room, heat can enter the room easily from a heated adjacent room (e.g a dining room may not have a radiator, but would receive heat from the heated living room through a large open archway).

If the heating system in the unit works, but there is some question whether a room without a heat source would receive adequate indirect heat, check "Inconclusive" and verify adequacy from tenant or owner (e.g., unheated bedroom at the end of a long hallway).

How to determine the capability of the heating system: If the unit is occupied, usually the quickest way to determine the capability of the heating system over time is to question the tenant. If the unit is not occupied, or the tenant has not lived in the unit during the months when heat would be needed, check "Inclusive." It will be necessary to question the owner on this point after the inspection has been completed and, if possible, to question other tenants (if it is a multi-unit structure) about the adequacy of heat provided. Under some circumstances, the adequacy of heat can be determined by a simple comparison of the size of the heating system to the area to be heated. For example, a small permanently installed space heater in a living room is probably inadequate for heating anything larger than a relatively small apartment.

7.2 Safety of Heating Equipment

Examples of "unvented fuel burning space heaters" are: portable kerosene units; unvented open flame portable units.

"Other unsafe conditions" include: breakage or damage to heating system such that there is a potential for fire or other threats to safety; improper connection of flues allowing exhaust gases to enter the living area; improper installation of equipment (e.g., proximity of fuel tank to heat source, absence of safety devices); indications of improper use of equipment (e.g., evidence of heavy build-up of soot, creosote, or other substance in the chimney); disintegrating equipment; combustible materials near heat source or flue. See Inspection Manual for a more detailed discussion of the inspection of safety aspects of the heating systems.

If you are unable to gain access to the primary heating system in the unit check "Inconclusive." Contact the owner or manager for verification of safety of the system. If the system has passed a recent local inspection, check "Pass." This applies especially to units in which heat is provided by a large scale, complex central heating system that serves multiple units (e.g., a boiler in the basement of a large apartment building). In most cases, a large scale heating system for a multi-unit building will be subject to periodic safety inspections by a local public agency. Check with the owner or manager to determine the date and outcome of the last such inspection, or look for an inspection certificate posted on the heating system.

7.3 Ventilation and Adequacy of Cooling

If the tenant is present and has occupied the unit during the summer months, inquire about the adequacy of air flow. If the tenant is not present or has not occupied the unit during the summer months, test a sample of windows to see that they open (see Inspection Manual for instruction).

"Working cooling equipment" includes: central (fan) ventilation system; evaporative cooling system; room or central air conditioning.

Check "Inconclusive" if there are no openable windows and it is impossible, or inappropriate, to test whether a cooling system works. Check with other tenants in the building (in a multi-unit structure) and with the owner or manager for verification of the adequacy of ventilation and cooling.

7.4 Water Heater

"Location presents hazard" means that the gas or oil water heater is located in living areas or closets where safety hazards may exist (e.g., water heater located in very cluttered closet with cloth and paper items stacked against it). Gas water heaters in bedrooms or other living areas must have safety dividers or shields.

Water heaters must have a temperature-pressure relief valve and discharge line (directed toward the floor or outside of the living area) as a safeguard against build up of steam if the water heater malfunctions. If not, they are not properly equipped and shall fail.

To pass, gas or oil fired water heaters must be vented into a properly installed chimney or flue leading outside. Electric water heaters do not require venting.

If it is impossible to view the water heater, check "Inconclusive." Obtain verification of safety of system from owner or manager.

Check "Pass" if the water heater has passed a local inspection. This applies primarily to hot water that is supplied by a large scale complex water heating system that serves multiple units (e.g., water heating system in large apartment building). Check in the same manner described for heating system safety, item 7.2, above.

7.5 Water Supply

If the structure is connected to a city or town water system, check "Pass." If the structure has a private water supply (usually in rural areas) inquire into the nature of the supply (probably from the owner) and whether it is approvable by an appropriate public agency.

General note: If items 7.5, 7.6, or 7.7 are checked "Inconclusive," check with owner or manager for verification of adequacy.

7.6 Plumbing

"Major leaks" means that main water drain and feed pipes (often located in the basement) are seriously leaking. (Leaks present at specific facilities have already been evaluated under the checklist items for "Bathroom" and "Kitchen.")

"Corrosion" (causing serious and persistent levels of rust or contamination in the drinking water) can be determined by observing the color of the drinking water at several taps. Badly corroded pipes will produce noticeably brownish water. If the tenant is currently occupying the unit, he or she should be able to provide information about the persistence of this condition. (Make sure that the "rusty water" is not a temporary condition caused by city or town maintenance of main water lines.) See general note under 7.5.

7.7 Sewer Connection

If the structure is connected to the city or town sewer system, check "Pass." If the structure has its own private disposal system (e.g., septic field), inquire into the nature of the system and determine whether this type of system can meet appropriate health and safety regulations.

The following conditions constitute "evidence of sewer back up": strong sewer gas smell in the basement or outside of unit; numerous clogged or very slow drains; marshy areas outside of unit above septic field. See general note under 7.5.

7. Heating and Plumbing

For each numbered item, check one box only.

Item No. Description	Decision			If Fail, what repairs are necessary? If Inconclusive, give details. If Pass with comments, give details.	If Fail or Inconclusive, date (mm/dd/yyyy) of final approval
	Yes, Pass	No, Fail	Inconclusive		
7.1 Adequacy of Heating Equipment Is the heating equipment capable of providing adequate heat (either directly or indirectly) to all rooms used for living?	☐	☐	☐		
7.2 Safety of Heating Equipment Is the unit free from unvented fuel burning space heaters or any other types of unsafe heating conditions?	☐	☐	☐		
7.3 Ventilation and Adequacy of Cooling Does the unit have adequate ventilation and cooling by means of openable windows or a working cooling system?	☐	☐	☐		
7.4 Water Heater Is the water heater located, equipped, and installed in a safe manner?	☐	☐	☐		
7.5 Water Supply Is the unit served by an approvable public or private sanitary water supply?	☐	☐	☐		
7.6 Plumbing Is plumbing free from major leaks or corrosion that causes serious and persistent levels of rust or contamination of the drinking water?	☐	☐	☐		
7.7 Sewer Connection Is plumbing connected to an approvable public or private disposal system, and is it free from sewer back-up?	☐	☐	☐		

Additional Comments: (Give Item Number)

Comments continued on a separate page   Yes ☐   No ☐

8. General Health and Safety

8.1 Access to Unit

"Through another unit" means that access to the unit Is only possible by means of passage through another dwelling unit.

8.2 Exits

"Acceptable fire exit" means that the building must have an alternative means of exit that meets local or State regulations in case of fire; this could include:

An openable window if the unit is on the first floor or second floor or easily accessible to the ground.

A back door opening on to a porch with a stairway leading to the ground.

Fire escape, fire ladder, or fire stairs.

"Blocked" means that the exit is not useable due to conditions such as debris, storage, door or window nailed shut, broken lock.

Important note: The HA has the final responsibility for deciding whether the type of emergency exit Is acceptable, although the tenant should assist in making the decision.

8.3 Evidence of Infestation

"Presence of rats, or severe infestation by mice or vermin" (such as roaches) is evidenced by: rat holes; droppings; rat runs; numerous settings of rat poison. If the unit is occupied, ask the tenant,

8.4 Garbage and Debris

"Heavy accumulation" means large piles of trash and garbage, discarded furniture, and other debris (not temporarily stored awaiting removal) that might harbor rodents, This may occur inside the unit, in common areas, or outside. It usually means a level of accumulation beyond the capacity of an individual to pick up within an hour or two.

8.5 Refuse Disposal

"Adequate covered facilities" includes: trash cans with covers, garbage chutes, "dumpsters" (i.e., large scale refuse boxes with lids); trash bags (if approvable by local public agency). "Approvable by local public agency" means that the local Health and Sanitation Department (city, town or county) approves the type of facility in use. Note: During the period when the HA is setting up its inspection program, it will check with the local health and sanitation department to determine which types of facilities are acceptable and include this in the inspection requirements.

If the unit is vacant and there are no adequate covered facilities present, check "Inconclusive." Contact the owner or manager for verification of facilities provided when the unit is occupied.

8.6 Interior Stairs and Common Halls

"Loose, broken, or missing steps" should fail if they present a serious risk of tripping or falling.

A handrail is required on extended sections of stairs (generally four or more consecutive steps). A railing is required on unprotected heights such as around stairwells.

"Other hazards" would be conditions such as bare electrical wires and tripping hazards.

Housing Choice Voucher Units If the unit was built January 1, 1978, or after, no child under six will occupy or currently occupies it, is a 0-BR, elderly or handicapped unit with no children under six on the lease or expected, has been certified lead-based paint free by a certified lead-based paint inspector (no lead-based paint present or no lead-based paint present after removal of lead-based paint.), check NA and do not inspect painted surfaces.

This requirement applies to all painted surfaces (building components) within the unit. (Do not include tenant belongings). Surfaces to receive a visual assessment for deteriorated paint include walls, floors, ceilings, built in cabinets (sink bases), baseboards, doors, door frames, windows systems including

mullions, sills, or frames and any other painted building component within the unit. Deteriorated paint includes any painted surface that is peeling, chipping, chalking, cracking, damaged or otherwise separated from the substrate.

All deteriorated paint surfaces **more than 2 sq. ft. in any one interior room or space, or more than 10% of the total surface area of an interior type of component with a small surface area (i.e., window sills, baseboards, and trim)** must be stabilized (corrected) in accordance with all safe work practice requirements and clearance is required. **If the deteriorated painted surface is less than 2 sq. ft. or less than 10% of the component, only stabilization is required. Clearance testing is not required.** Stabilization means removal of deteriorated paint, repair of the substrate, and application of a new protective coating or paint. Lead-Based Paint Owner Certification is required following stabilization activities, except for *de minimis level* repairs.

8.7 Other Interior Hazards

Examples of other hazards might be: a broken bathroom fixture with a sharp edge in a location where it represents a hazard; a protruding nail in a doorway.

8.8 Elevators

Note: At the time the HA is setting up its inspection program, it will determine local licensing practices for elevators. Inspectors should then be aware of these practices in evaluating this item (e.g., check inspection date). If no elevator check "Not Applicable."

8.9 Interior Air Quality

If the inspector has any questions about whether an existing poor air quality condition should be considered dangerous, he or she should check with the local Health and Safety Department (city, town or county).

8.10 Site and Neighborhood Conditions

Examples of conditions that would "seriously and continuously endanger the health or safety of the residents" are:

other buildings on, or near the property, that pose serious hazards (e.g., dilapidated shed or garage with potential for structural collapse),

evidence of flooding or major drainage problems,

evidence of mud slides or large land settlement or collapse,

proximity to open sewage,

unprotected heights (cliffs, quarries, mines, sandpits),

fire hazards,

abnormal air pollution or smoke which continues throughout the year and is determined to seriously endanger health, and

continuous or excessive vibration of vehicular traffic (if the unit is occupied, ask the tenant).

8.11 Lead-Based Paint: Owner Certification

If the owner is required to correct any lead-based paint hazards at the property including deteriorated paint or other hazards identified by a visual assessor, a certified lead-based paint risk assessor, or certified lead-based paint inspector, the PHA must obtain certification that the work has been done in accordance with all applicable requirements of 24 CFR Part 35. The Lead-Based Paint Owner Certification must be received by the PHA before the execution of the HAP contract or within the time period stated by the PHA in the owner HQS violation notice. Receipt of the completed and signed Lead-Based Paint Owner Certification signifies that all HQS lead-based paint requirements have been met and no re-inspection by the HQS inspector is required.

8. General Health and Safety

For each numbered item, check one box only.

Item No. Description	Decision			If Fail, what repairs are necessary? If Inconclusive, give details. If Pass with comments, give details.	If Fail or Inconclusive, date (mm/dd/yyyy) of final approval
	Yes, Pass	No, Fail	Inconclusive		
8.1 Access to Unit Can the unit be entered without having to go through another unit?	☐	☐			
8.2 Exits Is there an acceptable fire exit from this building that is not blocked?	☐	☐			
8.3 Evidence of Infestation Is the unit free from rats or severe infestation by mice or vermin?	☐	☐			
8.4 Garbage and Debris Is the unit free from heavy accumulation of garbage or debris inside and outside?	☐	☐			
8.5 Refuse Disposal Are there adequate covered facilities for temporary storage and disposal of food wastes, and are they approvable by a local agency?	☐	☐	☐		
8.6 Interior Stairs and Common Halls Are interior stairs and common halls free from hazards to the occupant because of loose, broken, or missing steps on stairways; absent or insecure railings; inadequate lighting; or other hazards?	☐	☐	☐		
8.7 Other Interior Hazards Is the interior of the unit free from any other hazard not specifically identified previously?	☐	☐			
8.8 Elevators Where local practice requires, do all elevators have a current inspection certificate? If local practice does not require this, are they working and safe?	☐	☐	☐	☐ Not Applicable	
8.9 Interior Air Quality Is the unit free from abnormally high levels of air pollution from vehicular exhaust, sewer gas, fuel gas, dust, or other pollutants?	☐	☐			
8.10 Site and Neighborhood Conditions Are the site and immediate neighborhood free from conditions which would seriously and continuously endanger the health or safety of the residents?	☐	☐			
8.11 Lead-Based Paint: Owner Certification If the owner of the unit is required to correct any deteriorated paint or lead-based paint hazards at the property, has the Lead-Based Paint Owner's Certification been completed, and received by the PHA? If the owner was not required to correct any deteriorated paint or lead-based paint hazards, check NA.	☐	☐		☐ Not Applicable	

Additional Comments: (Give Item Number)

Comments continued on a separate page   Yes ☐   No ☐

Special Amenities (Optional)
This Section is for optional use of the HA. It is designed to collect additional information about other positive features of the unit that may be present. Although the features listed below are not included in the Housing Quality Standards, the tenant and HA may wish to take them into consideration in decisions about renting the unit and the reasonableness of the rent.
Check/list any positive features found in relation to the unit.

1. Living Room

☐ High quality floors or wall coverings

☐ Working fireplace or stove

☐ Balcony, patio, deck, porch

☐ Special windows or doors

☐ Exceptional size relative to needs of family

☐ Other: (Specify)

2. Kitchen

☐ Dishwasher

☐ Separate freezer

☐ Garbage disposal

☐ Eating counter/breakfast nook

☐ Pantry or abundant shelving or cabinets

☐ Double oven/self cleaning oven, microwave

☐ Double sink

☐ High quality cabinets

☐ Abundant counter-top space

☐ Modern appliance(s)

☐ Exceptional size relative to needs of family

☐ Other: (Specify)

3. Other Rooms Used for Living

☐ High quality floors or wall coverings

☐ Working fireplace or stove

☐ Balcony, patio, deck, porch

☐ Special windows or doors

☐ Exceptional size relative to needs of family

☐ Other: (Specify)

4. Bath

☐ Special feature shower head

☐ Built-in heat lamp

☐ Large mirrors

☐ Glass door on shower/tub

☐ Separate dressing room

☐ Double sink or special lavatory

☐ Exceptional size relative to needs of family

☐ Other: (Specify)

5. Overall Characteristics

☐ Storm windows and doors

☐ Other forms of weatherization (e.g., insulation, weather stripping)

☐ Screen doors or windows

☐ Good upkeep of grounds (i.e., site cleanliness, landscaping, condition of lawn)

☐ Garage or parking facilities

☐ Driveway

☐ Large yard

☐ Good maintenance of building exterior

☐ Other: (Specify)

6. Disabled Accessibility
Unit is accessible to a particular disability.   ☐ Yes ☐ No
Disability _____

D. Questions to ask the Tenant (Optional)
1. Does the owner make repairs when asked?   Yes ☐   No ☐
2. How many people live there? _____
3. How much money do you pay to the owner/agent for rent? $ _____
4. Do you pay for anything else? (specify) _____
5. Who owns the range and refrigerator? (insert O = Owner or T = Tenant) Range _____   Refrigerator _____   Microwave _____
6. Is there anything else you want to tell us? (specify) _____

Everything U Need to Know...™

Inspection Summary (Optional)

Provide a summary description of each item which resulted in a rating of **Fail** or **Pass with Comments**.

Tenant ID No.	Inspector	Date of Inspection	Address of Inspected Unit

Type of Inspection ☐ Initial ☐ Special ☐ Reinspection

Item Number	Reason for "Fail" or "Pass with Comments" Rating

Comments continued on a separate page   Yes ☐   No ☐

Tenancy Addendum for Lease Agreement

Tenancy Addendum
Section 8 Tenant-Based Assistance
Housing Choice Voucher Program
(To be attached to Tenant Lease)

U.S. Department of Housing and Urban Development
Office of Public and Indian Housing

OMB Approval No. 2577-0169
(exp. 07/31/2007)

1. **Section 8 Voucher Program**

   a. The owner is leasing the contract unit to the tenant for occupancy by the tenant's family with assistance for a tenancy under the Section 8 housing choice voucher program (voucher program) of the United States Department of Housing and Urban Development (HUD).

   b. The owner has entered into a Housing Assistance Payments Contract (HAP contract) with the PHA under the voucher program. Under the HAP contract, the PHA will make housing assistance payments to the owner to assist the tenant in leasing the unit from the owner.

2. **Lease**

   a. The owner has given the PHA a copy of the lease, including any revisions agreed by the owner and the tenant. The owner certifies that the terms of the lease are in accordance with all provisions of the HAP contract and that the lease includes the tenancy addendum.

   b. The tenant shall have the right to enforce the tenancy addendum against the owner. If there is any conflict between the tenancy addendum and any other provisions of the lease, the language of the tenancy addendum shall control.

3. **Use of Contract Unit**

   a. During the lease term, the family will reside in the contract unit with assistance under the voucher program.

   b. The composition of the household must be approved by the PHA. The family must promptly inform the PHA of the birth, adoption or court-awarded custody of a child. Other persons may not be added to the household without prior written approval of the owner and the PHA.

   c. The contract unit may only be used for residence by the PHA-approved household members. The unit must be the family's only residence. Members of the household may engage in legal profit making activities incidental to primary use of the unit for residence by members of the family.

   d. The tenant may not sublease or let the unit.

   e. The tenant may not assign the lease or transfer the unit.

4. **Rent to Owner**

   a. The initial rent to owner may not exceed the amount approved by the PHA in accordance with HUD requirements.

   b. Changes in the rent to owner shall be determined by the provisions of the lease. However, the owner may not raise the rent during the initial term of the lease.

   c. During the term of the lease (including the initial term of the lease and any extension term), the rent to owner may at no time exceed:

   (1) The reasonable rent for the unit as most recently determined or redetermined by the PHA in accordance with HUD requirements, or

   (2) Rent charged by the owner for comparable unassisted units in the premises.

5. **Family Payment to Owner**

   a. The family is responsible for paying the owner any portion of the rent to owner that is not covered by the PHA housing assistance payment.

   b. Each month, the PHA will make a housing assistance payment to the owner on behalf of the family in accordance with the HAP contract. The amount of the monthly housing assistance payment will be determined by the PHA in accordance with HUD requirements for a tenancy under the Section 8 voucher program.

   c. The monthly housing assistance payment shall be credited against the monthly rent to owner for the contract unit.

   d. The tenant is not responsible for paying the portion of rent to owner covered by the PHA housing assistance payment under the HAP contract between the owner and the PHA. A PHA failure to pay the housing assistance payment to the owner is not a violation of the lease. The owner may not terminate the tenancy for nonpayment of the PHA housing assistance payment.

   e. The owner may not charge or accept, from the family or from any other source, any payment for rent of the unit in addition to the rent to owner. Rent to owner includes all housing services, maintenance, utilities and appliances to be provided and paid by the owner in accordance with the lease.

   f. The owner must immediately return any excess rent payment to the tenant.

6. **Other Fees and Charges**

   a. Rent to owner does not include cost of any meals or supportive services or furniture which may be provided by the owner.

   b. The owner may not require the tenant or family members to pay charges for any meals or supportive services or furniture which may be provided by the owner. Nonpayment of any such charges is not grounds for termination of tenancy.

   c. The owner may not charge the tenant extra amounts for items customarily included in rent to owner in the locality, or provided at no additional cost to unsubsidized tenants in the premises.

7. **Maintenance, Utilities, and Other Services**
   a. **Maintenance**
      (1) The owner must maintain the unit and premises in accordance with the HQS.
      (2) Maintenance and replacement (including redecoration) must be in accordance with the standard practice for the building concerned as established by the owner.

   b. **Utilities and appliances**
      (1) The owner must provide all utilities needed to comply with the HQS.
      (2) The owner is not responsible for a breach of the HQS caused by the tenant's failure to:
         (a) Pay for any utilities that are to be paid by the tenant.
         (b) Provide and maintain any appliances that are to be provided by the tenant.
   c. **Family damage**. The owner is not responsible for a breach of the HQS because of damages beyond normal wear and tear caused by any member of the household or by a guest.
   d. **Housing services**. The owner must provide all housing services as agreed to in the lease.

8. **Termination of Tenancy by Owner**
   a. **Requirements**. The owner may only terminate the tenancy in accordance with the lease and HUD requirements.
   b. **Grounds**. During the term of the lease (the initial term of the lease or any extension term), the owner may only terminate the tenancy because of:
      (1) Serious or repeated violation of the lease;
      (2) Violation of Federal, State, or local law that imposes obligations on the tenant in connection with the occupancy or use of the unit and the premises;
      (3) Criminal activity or alcohol abuse (as provided in paragraph c); or
      (4) Other good cause (as provided in paragraph d).
   c. **Criminal activity or alcohol abuse.**
      (1) The owner may terminate the tenancy during the term of the lease if any member of the household, a guest or another person under a resident's control commits any of the following types of criminal activity:
         (a) Any criminal activity that threatens the health or safety of, or the right to peaceful enjoyment of the premises by, other residents (including

property management staff residing on the premises);
         (b) Any criminal activity that threatens the health or safety of, or the right to peaceful enjoyment of their residences by, persons residing in the immediate vicinity of the premises;
         (c) Any violent criminal activity on or near the premises; or
         (d) Any drug-related criminal activity on or near the premises.
      (2) The owner may terminate the tenancy during the term of the lease if any member of the household is:
         (a) Fleeing to avoid prosecution, or custody or confinement after conviction, for a crime, or attempt to commit a crime, that is a felony under the laws of the place from which the individual flees, or that, in the case of the State of New Jersey, is a high misdemeanor; or
         (b) Violating a condition of probation or parole under Federal or State law.
      (3) The owner may terminate the tenancy for criminal activity by a household member in accordance with this section if the owner determines that the household member has committed the criminal activity, regardless of whether the household member has been arrested or convicted for such activity.
      (4) The owner may terminate the tenancy during the term of the lease if any member of the household has engaged in abuse of alcohol that threatens the health, safety or right to peaceful enjoyment of the premises by other residents.

   d. **Other good cause for termination of tenancy**
      (1) During the initial lease term, other good cause for termination of tenancy must be something the family did or failed to do.
      (2) During the initial lease term or during any extension term, other good cause includes:
         (a) Disturbance of neighbors,
         (b) Destruction of property, or
         (c) Living or housekeeping habits that cause damage to the unit or premises.
      (3) After the initial lease term, such good cause includes:
         (a) The tenant's failure to accept the owner's offer of a new lease or revision;

(b)   The owner's desire to use the unit for personal or family use or for a purpose other than use as a residential rental unit; or

(c)   A business or economic reason for termination of the tenancy (such as sale of the property, renovation of the unit, the owner's desire to rent the unit for a higher rent).

e. Protections for Victims of Abuse.

(1)   An incident or incidents of actual or threatened domestic violence, dating violence, or stalking will not be construed as serious or repeated violations of the lease or other "good cause" for termination of the assistance, tenancy, or occupancy rights of such a victim.

(2)   Criminal activity directly relating to abuse, engaged in by a member of a tenant's household or any guest or other person under the tenant's control, shall not be cause for termination of assistance, tenancy, or occupancy rights if the tenant or an immediate member of the tenant's family is the victim or threatened victim of domestic violence, dating violence or stalking.

(3)   Notwithstanding any restrictions on admission, occupancy, or terminations of occupancy or assistance, or any Federal, State or local law to the contrary, a PHA, owner or manager may "bifurcate" a lease, or otherwise remove a household member from a lease, without regard to whether a household member is a signatory to the lease, in order to evict, remove, terminate occupancy rights, or terminate assistance to any individual who is a tenant or lawful occupant and who engages in criminal acts of physical violence against family members or others. This action may be taken without evicting, removing, terminating assistance to, or otherwise penalizing the victim of the violence who is also a tenant or lawful occupant. Such eviction, removal, termination of occupancy rights, or termination of assistance shall be effected in accordance with the procedures prescribed by Federal, State, and

local law for the termination of leases or assistance under the housing choice voucher program.

(4)   Nothing in this section may be construed to limit the authority of a public housing agency, owner, or manager, when notified, to honor court orders addressing rights of access or control of the property, including civil protection orders issued to protect the victim and issued to address the distribution or possession of property among the household members in cases where a family breaks up.

(5)   Nothing in this section limits any otherwise available authority of an owner or manager to evict or the public housing agency to terminate assistance to a tenant for any violation of a lease not premised on the act or acts of violence in question against the tenant or a member of the tenant's household, provided that the owner, manager, or public housing agency does not subject an individual who is or has been a victim of domestic violence, dating violence, or stalking to a more demanding standard than other tenants in determining whether to evict or terminate.

(6)   Nothing in this section may be construed to limit the authority of an owner or manager to evict, or the public housing agency to terminate assistance, to any tenant if the owner, manager, or public housing agency can demonstrate an actual and imminent threat to other tenants or those employed at or providing service to the property if the tenant is not evicted or terminated from assistance.

(7)   Nothing in this section shall be construed to supersede any provision of any Federal, State, or local law that provides greater protection than this section for victims of domestic violence, dating violence, or stalking.

f.   **Eviction by court action**. The owner may only evict the tenant by a court action.

g. **Owner notice of grounds**

(1) At or before the beginning of a court action to evict the tenant, the owner must give the tenant a notice that specifies the grounds for termination of tenancy. The notice may be included in or combined with any owner eviction notice.

(2) The owner must give the PHA a copy of any owner eviction notice at the same time the owner notifies the tenant.

(3) Eviction notice means a notice to vacate, or a complaint or other initial pleading used to begin an eviction action under State or local law.

9. **Lease: Relation to HAP Contract**

If the HAP contract terminates for any reason, the lease terminates automatically.

10. **PHA Termination of Assistance**

The PHA may terminate program assistance for the family for any grounds authorized in accordance with HUD requirements. If the PHA terminates program assistance for the family, the lease terminates automatically.

11. **Family Move Out**

The tenant must notify the PHA and the owner before the family moves out of the unit.

12. **Security Deposit**

a. The owner may collect a security deposit from the tenant. (However, the PHA may prohibit the owner from collecting a security deposit in excess of private market practice, or in excess of amounts charged by the owner to unassisted tenants. Any such PHA-required restriction must be specified in the HAP contract.)

b. When the family moves out of the contract unit, the owner, subject to State and local law, may use the security deposit, including any interest on the deposit, as reimbursement for any unpaid rent payable by the tenant, any damages to the unit or any other amounts that the tenant owes under the lease.

c. The owner must give the tenant a list of all items charged against the security deposit, and the amount of each item. After deducting the amount, if any, used to reimburse the owner, the owner must promptly refund the full amount of the unused balance to the tenant.

d. If the security deposit is not sufficient to cover amounts the tenant owes under the lease, the owner may collect the balance from the tenant.

13. **Prohibition of Discrimination**

In accordance with applicable equal opportunity statutes, Executive Orders, and regulations, the owner must not discriminate against any person because of race, color, religion, sex, national origin, age, familial status or disability in connection with the lease.

14. **Conflict with Other Provisions of Lease**

a. The terms of the tenancy addendum are prescribed by HUD in accordance with Federal law and regulation, as a condition for Federal assistance to the tenant and tenant's family under the Section 8 voucher program.

b. In case of any conflict between the provisions of the tenancy addendum as required by HUD, and any other provisions of the lease or any other agreement between the owner and the tenant, the requirements of the HUD-required tenancy addendum shall control.

15. **Changes in Lease or Rent**

a. The tenant and the owner may not make any change in the tenancy addendum. However, if the tenant and the owner agree to any other changes in the lease, such changes must be in writing, and the owner must immediately give the PHA a copy of such changes. The lease, including any changes, must be in accordance with the requirements of the tenancy addendum.

b. In the following cases, tenant-based assistance shall not be continued unless the PHA has approved a new tenancy in accordance with program requirements and has executed a new HAP contract with the owner:

(1) If there are any changes in lease requirements governing tenant or owner responsibilities for utilities or appliances;

(2) If there are any changes in lease provisions governing the term of the lease;

(3) If the family moves to a new unit, even if the unit is in the same building or complex.

c. PHA approval of the tenancy, and execution of a new HAP contract, are not required for agreed changes in the lease other than as specified in paragraph b.

d. The owner must notify the PHA of any changes in the amount of the rent to owner at least sixty days before any such changes go into effect, and the amount of the rent to owner following any such agreed change may not exceed the reasonable rent for the unit as most recently determined or redetermined by the PHA in accordance with HUD requirements.

16. **Notices**

Any notice under the lease by the tenant to the owner or by the owner to the tenant must be in writing.

17. **Definitions**

Contract unit. The housing unit rented by the tenant with assistance under the program.

Family. The persons who may reside in the unit with assistance under the program.

HAP contract. The housing assistance payments contract between the PHA and the owner. The PHA pays housing assistance payments to the owner in accordance with the HAP contract.

Household. The persons who may reside in the contract unit. The household consists of the family and any PHA-approved live-in aide. (A live-in aide is a person who resides in the unit to provide necessary supportive services for a member of the family who is a person with disabilities.)

Housing quality standards (HQS). The HUD minimum quality standards for housing assisted under the Section 8 tenant-based programs.

HUD. The U.S. Department of Housing and Urban Development.

HUD requirements. HUD requirements for the Section 8 program. HUD requirements are issued by HUD headquarters, as regulations, Federal Register notices or other binding program directives.

Lease. The written agreement between the owner and the tenant for the lease of the contract unit to the tenant. The lease includes the tenancy addendum prescribed by HUD.

PHA. Public Housing Agency.

Premises. The building or complex in which the contract unit is located, including common areas and grounds.

Program. The Section 8 housing choice voucher program.

Rent to owner. The total monthly rent payable to the owner for the contract unit. The rent to owner is the sum of the portion of rent payable by the tenant plus the PHA housing assistance payment to the owner.

Section 8. Section 8 of the United States Housing Act of 1937 (42 United States Code 1437f).

Tenant. The family member (or members) who leases the unit from the owner.

Voucher program. The Section 8 housing choice voucher program. Under this program, HUD provides funds to an PHA for rent subsidy on behalf of eligible families. The tenancy under the lease will be assisted with rent subsidy for a tenancy under the voucher program

form **HUD-52641-A(1/2007)**
ref Handbook 7420.8

Tenancy Addendum for Lease Agreement (Manufactured Homes)

Tenancy Addendum
Manufactured Home Space Rental
Section 8 Tenant-Based Assistance
Housing Choice Voucher Program
(To be attached to Tenant Lease)

**U.S. Department of Housing
and Urban Development**
Office of Public and Indian Housing

Tenancy Addendum

1. **Section 8 Voucher Program**

   a. The owner has leased the manufactured home space (space) to the tenant for occupancy by the tenant's family with assistance for a tenancy under the Section 8 housing choice voucher program (voucher program) of the United States Department of Housing and Urban Development (HUD). During the term of the lease, a manufactured home owned by the family will be located on the space. The family will reside in the manufactured home with assistance under the voucher program.

   b. The owner has entered into a Housing Assistance Payments Contract (HAP contract) with the PHA under the voucher program. Under the HAP contract, the PHA will make housing assistance payments to the owner to help the family pay the rent for the space.

2. **Lease**

   a. The owner has given the PHA a copy of the lease, including any revisions agreed by the owner and the tenant. The owner certifies that the terms of the lease are in accordance with all provisions of the HAP contract, and that the lease includes the tenancy addendum.

   b. The tenant shall have the right to enforce the tenancy addendum against the owner. If there is any conflict between the tenancy addendum and any other provisions of the lease, the language of the tenancy addendum shall control.

3. **Use of Manufactured Home**

   a. During the lease term, the family will reside in the manufactured home located on the space with assistance under the voucher program.

   b. The composition of the household must be approved by the PHA. The family must promptly inform the PHA of the birth, adoption or court-awarded custody of a child. Other persons may not be added to the household without prior written approval of the owner and the PHA.

   c. The manufactured home space may only be used for residence by the PHA-approved household members. The manufactured home must be the family's only residence. Members of the family may engage in legal profit-making activities incidental to primary use of the manufactured home and space for residence by members of the family.

   d. The tenant may not sublease or let the manufactured home or the space.

   e. The tenant may not assign the lease or transfer the space.

4. **Rent to Owner**

   a. The initial rent to owner for the space may not exceed the amount approved by the PHA in accordance with HUD requirements.

   b. Changes in the rent to owner for the space shall be determined by the provisions of the lease. However, the owner may not raise the rent during the initial term of the lease.

   c. During the term of the lease (including the initial term of the lease and any extension term), the rent to owner for the space may at no time exceed:

      (1) The reasonable rent for the space as most recently determined or redetermined by the PHA in accordance with HUD requirements.

      (2) Rent charged by the owner for comparable unassisted spaces in the manufactured home park.

5. **Family Payment to Owner**

   a. The family is responsible for paying the owner any portion of the rent to owner that is not covered by the PHA housing assistance payment.

   b. Each month, the PHA will make a housing assistance payment to the owner on behalf of the family in accordance with the HAP contract. The amount of the monthly housing assistance payment will be determined by the PHA in accordance with HUD requirements for a manufactured home space tenancy under the Section 8 voucher program.

   c. The monthly housing assistance payment shall be credited against the monthly rent to owner for the space.

   d. The tenant is not responsible for paying the portion of rent to owner covered by the PHA housing assistance payment under the HAP contract between the owner and the PHA. A PHA failure to pay the housing assistance payment to the owner is not a violation of the lease. The owner may not terminate the tenancy for nonpayment of the PHA housing assistance payment.

   e. The owner may not charge or accept, from the family or from any other source, any payment for rent of the space in addition to the rent to owner. The rent to owner for the space includes owner management and maintenance charges for the space, and owner-paid utilities. However, rent to owner does not include tenant-paid utilities.

   f. The owner must immediately return any excess rent payment to the tenant.

6. **Other Fees and Charges**

   a. Rent to owner does not include cost of any meals or supportive services or furniture which may be provided by the owner.

   b. The owner may not require the tenant or family members to pay charges for any meals or supportive services or furniture which may be provided by the owner. Nonpayment of any such charges is not grounds for termination of tenancy.

   c. The owner may not charge the tenant extra amounts for items customarily included in rent to owner in the locality, or provided at no additional cost to unsubsidized tenants in the premises.

7. **Maintenance, Utilities, and Other Services**

a. **Maintenance**

(1) The manufactured home park and the space shall be operated in accordance with the housing quality standards (HQS). The owner shall provide all maintenance and management services and facilities necessary for compliance with the HQS, including: trash collection and facilities for disposal of waste and refuse. However, the owner is not required to maintain or repair the family's manufactured home.

(2) The owner shall provide adequate maintenance of roads, walkways and other common areas and facilities, and shall assure that the family has adequate access to the space.

b. **Utilities and appliances**

(1) The owner must provide sources and lines for supply of all utilities needed to comply with the HQS, including water, electricity and other necessary utilities.

(2) The owner is not responsible for a breach of the HQS caused by the tenant's failure to:

(a) Pay for any utilities that are to be paid by the tenant.

(b) Provide and maintain any appliances that are to be provided by the tenant.

c. **Family damage**. The owner is not responsible for a breach of HQS because of damages to the manufactured home by a member of the household.

8. **Termination of Tenancy by Owner**

a. **Requirements.** The owner may only terminate the tenancy in accordance with the lease and HUD requirements.

b. **Grounds.** During the term of the lease (the initial term of the lease or any extension term), the owner may only terminate the tenancy because of:

(1) Serious or repeated violation of the lease;

(2) Violation of Federal, State, or local law that imposes obligations on the tenant in connection with the occupancy or use of the space and the manufactured home park;

(3) Criminal activity or alcohol abuse (as provided in paragraph c); or

(4) Other good cause (as provided in paragraph d).

c. **Criminal activity or alcohol abuse.**

(1) The owner may terminate the tenancy during the term of the lease if any member of the household, a guest or another person under a resident's control commits any of the following types of criminal activity:

(a) Any criminal activity that threatens the health or safety of, or the right to peaceful enjoyment of the manufactured home park by, other residents (including property management staff residing in the manufactured home park);

(b) Any criminal activity that threatens the health or safety of, or the right to peaceful enjoyment of their residences by, persons residing in the immediate vicinity of the manufactured home park;

(c) Any violent criminal activity on or near the manufactured home park; or

(d) Any drug-related criminal activity on or near the manufactured home park.

(2) The owner may terminate the tenancy during the term of the lease if any member of the household is:

(a) Fleeing to avoid prosecution, or custody or confinement after conviction, for a crime, or attempt to commit a crime, that is a felony under the laws of the place from which the individual flees, or that, in the case of the State of New Jersey, is a high misdemeanor; or

(b) Violating a condition of probation or parole under Federal or State law.

(3) The owner may terminate the tenancy for criminal activity by a household member in accordance with this section if the owner determines that the household member has committed the criminal activity, regardless of whether the household member has been arrested or convicted for such activity.

(4) The owner may terminate the tenancy during the term of the lease if any member of the household has engaged in abuse of alcohol that threatens the health, safety or right to peaceful enjoyment of the manufactured home park by other residents.

d. **Other good cause for termination of tenancy**

(1) During the initial lease term, other good cause for termination of tenancy must be something the family did or failed to do.

(2) During the initial lease term or during any extension term, other good cause includes:

(a) Disturbance of neighbors,

(b) Destruction of property, or

(c) Living or housekeeping habits that cause damage to the manufactured home, the space or the manufactured home park.

(3) After the initial lease term, such good cause includes:

(a) The tenant's failure to accept the owner's offer of a new lease or revision;

(b) The owner's desire to use the space for personal or family use or for a purpose other than residential rental use; or

(c) A business or economic reason for termination of the tenancy (such as sale of the property, renovation of the manufactured home park, the owner's desire to rent the space for a higher rent).

e. **Eviction by court action.** The owner may only evict the tenant from the space by a court action.

f. **Owner notice of grounds**

(1) The owner must give the tenant a notice that specifies the grounds for termination of tenancy during the term of the lease. The tenancy does not terminate before the owner has given this notice to the tenant.

(2) The notice must be given at or before commencement of the eviction action. The notice may be included in or combined with any owner eviction notice.

(3) The owner must give the PHA a copy of any owner eviction notice at the same time the owner notifies the tenant.

(4) Eviction notice means a notice to vacate, or a complaint or other initial pleading used to begin an eviction action under State or local law.

9. **Lease: Relation to HAP Contract**. If the HAP contract terminates for any reason, the lease terminates automatically.

10. **PHA Termination of Assistance**. The PHA may terminate program assistance for the family for any grounds authorized in accordance with HUD requirements. If the PHA terminates program assistance for the family, the lease terminates automatically.

11. **Family Move-Out**. The tenant must notify the PHA and the owner before the family moves out of the space.

12. **Security Deposit**

   a. The owner may collect a security deposit from the tenant. (However, the PHA may prohibit the owner from collecting a security deposit in excess of private market practice, or in excess of amounts charged by the owner to unassisted tenants. Any such PHA-required restriction must be specified in the HAP contract.)

   b. When the family moves out of the space, the owner, subject to State and local law, may use the security deposit, including any interest on the deposit, as reimbursement for any unpaid rent payable by the tenant, any damages or any other amounts that the tenant owes under the lease.

   c. The owner must give the tenant a list of all items charged against the security deposit, and the amount of each item. After deducting the amount, if any, used to reimburse the owner, the owner must promptly refund the full amount of the unused balance to the tenant.

   d. If the security deposit is not sufficient to cover amounts the tenant owes under the lease, the owner may collect the balance from the tenant.

13. **Prohibition of Discrimination**. In accordance with applicable equal opportunity statutes, Executive Orders, and regulations, the owner must not discriminate against any person because of race, color, religion, sex, national origin, age, familial status or disability in connection with the lease.

14. **Conflict with Other Provisions of Lease**

   a. The terms of the tenancy addendum are prescribed by HUD in accordance with Federal law and regulation, as a condition for Federal assistance to the tenant and tenant's family under the Section 8 voucher program.

   b. In case of any conflict between the provisions of the tenancy addendum as required by HUD, and any other provisions of the lease or any other agreement between the owner and the tenant, the requirements of the HUD-required tenancy addendum shall control.

15. **Changes in Lease or Rent**

   a. The tenant and the owner may not make any change in the tenancy addendum. However, if the tenant and the owner agree to any other changes in the lease, such changes must be in writing, and the owner must immediately give the PHA a copy of such changes. The lease, including any changes, must be in accordance with the requirements of the tenancy addendum.

   b. In the following cases, tenant-based assistance shall not be continued unless the PHA has approved a new tenancy in accordance with program requirements and has executed a new HAP contract with the owner:

      (1) If there are any changes in lease requirements governing tenant or owner responsibilities for utilities or appliances;

      (2) If there are any changes in lease provisions governing the term of the lease;

      (3) If the family moves to a new unit, even if the unit is in the same building or complex.

   c. PHA approval of the tenancy, and execution of a new HAP contract, are not required for agreed changes in the lease other than as specified in paragraph b.

   d. The owner must notify the PHA of any changes in the amount of the rent to owner at least sixty days before any such changes go into effect, and the amount of the rent to owner following any such agreed change may not exceed the reasonable rent for the space as most recently determined or redetermined by the PHA in accordance with HUD requirements.

16. **Notices**. Any notice under the lease by the tenant to the owner or by the owner to the tenant must be in writing.

17. **Definitions**

Family. The persons who may reside in the manufactured home located on the space with assistance under the program.

HAP contract. The housing assistance payments contract between the PHA and the owner. The PHA pays housing assistance payments to the owner in accordance with the HAP contract.

Household. The persons who may reside in the manufactured home located on the space. The household consists of the family and any PHA-approved live-in aide. (A live-in aide is a person who resides in the unit to provide necessary supportive services for a member of the family who is a person with disabilities.)

Housing quality standards (HQS). The HUD minimum quality standards for manufactured housing assisted under the Section 8 tenant-based programs.

HUD. The U.S. Department of Housing and Urban Development.

HUD requirements. HUD requirements for the Section 8 program. HUD requirements are issued by HUD headquarters, as regulations, Federal Register notices or other binding program directives.

Lease. The written agreement between the owner and the tenant for the lease of the space to the tenant. The lease includes the tenancy addendum prescribed by HUD.

Manufactured home park. The property on which the space is located, including common areas and grounds.

PHA. Public Housing Agency.

Program. The Section 8 housing choice voucher program.

Rent to owner. The total monthly rent payable to the owner for the space. The rent to owner is the sum of the portion of rent payable by the tenant plus the PHA housing assistance payment to the owner.

Section 8. Section 8 of the United States Housing Act of 1937 (42 United States Code 1437f).

Space (manufactured home space). The manufactured home space rented by the tenant with assistance under the program.

Tenant. The family member (or members) who leases the space from the owner.

Voucher program. The Section 8 housing choice voucher program. Under this program, HUD provides funds to a PHA for rent subsidy on behalf of eligible families. The tenancy under the lease will be assisted with rent subsidy for a tenancy under the voucher program.

Housing Assistance Payments (HAP) Contract

**Housing Assistance Payments Contract
(HAP Contract)
Section 8 Tenant-Based Assistance
Housing Choice Voucher Program**

**U.S. Department of Housing
and Urban Development**
Office of Public and Indian Housing

OMB Approval No. 2577-0169
(exp. 07/31/2007)

Instructions for use of HAP Contract

This form of Housing Assistance Payments Contract (HAP contract) is used to provide Section 8 tenant-based assistance under the housing choice voucher program (voucher program) of the U.S. Department of Housing and Urban Development (HUD). The main regulation for this program is 24 Code of Federal Regulations Part 982.

The local voucher program is administered by a public housing agency (PHA). The HAP contract is an agreement between the PHA and the owner of a unit occupied by an assisted family. The HAP contract has three parts:

Part A Contract information (fill-ins).
See section by section instructions.
Part B Body of contract
Part C Tenancy addendum

Use of this form

Use of this HAP contract is required by HUD. Modification of the HAP contract is not permitted. The HAP contract must be word-for-word in the form prescribed by HUD.
However, the PHA may choose to add the following:

> Language that prohibits the owner from collecting a security deposit in excess of private market practice, or in excess of amounts charged by the owner to unassisted tenants. Such a prohibition must be added to Part A of the HAP contract.

> Language that defines when the housing assistance payment by the PHA is deemed received by the owner (e.g., upon mailing by the PHA or actual receipt by the owner). Such language must be added to Part A of the HAP contract.

To prepare the HAP contract, fill in all contract information in Part A of the contract. Part A must then be executed by the owner and the PHA.

Use for special housing types

In addition to use for the basic Section 8 voucher program, this form must also be used for the following "special housing types" which are voucher program variants for special needs (see 24 CFR Part 982, Subpart M): (1) single room occupancy (SRO) housing; (2) congregate housing; (3) group home; (4) shared housing; and (5) manufactured home rental by a family that leases the manufactured home and space. When this form is used for a special housing type, the special housing type shall be specified in Part A of the HAP contract, as follows: "This HAP contract is used for the following special housing type under HUD regulations for the Section 8 voucher program: (Insert Name of Special Housing type)."

However, this form may not be used for the following special housing types: (1) manufactured home space rental by a family that owns the manufactured home and leases only the space; (2) cooperative housing; and (3) the homeownership option under Section 8(y) of the United States Housing Act of 1937 (42 U.S.C. 1437f(y)).

How to fill in Part A
Section by Section Instructions

Section 2: **Tenant**
Enter full name of tenant.

Section 3. **Contract Unit**
Enter address of unit, including apartment number, if any.

Section 4. **Household Members**
Enter full names of all PHA-approved household members. Specify if any such person is a live-in aide, which is a person approved by the PHA to reside in the unit to provide supportive services for a family member who is a person with disabilities.

Section 5. **Initial Lease Term**
Enter first date and last date of initial lease term.

The initial lease term must be for at least one year. However, the PHA may approve a shorter initial lease term if the PHA determines that:

- Such shorter term would improve housing opportunities for the tenant, **and**

- Such shorter term is the prevailing local market practice.

Section 6. **Initial Rent to Owner**

Enter the amount of the monthly rent to owner during the initial lease term. The PHA must determine that the rent to owner is reasonable in comparison to rent for other comparable unassisted units. During the initial lease term, the owner may not raise the rent to owner.

Section 7. **Housing Assistance Payment**

Enter the initial amount of the monthly housing assistance payment.

Section 8. **Utilities and Appliances**.
The lease and the HAP contract must specify what utilities and appliances are to be supplied by the owner, and what utilities and appliances are to be supplied by the tenant. Fill in section 8 to show who is responsible to provide or pay for utilities and appliances.

Housing Assistance Payments Contract (HAP Contract)
Section 8 Tenant-Based Assistance
Housing Choice Voucher Program

U.S. Department of Housing and Urban Development
Office of Public and Indian Housing

OMB Approval No. 2577-0169
(exp. 07/31/2007)

Part A of the HAP Contract: Contract Information

(To prepare the contract, fill out all contract information in Part A.)

1. **Contents of Contract**
   This HAP contract has three parts:

   Part A: Contract Information
   Part B: Body of Contract
   Part C: Tenancy Addendum

2. **Tenant**

3. **Contract Unit**

4. **Household**

   The following persons may reside in the unit. Other persons may not be added to the household without prior written approval of the owner and the PHA.

5. **Initial Lease Term**

   The initial lease term begins on (mm/dd/yyyy): _____

   The initial lease term ends on (mm/dd/yyyy): _____

6. **Initial Rent to Owner**

   The initial rent to owner is: $ _____
   During the initial lease term, the owner may not raise the rent to owner.

7. **Initial Housing Assistance Payment**

   The HAP contract term commences on the first day of the initial lease term. At the beginning of the HAP contract term, the amount of the housing assistance payment by the PHA to the owner is $ _____ per month.
   The amount of the monthly housing assistance payment by the PHA to the owner is subject to change during the HAP contract term in accordance with HUD requirements.

269

8. Utilities and Appliances

The owner shall provide or pay for the utilities and appliances indicated below by an "O". The tenant shall provide or pay for the utilities and appliances indicated below by a "T". Unless otherwise specified below, the owner shall pay for all utilities and appliances provided by the owner.

Item	Specify fuel type				Provided by	Paid by
Heating	☐ Natural gas	☐ Bottle gas	☐ Oil or Electric	☐ Coal or Other		
Cooking	☐ Natural gas	☐ Bottle gas	☐ Oil or Electric	☐ Coal or Other		
Water Heating	☐ Natural gas	☐ Bottle gas	☐ Oil or Electric	☐ Coal or Other		
Other Electric						
Water						
Sewer						
Trash Collection						
Air Conditioning						
Refrigerator						
Range/Microwave						
Other (specify)						

Signatures:

Public Housing Agency   **Owner**

_____   _____
Print or Type Name of PHA   Print or Type Name of Owner

_____   _____
Signature   Signature

_____   _____
Print or Type Name and Title of Signatory   Print or Type Name and Title of Signatory

_____   _____
Date (mm/dd/yyyy)   Date (mm/dd/yyyy)

Mail Payments to:

_____
Name

_____
Address (street, city, State, Zip)

form **HUD-52641** (1/2007)
ref Handbook 7420.8

Housing Assistance Payments Contract (HAP Contract)
Section 8 Tenant-Based Assistance
Housing Choice Voucher Program

U.S. Department of Housing
and Urban Development
Office of Public and Indian Housing

OMB Approval No. 2577-0169
(exp. 07/31/2007)

Part B of HAP Contract: Body of Contract

1. **Purpose**

   a. This is a HAP contract between the PHA and the owner. The HAP contract is entered to provide assistance for the family under the Section 8 voucher program (see HUD program regulations at 24 Code of Federal Regulations Part 982).

   b. The HAP contract only applies to the household and contract unit specified in Part A of the HAP contract.

   c. During the HAP contract term, the PHA will pay housing assistance payments to the owner in accordance with the HAP contract.

   d. The family will reside in the contract unit with assistance under the Section 8 voucher program. The housing assistance payments by the PHA assist the tenant to lease the contract unit from the owner for occupancy by the family.

2. **Lease of Contract Unit**

   a. The owner has leased the contract unit to the tenant for occupancy by the family with assistance under the Section 8 voucher program.

   b. The PHA has approved leasing of the unit in accordance with requirements of the Section 8 voucher program.

   c. The lease for the contract unit must include word-for-word all provisions of the tenancy addendum required by HUD (Part C of the HAP contract).

   d. The owner certifies that:

      (1) The owner and the tenant have entered into a lease of the contract unit that includes all provisions of the tenancy addendum.

      (2) The lease is in a standard form that is used in the locality by the owner and that is generally used for other unassisted tenants in the premises.

      (3) The lease is consistent with State and local law.

   e. The owner is responsible for screening the family's behavior or suitability for tenancy. The PHA is not responsible for such screening. The PHA has no liability or responsibility to the owner or other persons for the family's behavior or the family's conduct in tenancy.

3. **Maintenance, Utilities, and Other Services**

   a. The owner must maintain the contract unit and premises in accordance with the housing quality standards (HQS).

   b. The owner must provide all utilities needed to comply with the HQS.

   c. If the owner does not maintain the contract unit in accordance with the HQS, or fails to provide all utilities needed to comply with the HQS, the PHA may exercise any available remedies. PHA remedies for such breach include recovery of overpayments, suspension of housing assistance payments, abatement or other reduction of housing assistance payments, termination of housing assistance payments, and termination of the HAP contract. The PHA may not exercise such remedies against the owner because of an HQS breach for which the family is responsible, and that is not caused by the owner.

   d. The PHA shall not make any housing assistance payments if the contract unit does not meet the HQS, unless the owner corrects the defect within the period specified by the PHA and the PHA verifies the correction. If a defect is life threatening, the owner must correct the defect within no more than 24 hours. For other defects, the owner must correct the defect within the period specified by the PHA.

   e. The PHA may inspect the contract unit and premises at such times as the PHA determines necessary, to ensure that the unit is in accordance with the HQS.

   f. The PHA must notify the owner of any HQS defects shown by the inspection.

   g. The owner must provide all housing services as agreed to in the lease.

4. **Term of HAP Contract**

   a. **Relation to lease term**. The term of the HAP contract begins on the first day of the initial term of the lease, and terminates on the last day of the term of the lease (including the initial lease term and any extensions).

   b. When HAP contract terminates.

      (1) The HAP contract terminates automatically if the lease is terminated by the owner or the tenant.

      (2) The PHA may terminate program assistance for the family for any grounds authorized in accordance with HUD requirements. If the PHA terminates program assistance for the family, the HAP contract terminates automatically.

      (3) If the family moves from the contract unit, the HAP contract terminates automatically.

      (4) The HAP contract terminates automatically 180 calendar days after the last housing assistance payment to the owner.

      (5) The PHA may terminate the HAP contract if the PHA determines, in accordance with HUD requirements, that available program funding is not sufficient to support continued assistance for families in the program.

---

form **HUD-52641** (1/2007)
ref Handbook 7420.8

(6) The PHA may terminate the HAP contract if the PHA determines that the contract unit does not provide adequate space in accordance with the HQS because of an increase in family size or a change in family composition.

(7) If the family breaks up, the PHA may terminate the HAP contract, or may continue housing assistance payments on behalf of family members who remain in the contract unit.

(8) The PHA may terminate the HAP contract if the PHA determines that the unit does not meet all requirements of the HQS, or determines that the owner has otherwise breached the HAP contract.

5. **Provision and Payment for Utilities and Appliances**

a. The lease must specify what utilities are to be provided or paid by the owner or the tenant.

b. The lease must specify what appliances are to be provided or paid by the owner or the tenant.

c. Part A of the HAP contract specifies what utilities and appliances are to be provided or paid by the owner or the tenant. The lease shall be consistent with the HAP contract.

6. **Rent to Owner: Reasonable Rent**

a. During the HAP contract term, the rent to owner may at no time exceed the reasonable rent for the contract unit as most recently determined or redetermined by the PHA in accordance with HUD requirements.

b. The PHA must determine whether the rent to owner is reasonable in comparison to rent for other comparable unassisted units. To make this determination, the PHA must consider:

(1) The location, quality, size, unit type, and age of the contract unit; and

(2) Any amenities, housing services, maintenance and utilities provided and paid by the owner.

c. The PHA must redetermine the reasonable rent when required in accordance with HUD requirements. The PHA may redetermine the reasonable rent at any time.

d. During the HAP contract term, the rent to owner may not exceed rent charged by the owner for comparable unassisted units in the premises. The owner must give the PHA any information requested by the PHA on rents charged by the owner for other units in the premises or elsewhere.

7. **PHA Payment to Owner**

a. When paid

(1) During the term of the HAP contract, the PHA must make monthly housing assistance payments to the owner on behalf of the family at the beginning of each month.

(2) The PHA must pay housing assistance payments promptly when due to the owner.

(3) If housing assistance payments are not paid promptly when due after the first two calendar months of the HAP contract term, the PHA shall pay the owner penalties in accordance with generally accepted practices and law, as applicable in the local housing market, governing penalties for late payment by a tenant. However, the PHA shall not be obligated to pay any late payment penalty if HUD determines that late payment by the PHA is due to factors beyond the PHA's control. Moreover, the PHA shall not be obligated to pay any late payment penalty if housing assistance payments by the PHA are delayed or denied as a remedy for owner breach of the HAP contract (including any of the following PHA remedies: recovery of overpayments, suspension of housing assistance payments, abatement or reduction of housing assistance payments, termination of housing assistance payments and termination of the contract).

(4) Housing assistance payments shall only be paid to the owner while the family is residing in the contract unit during the term of the HAP contract. The PHA shall not pay a housing assistance payment to the owner for any month after the month when the family moves out.

b. **Owner compliance with HAP contract**. Unless the owner has complied with all provisions of the HAP contract, the owner does not have a right to receive housing assistance payments under the HAP contract.

c. **Amount of PHA payment to owner**

(1) The amount of the monthly PHA housing assistance payment to the owner shall be determined by the PHA in accordance with HUD requirements for a tenancy under the voucher program.

(2) The amount of the PHA housing assistance payment is subject to change during the HAP contract term in accordance with HUD requirements. The PHA must notify the family and the owner of any changes in the amount of the housing assistance payment.

(3) The housing assistance payment for the first month of the HAP contract term shall be prorated for a partial month.

d. **Application of payment**. The monthly housing assistance payment shall be credited against the monthly rent to owner for the contract unit.

e. **Limit of PHA responsibility**.

(1) The PHA is only responsible for making housing assistance payments to the owner in accordance with the HAP contract and HUD requirements for a tenancy under the voucher program.

(2) The PHA shall not pay any portion of the rent to owner in excess of the housing assistance payment. The PHA shall not pay any other claim by the owner against the family.

f. **Overpayment to owner**. If the PHA determines that the owner is not entitled to the housing assistance payment or any part of it, the PHA, in addition to other remedies, may deduct the amount of the overpayment from any amounts due the owner (including amounts due under any other Section 8 assistance contract).

8. **Owner Certification**

During the term of this contract, the owner certifies that:

a. The owner is maintaining the contract unit and premises in accordance with the HQS.

b. The contract unit is leased to the tenant. The lease includes the tenancy addendum (Part C of the HAP contract), and is in accordance with the HAP contract and program requirements. The owner has provided the lease to the PHA, including any revisions of the lease.

c. The rent to owner does not exceed rents charged by the owner for rental of comparable unassisted units in the premises.

d. Except for the rent to owner, the owner has not received and will not receive any payments or other consideration (from the family, the PHA, HUD, or any other public or private source) for rental of the contract unit during the HAP contract term.

e. The family does not own or have any interest in the contract unit.

f. To the best of the owner's knowledge, the members of the family reside in the contract unit, and the unit is the family's only residence.

g. The owner (including a principal or other interested party) is not the parent, child, grandparent, grandchild, sister, or brother of any member of the family, unless the PHA has determined (and has notified the owner and the family of such determination) that approving rental of the unit, notwithstanding such relationship, would provide reasonable accommodation for a family member who is a person with disabilities.

9. **Prohibition of Discrimination**. In accordance with applicable equal opportunity statutes, Executive Orders, and regulations:

a. The owner must not discriminate against any person because of race, color, religion, sex, national origin, age, familial status, or disability in connection with the HAP contract.

b. The owner must cooperate with the PHA and HUD in conducting equal opportunity compliance reviews and complaint investigations in connection with the HAP contract.

10. **Owner's Breach of HAP Contract**

a. Any of the following actions by the owner (including a principal or other interested party) is a breach of the HAP contract by the owner:

   (1) If the owner has violated any obligation under the HAP contract, including the owner's obligation to maintain the unit in accordance with the HQS.

   (2) If the owner has violated any obligation under any other housing assistance payments contract under Section 8.

   (3) If the owner has committed fraud, bribery or any other corrupt or criminal act in connection with any Federal housing assistance program.

   (4) For projects with mortgages insured by HUD or loans made by HUD, if the owner has failed to comply with the regulations for the applicable mortgage insurance or loan program, with the mortgage or mortgage note, or with the regulatory agreement; or if the owner has committed fraud, bribery or any other corrupt or criminal act in connection with the mortgage or loan.

   (5) If the owner has engaged in any drug-related criminal activity or any violent criminal activity.

b. If the PHA determines that a breach has occurred, the PHA may exercise any of its rights and remedies under the HAP contract, or any other available rights and remedies for such breach. The PHA shall notify the owner of such determination, including a brief statement of the reasons for the determination. The notice by the PHA to the owner may require the owner to take corrective action, as verified or determined by the PHA, by a deadline prescribed in the notice.

c. The PHA's rights and remedies for owner breach of the HAP contract include recovery of overpayments, suspension of housing assistance payments, abatement or other reduction of housing assistance payments, termination of housing assistance payments, and termination of the HAP contract.

d. The PHA may seek and obtain additional relief by judicial order or action, including specific performance, other injunctive relief or order for damages.

e. Even if the family continues to live in the contract unit, the PHA may exercise any rights and remedies for owner breach of the HAP contract.

f. The PHA's exercise or non-exercise of any right or remedy for owner breach of the HAP contract is not a waiver of the right to exercise that or any other right or remedy at any time.

11. **PHA and HUD Access to Premises and Owner's Records**

a. The owner must provide any information pertinent to the HAP contract that the PHA or HUD may reasonably require.

b. The PHA, HUD and the Comptroller General of the United States shall have full and free access to the contract unit and the premises, and to all accounts and other records of the owner that are relevant to the HAP contract, including the right to examine or audit the records and to make copies.

c. The owner must grant such access to computerized or other electronic records, and to any computers, equipment or facilities containing such records, and must provide any information or assistance needed to access the records.

12. **Exclusion of Third Party Rights**

a. The family is not a party to or third party beneficiary of Part B of the HAP contract. The family may not enforce any provision of Part B, and may not exercise any right or remedy against the owner or PHA under Part B.

b. The tenant or the PHA may enforce the tenancy addendum (Part C of the HAP contract) against the owner, and may exercise any right or remedy against the owner under the tenancy addendum.

c. The PHA does not assume any responsibility for injury to, or any liability to, any person injured as a result of the owner's action or failure to act in connection with management of the contract unit or the premises or with implementation of the HAP contract, or as a result of any other action or failure to act by the owner.

d. The owner is not the agent of the PHA, and the HAP contract does not create or affect any relationship between the PHA and any lender to the owner or any suppliers, employees, contractors or subcontractors used by the owner in connection with management of the contract unit or the premises or with implementation of the HAP contract.

13. **Conflict of Interest**

a. "Covered individual" means a person or entity who is a member of any of the following classes:

(1) Any present or former member or officer of the PHA (except a PHA commissioner who is a participant in the program);

(2) Any employee of the PHA, or any contractor, sub-contractor or agent of the PHA, who formulates policy or who influences decisions with respect to the program;

(3) Any public official, member of a governing body, or State or local legislator, who exercises functions or responsibilities with respect to the program; or

(4) Any member of the Congress of the United States.

b. A covered individual may not have any direct or indirect interest in the HAP contract or in any benefits or payments under the contract (including the interest of an immediate family member of such covered individual) while such person is a covered individual or during one year thereafter.

c. "Immediate family member" means the spouse, parent (including a stepparent), child (including a stepchild), grandparent, grandchild, sister or brother (including a stepsister or stepbrother) of any covered individual.

d. The owner certifies and is responsible for assuring that no person or entity has or will have a prohibited interest, at execution of the HAP contract, or at any time during the HAP contract term.

e. If a prohibited interest occurs, the owner shall promptly and fully disclose such interest to the PHA and HUD.

f. The conflict of interest prohibition under this section may be waived by the HUD field office for good cause.

g. No member of or delegate to the Congress of the United States or resident commissioner shall be admitted to any share or part of the HAP contract or to any benefits which may arise from it.

14. **Assignment of the HAP Contract**

a. The owner may not assign the HAP contract to a new owner without the prior written consent of the PHA.

b. If the owner requests PHA consent to assign the HAP contract to a new owner, the owner shall supply any information as required by the PHA pertinent to the proposed assignment.

c. The HAP contract may not be assigned to a new owner that is debarred, suspended or subject to a limited denial of participation under HUD regulations (see 24 Code of Federal Regulations Part 24).

d. The HAP contract may not be assigned to a new owner if HUD has prohibited such assignment because:

(1) The Federal government has instituted an administrative or judicial action against the owner or proposed new owner for violation of the Fair Housing Act or other Federal equal opportunity requirements, and such action is pending; or

(2) A court or administrative agency has determined that the owner or proposed new owner violated the Fair Housing Act or other Federal equal opportunity requirements.

e. The HAP contract may not be assigned to a new owner if the new owner (including a principal or other interested party) is the parent, child, grandparent,

grandchild, sister or brother of any member of the family, unless the PHA has determined (and has notified the family of such determination) that approving the assignment, notwithstanding such relationship, would provide reasonable accommodation for a family member who is a person with disabilities.

f. The PHA may deny approval to assign the HAP contract if the owner or proposed new owner (including a principal or other interested party):

(1) Has violated obligations under a housing assistance payments contract under Section 8;

(2) Has committed fraud, bribery or any other corrupt or criminal act in connection with any Federal housing program;

(3) Has engaged in any drug-related criminal activity or any violent criminal activity;

(4) Has a history or practice of non-compliance with the HQS for units leased under the Section 8 tenant-based programs, or non-compliance with applicable housing standards for units leased with project-based Section 8 assistance or for units leased under any other Federal housing program;

(5) Has a history or practice of failing to terminate tenancy of tenants assisted under any Federally assisted housing program for activity engaged in by the tenant, any member of the household, a guest or another person under the control of any member of the household that:

(a) Threatens the right to peaceful enjoyment of the premises by other residents;

(b) Threatens the health or safety of other residents, of employees of the PHA, or of owner employees or other persons engaged in management of the housing;

(c) Threatens the health or safety of, or the right to peaceful enjoyment of their residents by, persons residing in the immediate vicinity of the premises; or

(d) Is drug-related criminal activity or violent criminal activity;

(6) Has a history or practice of renting units that fail to meet State or local housing codes; or

(7) Has not paid State or local real estate taxes, fines or assessments.

g. The new owner must agree to be bound by and comply with the HAP contract. The agreement must be in writing, and in a form acceptable to the PHA. The new owner must give the PHA a copy of the executed agreement.

15. **Written Notices**. Any notice by the PHA or the owner in connection with this contract must be in writing.

16. **Entire Agreement: Interpretation**

a. The HAP contract contains the entire agreement between the owner and the PHA.

b. The HAP contract shall be interpreted and implemented in accordance with HUD requirements, including the HUD program regulations at 24 Code of Federal Regulations Part 982.

Housing Assistance Payments Contract (HAP Contract)
Section 8 Tenant-Based Assistance
Housing Choice Voucher Program

U.S. Department of Housing and Urban Development
Office of Public and Indian Housing

OMB Approval No. 2577-0169
(exp. 07/31/2007)

Part C of HAP Contract: Tenancy Addendum

1. **Section 8 Voucher Program**
   a. The owner is leasing the contract unit to the tenant for occupancy by the tenant's family with assistance for a tenancy under the Section 8 housing choice voucher program (voucher program) of the United States Department of Housing and Urban Development (HUD).
   b. The owner has entered into a Housing Assistance Payments Contract (HAP contract) with the PHA under the voucher program. Under the HAP contract, the PHA will make housing assistance payments to the owner to assist the tenant in leasing the unit from the owner.

2. **Lease**
   a. The owner has given the PHA a copy of the lease, including any revisions agreed by the owner and the tenant. The owner certifies that the terms of the lease are in accordance with all provisions of the HAP contract and that the lease includes the tenancy addendum.
   b. The tenant shall have the right to enforce the tenancy addendum against the owner. If there is any conflict between the tenancy addendum and any other provisions of the lease, the language of the tenancy addendum shall control.

3. **Use of Contract Unit**
   a. During the lease term, the family will reside in the contract unit with assistance under the voucher program.
   b. The composition of the household must be approved by the PHA. The family must promptly inform the PHA of the birth, adoption or court-awarded custody of a child. Other persons may not be added to the household without prior written approval of the owner and the PHA.
   c. The contract unit may only be used for residence by the PHA-approved household members. The unit must be the family's only residence. Members of the household may engage in legal profit making activities incidental to primary use of the unit for residence by members of the family.
   d. The tenant may not sublease or let the unit.
   e. The tenant may not assign the lease or transfer the unit.

4. **Rent to Owner**
   a. The initial rent to owner may not exceed the amount approved by the PHA in accordance with HUD requirements.
   b. Changes in the rent to owner shall be determined by the provisions of the lease. However, the owner may not raise the rent during the initial term of the lease.

   c. During the term of the lease (including the initial term of the lease and any extension term), the rent to owner may at no time exceed:
      (1) The reasonable rent for the unit as most recently determined or redetermined by the PHA in accordance with HUD requirements, or
      (2) Rent charged by the owner for comparable unassisted units in the premises.

5. **Family Payment to Owner**
   a. The family is responsible for paying the owner any portion of the rent to owner that is not covered by the PHA housing assistance payment.
   b. Each month, the PHA will make a housing assistance payment to the owner on behalf of the family in accordance with the HAP contract. The amount of the monthly housing assistance payment will be determined by the PHA in accordance with HUD requirements for a tenancy under the Section 8 voucher program.
   c. The monthly housing assistance payment shall be credited against the monthly rent to owner for the contract unit.
   d. The tenant is not responsible for paying the portion of rent to owner covered by the PHA housing assistance payment under the HAP contract between the owner and the PHA. A PHA failure to pay the housing assistance payment to the owner is not a violation of the lease. The owner may not terminate the tenancy for nonpayment of the PHA housing assistance payment.
   e. The owner may not charge or accept, from the family or from any other source, any payment for rent of the unit in addition to the rent to owner. Rent to owner includes all housing services, maintenance, utilities and appliances to be provided and paid by the owner in accordance with the lease.
   f. The owner must immediately return any excess rent payment to the tenant.

6. **Other Fees and Charges**
   a. Rent to owner does not include cost of any meals or supportive services or furniture which may be provided by the owner.
   b. The owner may not require the tenant or family members to pay charges for any meals or supportive services or furniture which may be provided by the owner. Nonpayment of any such charges is not grounds for termination of tenancy.
   c. The owner may not charge the tenant extra amounts for items customarily included in rent to owner in the locality, or provided at no additional cost to unsubsidized tenants in the premises.

7. **Maintenance, Utilities, and Other Services**
   a. **Maintenance**

(1) The owner must maintain the unit and premises in accordance with the HQS.

(2) Maintenance and replacement (including redecoration) must be in accordance with the standard practice for the building concerned as established by the owner.

b. **Utilities and appliances**

(1) The owner must provide all utilities needed to comply with the HQS.

(2) The owner is not responsible for a breach of the HQS caused by the tenant's failure to:

  (a) Pay for any utilities that are to be paid by the tenant.

  (b) Provide and maintain any appliances that are to be provided by the tenant.

c. **Family damage**. The owner is not responsible for a breach of the HQS because of damages beyond normal wear and tear caused by any member of the household or by a guest.

d. **Housing services**. The owner must provide all housing services as agreed to in the lease.

8. **Termination of Tenancy by Owner**

a. **Requirements**. The owner may only terminate the tenancy in accordance with the lease and HUD requirements.

b. **Grounds**. During the term of the lease (the initial term of the lease or any extension term), the owner may only terminate the tenancy because of:

(1) Serious or repeated violation of the lease;

(2) Violation of Federal, State, or local law that imposes obligations on the tenant in connection with the occupancy or use of the unit and the premises;

(3) Criminal activity or alcohol abuse (as provided in paragraph c); or

(4) Other good cause (as provided in paragraph d).

c. **Criminal activity or alcohol abuse.**

(1) The owner may terminate the tenancy during the term of the lease if any member of the household, a guest or another person under a resident's control commits any of the following types of criminal activity:

  (a) Any criminal activity that threatens the health or safety of, or the right to peaceful enjoyment of the premises by, other residents (including property management staff residing on the premises);

  (b) Any criminal activity that threatens the health or safety of, or the right to peaceful enjoyment of their residences by, persons residing in the immediate vicinity of the premises;

  (c) Any violent criminal activity on or near the premises; or

  (d) Any drug-related criminal activity on or near the premises.

(2) The owner may terminate the tenancy during the term of the lease if any member of the household is:

  (a) Fleeing to avoid prosecution, or custody or confinement after conviction, for a crime, or attempt to commit a crime, that is a felony under the laws of the place from which the individual flees, or that, in the case of the State of New Jersey, is a high misdemeanor; or

  (b) Violating a condition of probation or parole under Federal or State law.

(3) The owner may terminate the tenancy for criminal activity by a household member in accordance with this section if the owner determines that the household member has committed the criminal activity, regardless of whether the household member has been arrested or convicted for such activity.

(4) The owner may terminate the tenancy during the term of the lease if any member of the household has engaged in abuse of alcohol that threatens the health, safety or right to peaceful enjoyment of the premises by other residents.

d. **Other good cause for termination of tenancy**

(1) During the initial lease term, other good cause for termination of tenancy must be something the family did or failed to do.

(2) During the initial lease term or during any extension term, other good cause includes:

  (a) Disturbance of neighbors,

  (b) Destruction of property, or

  (c) Living or housekeeping habits that cause damage to the unit or premises.

(3) After the initial lease term, such good cause includes:

  (a) The tenant's failure to accept the owner's offer of a new lease or revision;

  (b) The owner's desire to use the unit for personal or family use or for a purpose other than use as a residential rental unit; or

  (c) A business or economic reason for termination of the tenancy (such as sale of the property, renovation of the unit, the owner's desire to rent the unit for a higher rent).

e. **Protections for Victims of Abuse.**

(1) An incident or incidents of actual or threatened domestic violence, dating violence, or stalking will not be construed as serious or repeated violations of the lease or other "good cause" for termination of the assistance, tenancy, or occupancy rights of such a victim.

(2) Criminal activity directly relating to abuse, engaged in by a member of a tenant's household or any guest or other person under the tenant's control,

form **HUD-52641** (1/2007)
ref Handbook 7420.8

shall not be cause for termination of assistance, tenancy, or occupancy rights if the tenant or an immediate member of the tenant's family is the victim or threatened victim of domestic violence, dating violence, or stalking.

(3) Notwithstanding any restrictions on admission, occupancy, or terminations of occupancy or assistance, or any Federal, State or local law to the contrary, a PHA, owner or manager may "bifurcate" a lease, or otherwise remove a household member from a lease, without regard to whether a household member is a signatory to the lease, in order to evict, remove, terminate occupancy rights, or terminate assistance to any individual who is a tenant or lawful occupant and who engages in criminal acts of physical violence against family members or others. This action may be taken without evicting, removing, terminating assistance to, or otherwise penalizing the victim of the violence who is also a tenant or lawful occupant. Such eviction, removal, termination of occupancy rights, or termination of assistance shall be effected in accordance with the procedures prescribed by Federal, State, and local law for the termination of leases or assistance under the housing choice voucher program.

(4) Nothing in this section may be construed to limit the authority of a public housing agency, owner, or manager, when notified, to honor court orders addressing rights of access or control of the property, including civil protection orders issued to protect the victim and issued to address the distribution or possession of property among the household members in cases where a family breaks up.

(5) Nothing in this section limits any otherwise available authority of an owner or manager to evict or the public housing agency to terminate assistance to a tenant for any violation of a lease not premised on the act or acts of violence in question against the tenant or a member of the tenant's household, provided that the owner, manager, or public housing agency does not subject an individual who is or has been a victim of domestic violence, dating violence, or stalking to a more demanding standard than other tenants in determining whether to evict or terminate.

(6) Nothing in this section may be construed to limit the authority of an owner or manager to evict, or the public housing agency to terminate assistance, to any tenant if the owner, manager, or public housing agency can demonstrate an actual and imminent threat to other tenants or those employed at or providing service to the property if the tenant is not evicted or terminated from assistance.

(7) Nothing in this section shall be construed to supersede any provision of any Federal, State, or local law that provides greater protection than this section for victims of domestic violence, dating violence, or stalking.

f. **Eviction by court action**. The owner may only evict the tenant by a court action.

g. **Owner notice of grounds**

   (1) At or before the beginning of a court action to evict the tenant, the owner must give the tenant a notice that specifies the grounds for termination of tenancy. The notice may be included in or combined with any owner eviction notice.

   (2) The owner must give the PHA a copy of any owner eviction notice at the same time the owner notifies the tenant.

   (3) Eviction notice means a notice to vacate, or a complaint or other initial pleading used to begin an eviction action under State or local law.

9. **Lease: Relation to HAP Contract**

If the HAP contract terminates for any reason, the lease terminates automatically.

10. **PHA Termination of Assistance**

The PHA may terminate program assistance for the family for any grounds authorized in accordance with HUD requirements. If the PHA terminates program assistance for the family, the lease terminates automatically.

11. **Family Move Out**

The tenant must notify the PHA and the owner before the family moves out of the unit.

12. **Security Deposit**

a. The owner may collect a security deposit from the tenant. (However, the PHA may prohibit the owner from collecting a security deposit in excess of private market practice, or in excess of amounts charged by the owner to unassisted tenants. Any such PHA-required restriction must be specified in the HAP contract.)

b. When the family moves out of the contract unit, the owner, subject to State and local law, may use the security deposit, including any interest on the deposit, as reimbursement for any unpaid rent payable by the tenant, any damages to the unit or any other amounts that the tenant owes under the lease.

c. The owner must give the tenant a list of all items charged against the security deposit, and the amount of each item. After deducting the amount, if any, used to reimburse the owner, the owner must promptly refund the full amount of the unused balance to the tenant.

d. If the security deposit is not sufficient to cover amounts the tenant owes under the lease, the owner may collect the balance from the tenant.

13. **Prohibition of Discrimination**

In accordance with applicable equal opportunity statutes, Executive Orders, and regulations, the owner must not discriminate against any person because of race, color, religion, sex, national origin, age, familial status or disability in connection with the lease.

14. **Conflict with Other Provisions of Lease**

a. The terms of the tenancy addendum are prescribed by HUD in accordance with Federal law and regulation, as a condition for Federal assistance to the tenant and tenant's family under the Section 8 voucher program.

b. In case of any conflict between the provisions of the tenancy addendum as required by HUD, and any other provisions of the lease or any other agreement between the owner and the tenant, the requirements of the HUD-required tenancy addendum shall control.

15. Changes in Lease or Rent

a. The tenant and the owner may not make any change in the tenancy addendum. However, if the tenant and the owner agree to any other changes in the lease, such changes must be in writing, and the owner must immediately give the PHA a copy of such changes. The lease, including any changes, must be in accordance with the requirements of the tenancy addendum.

b. In the following cases, tenant-based assistance shall not be continued unless the PHA has approved a new tenancy in accordance with program requirements and has executed a new HAP contract with the owner:

   (1) If there are any changes in lease requirements governing tenant or owner responsibilities for utilities or appliances;

   (2) If there are any changes in lease provisions governing the term of the lease;

   (3) If the family moves to a new unit, even if the unit is in the same building or complex.

c. PHA approval of the tenancy, and execution of a new HAP contract, are not required for agreed changes in the lease other than as specified in paragraph b.

d. The owner must notify the PHA of any changes in the amount of the rent to owner at least sixty days before any such changes go into effect, and the amount of the rent to owner following any such agreed change may not exceed the reasonable rent for the unit as most recently determined or redetermined by the PHA in accordance with HUD requirements.

16. Notices

Any notice under the lease by the tenant to the owner or by the owner to the tenant must be in writing.

17. Definitions

Contract unit. The housing unit rented by the tenant with assistance under the program.

Family. The persons who may reside in the unit with assistance under the program.

HAP contract. The housing assistance payments contract between the PHA and the owner. The PHA pays housing assistance payments to the owner in accordance with the HAP contract.

Household. The persons who may reside in the contract unit. The household consists of the family and any PHA-approved live-in aide. (A live-in aide is a person who resides in the unit to provide necessary supportive services for a member of the family who is a person with disabilities.)

Housing quality standards (HQS). The HUD minimum quality standards for housing assisted under the Section 8 tenant-based programs.

HUD. The U.S. Department of Housing and Urban Development.

HUD requirements. HUD requirements for the Section 8 program. HUD requirements are issued by HUD headquarters, as regulations, Federal Register notices or other binding program directives.

Lease. The written agreement between the owner and the tenant for the lease of the contract unit to the tenant. The lease includes the tenancy addendum prescribed by HUD.

PHA. Public Housing Agency.

Premises. The building or complex in which the contract unit is located, including common areas and grounds.

Program. The Section 8 housing choice voucher program.

Rent to owner. The total monthly rent payable to the owner for the contract unit. The rent to owner is the sum of the portion of rent payable by the tenant plus the PHA housing assistance payment to the owner.

Section 8. Section 8 of the United States Housing Act of 1937 (42 United States Code 1437f).

Tenant. The family member (or members) who leases the unit from the owner.

Voucher program. The Section 8 housing choice voucher program. Under this program, HUD provides funds to an PHA for rent subsidy on behalf of eligible families. The tenancy under the lease will be assisted with rent subsidy for a tenancy under the voucher program.

Housing Assistance Payments (HAP) Contract (Manufactured Homes)

Housing Assistance Payments Contract
Manufactured Home Space Rental
Section 8 Tenant-Based Assistance
Housing Choice Voucher Program

U.S. Department of Housing
and Urban Development
Office of Public and Indian Housing

Instructions for use of HAP Contract

This form of Housing Assistance Payments Contract (HAP contract) is used to provide Section 8 tenant-based rental assistance for manufactured home space rental by an eligible low-income family under the housing choice voucher program (voucher program) of the U.S. Department of Housing and Urban Development (HUD).

The main regulation for the voucher program is 24 Code of Federal Regulations Part 982. Assistance for manufactured home space rental is a "special housing type" in the voucher program. Special voucher program requirements for special housing types are described in Subpart M of Part 982.

The local voucher program is administered by a public housing agency (PHA). The HAP contract for manufactured home space rental is an agreement between the PHA and the owner of a manufactured home space leased by an assisted family (manufactured home space owner). The family owns a manufactured home. During the lease term, the family will occupy a manufactured home located on the leased space.

Use of this form

The HAP contract has three parts:

    Part A: Contract information (fill-ins).
    See section by section instructions.

    Part B: Body of contract

    Part C: Tenancy addendum

Use of this HAP contract is required by HUD. Modification of the HAP contract is not permitted. The HAP contract must be word-for-word in the form prescribed by HUD.

However, the PHA may choose to add the following:

  o Language that prohibits the owner from collecting a security deposit in excess of private market practice, or in excess of amounts charged by the owner to unassisted tenants. Such a prohibition must be added to Part A of the HAP contract.

  o Language that defines when the housing assistance payment by the PHA is deemed received by the owner (e.g., upon mailing by the PHA or upon actual receipt by the owner). Such language must be added to Part A of the HAP contract.

To prepare the HAP contract, fill in all contract information in Part A of the contract. Part A must then be executed by the manufactured home space owner and the PHA.

How to fill in Part A

Section by section instructions

Section 2: Tenant

Enter full name of tenant.

Section 3. Manufactured Home Space

Enter address and designation of manufactured home space.

Section 4. Household Members

Enter full names of all PHA-approved household members. Specify if any such person is a live-in aide – a person approved by the PHA to reside in the manufactured home to provide supportive services for a family member who is a person with disabilities.

Section 5. Initial Lease Term

Enter first date and last date of initial lease term.

The initial lease term must be for at least one year. However, the PHA may approve a shorter initial lease term if the PHA determines that:

  o Such shorter term would improve housing opportunities for the tenant, and

  o Such shorter term is the prevailing local market practice.

Section 6. Initial Space Rent

Enter the amount of the monthly rent to owner for the space during the initial lease term. The rent to owner includes owner maintenance and management charges for the space, and charges for owner-paid utilities. However, rent to owner does not include tenant-paid utilities.

The PHA must determine that the rent to owner for the space is reasonable in comparison to rent for other comparable unassisted spaces. During the initial lease term, the owner may not raise the rent to owner.

Section 7. Housing Assistance Payment

Enter the initial amount of the monthly housing assistance payment.

Section 8. Utilities

The lease and the HAP contract must specify what utilities are to be supplied by the owner, and what utilities are to be supplied by the tenant. Fill in section 8 to show who is responsible to provide or pay for utilities.

Housing Assistance Payments Contract
Manufactured Home Space Rental
Section 8 Tenant-Based Assistance
Housing Choice Voucher Program

**U.S. Department of Housing
and Urban Development**
Office of Public and Indian Housing

Part A of the HAP Contract: Contract Information

(To prepare the contract, fill out all contract information in Part A.)

1. **Contents of Contract**

    The purpose of this HAP contract is to assist the household to lease a manufactured home space (space) from the owner. The HAP contract has three parts:

    Part A: Contract Information

    Part B: Body of Contract

    Part C: Tenancy Addendum

2. **Tenant**

3. **Manufactured Home Space: Address and Designation**

4. **Household Members**

    The following persons may reside in the manufactured home and space. Other persons may not be added to the household without prior written approval of the owner and the PHA.

5. **Initial Lease Term**   (mm/dd/yyyy)

    The initial lease term begins on: _____

    The initial lease term ends on: _____

6. **Initial Space Rent**

    The initial rent to owner for the space is: $_____

    During the initial lease term, the owner may not raise the rent to owner.

7. **Initial Housing Assistance Payment**

    The HAP contract term commences on the first day of the initial lease term. At the beginning of the HAP contract term, the amount of the housing assistance payment by the PHA to the owner is $_____ per month.

    The amount of the monthly housing assistance payment by the PHA to the owner is subject to change during the HAP contract term in accordance with HUD requirements.

---

8. Utilities and Appliances

The owner shall provide or pay for the utilities and appliances indicated below by an "**O**". The tenant shall provide or pay for the utilities and appliances indicated below by a "**T**". Unless otherwise specified below, the owner shall pay for all utilities and appliances provided by the owner.

Item	Specify fuel type				Provided by	Paid by
Heating	☐ Natural gas	☐ Bottle gas	☐ Oil or Electric	☐ Coal or Other		
Cooking	☐ Natural gas	☐ Bottle gas	☐ Oil or Electric	☐ Coal or Other		
Water Heating	☐ Natural gas	☐ Bottle gas	☐ Oil or Electric	☐ Coal or Other		
Other Electric						
Water						
Sewer						
Trash Collection						
Air Conditioning					N/A	
Refrigerator					N/A	
Range/Microwave					N/A	
Other (specify)						

Signatures:

Public Housing Agency

_____
Print or Type Name of PHA

_____
Signature

_____
Print or Type Name and Title of Signatory

_____
Date (mm/dd/yyyy)

Owner

_____
Print or Type Name of Owner

_____
Signature

_____
Print or Type Name and Title of Signatory

_____
Date (mm/dd/yyyy)

Mail Payments to:

_____
Name

_____
Address (street, city, State, Zip)

form **HUD-52642** (3/2000)
ref Handbook 7420.8

Housing Assistance Payments Contract Manufactured Home Space Rental Section 8 Tenant-Based Assistance Housing Choice Voucher Program

U.S. Department of Housing and Urban Development
Office of Public and Indian Housing

Part B of HAP Contract: Body of Contract

1. **Purpose**

   a. This is a HAP contract between the PHA and the owner. The HAP contract is entered to help the family pay rent for the manufactured home space (space) described in Part A of the HAP contract with monthly assistance payments from the PHA under the Section 8 voucher program (see HUD program regulations at 24 Code of Federal Regulations Part 982).

   b. During the HAP contract term, the PHA will pay housing assistance payments to the owner in accordance with the HAP contract. The housing assistance payments by the PHA assist the tenant to lease the space from the owner. The HAP contract only applies to the space and household identified in Part A (including any PHA-approved changes in household composition in accordance with this contract).

2. **Lease of Manufactured Home Space**

   a. The PHA has approved the leasing of the space in accordance with requirements of the Section 8 voucher program.

   b. The lease for the space must include word-for-word all provisions of the tenancy addendum required by HUD (Part C of the HAP contract).

   c. The owner certifies that:

   (1) The owner and the tenant have entered into a lease for the space that includes all provisions of the tenancy addendum.

   (2) The lease is in a standard form that is used in the locality by the owner for rental of a manufactured home space and that is used for other unassisted tenants in the manufactured home park.

   (3) The lease is consistent with State and local law.

   d. The owner is responsible for screening the family's behavior or suitability for tenancy. The PHA is not responsible for such screening. The PHA has no liability or responsibility to the owner or other persons for the family's behavior or the family's conduct in tenancy.

3. **Housing Quality Standards**

   a. The PHA shall not make any housing assistance payments if the housing, including the space and the manufactured home, does not comply with the HQS, regardless of whether the failure is caused by the owner or by the household.

   b. The PHA may inspect the mobile home park, the space and the manufactured home at such times as the PHA determines necessary to ensure that the unit is in accordance with the HQS.

   c. The PHA must notify the owner and the tenant of any HQS defects shown by the inspection.

   d. The owner must provide all maintenance and management services for the space as agreed to in the lease.

4. **Term of HAP Contract**

   a. **Relation to lease term.** The term of the HAP contract begins on the first day of the initial term of the lease, and terminates on the last day of the term of the lease (including the initial lease term and any extensions).

   b. **When HAP contract terminates.**

   (1) The HAP contract terminates automatically if the lease is terminated by the owner or the tenant.

   (2) The PHA may terminate program assistance for the family for any grounds authorized in accordance with HUD requirements. If the PHA terminates program assistance for the family, the HAP contract terminates automatically.

   (3) The HAP contract terminates automatically if the family moves from the space, or if the family's manufactured home is removed from the space.

   (4) The HAP contract terminates automatically 180 calendar days after the last housing assistance payment to the owner.

   (5) The PHA may terminate the HAP contract if the PHA determines, in accordance with HUD requirements, that available program funding is not sufficient to support continued assistance for families in the program.

   (6) The PHA may terminate the HAP contract if the PHA determines that the manufactured home does not provide adequate space in accordance with the HQS because of an increase in family size or a change in family composition.

   (7) If the family breaks up, the PHA may terminate the HAP contract, or may continue housing assistance payments on behalf of family members who continue to reside in the manufactured home located on the space.

   (8) The PHA may terminate the HAP contract if the PHA determines that the housing does not comply with all requirements of the HQS, or determines that the owner has otherwise breached the HAP contract.

5. **Provision and Payment for Utilities**

   a. The lease must specify what utilities are to be provided or paid by the owner or the tenant.

   b. Part A of the HAP contract specifies what utilities are to be provided or paid by the owner or the tenant. The lease shall be consistent with the HAP contract.

6. **Rent to Owner: Reasonable Rent**

   a. During the HAP contract term, the rent to owner for the space may at no time exceed the reasonable rent as most recently determined or redetermined by the PHA in accordance with HUD requirements.

b. The PHA must determine whether the rent to owner is reasonable in comparison to rent for other comparable unassisted spaces. To make this determination, the PHA must consider:

(1) The location and size of the space,

(2) Any utilities provided or paid by the owner in connection with rental of the space, and

(3) Any services and maintenance provided by the owner in accordance with the lease.

c. The PHA must redetermine the reasonable rent when required in accordance with HUD requirements. The PHA may redetermine the reasonable rent at any time.

d. During the HAP contract term, the rent to owner may not exceed rent charged by the owner for comparable unassisted spaces in the manufactured home park. The owner must give the PHA any information requested by the PHA on rents charged by the owner for rental of other spaces in the manufactured home park or elsewhere.

7. **PHA Payment to Owner**

a. **When paid**

(1) During the term of the HAP contract, the PHA must make monthly housing assistance payments to the owner on behalf of the family at the beginning of each month.

(2) The PHA must pay housing assistance payments promptly when due to the owner.

(3) If housing assistance payments are not paid promptly when due after the first two calendar months of the HAP contract term, the PHA shall pay the owner penalties in accordance with generally accepted practices and law, as applicable in the local housing market, governing penalties for late payment by a tenant. However, the PHA shall not be obligated to pay any late payment penalty if HUD determines that late payment by the PHA is due to factors beyond the PHA's control. Moreover, the PHA shall not be obligated to pay any late payment penalty if housing assistance payments by the PHA are delayed or denied as a remedy for owner breach of the HAP contract (including any of the following PHA remedies: recovery of overpayments, suspension of housing assistance payments, abatement or reduction of housing assistance payments, termination of housing assistance payments and termination of the contract).

(4) Housing assistance payments shall only be paid to the owner while the family is residing in the manufactured home located on the space during the term of the HAP contract. The PHA shall not pay a housing assistance payment to the owner for any month after the month when the family moves from the space.

b. **Owner compliance with HAP contract.** Unless the owner has complied with all provisions of the HAP contract, the owner does not have a right to receive housing assistance payments under the HAP contract.

c. **Amount of PHA payment to owner**

(1) The amount of the monthly PHA housing assistance payment to the owner shall be determined by the PHA in accordance with HUD requirements for a manufactured home space tenancy under the voucher program.

(2) The amount of the PHA housing assistance payment is subject to change during the HAP contract term in accordance with HUD requirements. The PHA must notify the family and the owner of any changes in the amount of the housing assistance payment.

(3) The housing assistance payment for the first month of the HAP contract term shall be prorated for a partial month.

d. **Application of payment.** The monthly housing assistance payment shall be credited against the monthly rent to owner for the contract space.

e. **Limit of PHA responsibility.**

(1) The PHA is only responsible for making housing assistance payments to the owner in accordance with the HAP contract and HUD requirements for a manufactured home space tenancy assisted under the voucher program.

(2) The PHA shall not pay any portion of the rent to owner in excess of the housing assistance payment. The PHA shall not pay any other claim by the owner against the family.

f. **Overpayment to owner.** If the PHA determines that the owner is not entitled to the housing assistance payment or any part of it, the PHA, in addition to other remedies, may deduct the amount of the overpayment from any amounts due the owner (including amounts due under any other Section 8 assistance contract).

8. **Owner Certification.**

During the term of this contract, the owner certifies that:

a. The owner is operating the manufactured home park and the space in accordance with the housing quality standards (HQS), and is providing all maintenance and management services and facilities necessary for compliance with the HQS, including trash collection and facilities for disposal of waste and refuse.

b. The space is leased to the tenant. The lease includes the tenancy addendum for manufactured home space rental (Part C of the HAP contract), and is in accordance with the HAP contract and program requirements. The owner has provided the lease to the PHA, including any revisions of the lease.

c. The rent to owner does not exceed rents charged by the owner for rental of comparable unassisted spaces in the manufactured home park.

d. Except for the rent to owner, the owner has not received and will not receive any payments or other consideration (from the family, the PHA, HUD, or any other public or private source) for rental of the contract unit during the HAP contract term.

e. The family does not own or have any interest in the space.

f. To the best of the owner's knowledge, the members of the family reside in the manufactured home located on the space, and the manufactured home is the family's only residence.

g. The owner (including a principal or other interested party) is not the parent, child, grandparent, grandchild, sister, or brother of any member of the family, unless the PHA has determined (and has notified the owner and the family of such determination) that approving rental of the space, notwithstanding such relationship, would provide reasonable accommodation for a family member who is a person with disabilities.

9. **Prohibition of Discrimination.** In accordance with applicable equal opportunity statutes, Executive Orders, and regulations:

a. The owner must not discriminate against any person because of race, color, religion, sex, national origin, age, familial status, or disability in connection with the HAP contract.

b. The owner must cooperate with the PHA and HUD in conducting equal opportunity compliance reviews and complaint investigations in connection with the HAP contract.

10. **Owner's Breach of HAP Contract**

a. Any of the following actions by the owner (including a principal or other interested party) is a breach of the HAP contract by the owner:

(1) If the owner has violated any obligation under the HAP contract.

(2) If the owner has violated any obligation under any other housing assistance payments contract under Section 8.

(3) If the owner has committed fraud, bribery or any other corrupt or criminal act in connection with any Federal housing assistance program.

(4) For projects with mortgages insured by HUD or loans made by HUD, if the owner has failed to comply with the regulations for the applicable mortgage insurance or loan program, with the mortgage or mortgage note, or with the regulatory agreement; or if the owner has committed fraud, bribery or any other corrupt or criminal act in connection with the mortgage or loan.

(5) If the owner has engaged in any drug-related criminal activity or any violent criminal activity.

b. If the PHA determines that a breach has occurred, the PHA may exercise any of its rights and remedies under the HAP contract, or any other available rights and remedies for such breach. The PHA shall notify the owner of such determination, including a brief statement of the reasons for the determination. The notice by the PHA to the owner may require the owner to take corrective action, as verified or determined by the PHA, by a deadline prescribed in the notice.

c. The PHA's rights and remedies for owner breach of the HAP contract include recovery of overpayments, suspension of housing assistance payments, abatement or other reduction of housing assistance payments, termination of housing assistance payments, and termination of the HAP contract.

d. The PHA may seek and obtain additional relief by judicial order or action, including specific performance, other injunctive relief or order for damages.

e. Even if the family continues to live in the manufactured home, the PHA may exercise any rights and remedies for owner breach of the HAP contract.

f. The PHA's exercise or non-exercise of any right or remedy for owner breach of the HAP contract is not a waiver of the right to exercise that or any other right or remedy at any time.

11. **PHA and HUD Access to Premises and Owner's Records**

a. The owner must provide any information pertinent to the HAP contract that the PHA or HUD may reasonably require.

b. The PHA, HUD and the Comptroller General of the United States shall have full and free access to the manufactured home park, the space and the manufactured home, and to all accounts and other records of the owner that are relevant to the HAP contract, including the right to examine or audit the records and to make copies.

c. The owner must grant such access to computerized or other electronic records, and to any computers, equipment or facilities containing such records, and must provide any information or assistance needed to access the records.

12. **Exclusion of Third Party Rights**

a. The family is not a party to or third party beneficiary of Part B of the HAP contract. The family may not enforce any provision of Part B, and may not exercise any right or remedy against the owner or PHA under Part B.

b. The tenant or the PHA may enforce the tenancy addendum (Part C of the HAP contract) against the owner, and may exercise any right or remedy against the owner under the tenancy addendum.

c. The PHA does not assume any responsibility for injury to, or any liability to, any person injured as a result of the owner's action or failure to act in connection with management of the space or the manufactured home park, or in conjunction with implementation of the HAP contract, or as a result of any other action or failure to act by the owner.

d. The owner is not the agent of the PHA, and the HAP contract does not create or affect any relationship between the PHA and any lender to the owner or any suppliers, employees, contractors or subcontractors used by the owner in connection with management of the space or the manufactured home park, or with implementation of the HAP contract.

13. **Conflict of Interest**

a. "Covered individual" means a person or entity who is a member of any of the following classes:

(1) Any present or former member or officer of the PHA (except a PHA commissioner who is a participant in the program);

(2) Any employee of the PHA, or any contractor, subcontractor or agent of the PHA, who formulates policy or who influences decisions with respect to the program;

(3) Any public official, member of a governing body, or State or local legislator, who exercises functions or responsibilities with respect to the program; or

(4) Any member of the Congress of the United States.

b. A covered individual may not have any direct or indirect interest in the HAP contract or in any benefits or payments under the contract (including the interest of an immediate family member of such covered individual) while such person is a covered individual or during one year thereafter.

c. "Immediate family member" means the spouse, parent (including a stepparent), child (including a stepchild), grandparent, grandchild, sister or brother (including a stepsister or stepbrother) of any covered individual.

d. The owner certifies and is responsible for assuring that no person or entity has or will have a prohibited interest, at execution of the HAP contract, or at any time during the HAP contract term.

e. If a prohibited interest occurs, the owner shall promptly and fully disclose such interest to the PHA and HUD.

f. The conflict of interest prohibition under this section may be waived by the HUD field office for good cause.

g. No member of or delegate to the Congress of the United States or resident commissioner shall be admitted to any share or part of the HAP contract or to any benefits which may arise from it.

14. **Assignment of the HAP Contract**

a. The owner may not assign the HAP contract to a new owner without the prior written consent of the PHA.

b. If the owner requests PHA consent to assign the HAP contract to a new owner, the owner shall supply any information as required by the PHA pertinent to the proposed assignment.

c. The HAP contract may not be assigned to a new owner if the new owner (including a principal or other interested party) is debarred, suspended or subject to a limited denial of participation under HUD regulations (see 24 Code of Federal Regulations Part 24).

d. The HAP contract may not be assigned to a new owner if HUD has prohibited such assignment because:

(1) The Federal government has instituted an administrative or judicial action against the owner or proposed new owner for violation of the Fair Housing Act or other Federal equal opportunity requirements, and such action is pending; or

(2) A court or administrative agency has determined that the owner or proposed new owner violated the Fair Housing Act or other Federal equal opportunity requirements.

e. The HAP contract may not be assigned to a new owner if the new owner (including a principal or other interested party) is the parent, child, grandparent, grandchild, sister or brother of any member of the family, unless the PHA has determined (and has notified the family of such determination) that

approving the assignment, notwithstanding such relationship, would provide reasonable accommodation for a family member who is a person with disabilities.

f. The PHA may deny approval to assign the HAP contract if the owner or proposed new owner (including a principal or other interested party):

(1) Has violated obligations under a housing assistance payments contract under Section 8;

(2) Has committed fraud, bribery or any other corrupt or criminal act in connection with any Federal housing program;

(3) Has engaged in any drug-related criminal activity or any violent criminal activity;

(4) Has a history or practice of noncompliance with the HQS for units leased under the Section 8 tenant-based programs, or noncompliance with applicable housing standards for units leased with project-based Section 8 assistance or for units leased under any other Federal housing program;

(5) Has a history or practice of failing to terminate tenancy of tenants assisted under any federally assisted housing program for activity engaged in by the tenant, any member of the household, a guest or another person under the control of any member of the household that:

(a) Threatens the right to peaceful enjoyment of the premises by other residents;

(b) Threatens the health or safety of other residents, of employees of the PHA or of owner employees or other persons engaged in management of the housing;

(c) Threatens the health or safety of, or the right to peaceful enjoyment of their residences by, persons residing in the immediate vicinity of the premises; or

(d) Is drug-related criminal activity or violent criminal activity;

(6) Has a history or practice of renting spaces or units that fail to meet State or local housing codes; or

(7) Has not paid State or local real estate taxes, fines or assessments.

g. The new owner must agree to be bound by and comply with the HAP contract. The agreement must be in writing, and in a form acceptable to the PHA. The new owner must give the PHA a copy of the executed agreement.

15. **Written Notices.** Any notice by the PHA or the owner in connection with this contract must be in writing.

16. **Entire Agreement; Interpretation**

a. The HAP contract contains the entire agreement between the owner and the PHA.

b. The HAP contract shall be interpreted and implemented in accordance with HUD requirements, including the HUD program regulations at 24 Code of Federal Regulations Part 982.

Housing Assistance Payments Contract
Manufactured Home Space Rental
Section 8 Tenant-Based Assistance
Housing Choice Voucher Program

U.S. Department of Housing
and Urban Development
Office of Public and Indian Housing

Part C of HAP Contract: Tenancy Addendum

1. **Section 8 Voucher Program**

   a. The owner has leased the manufactured home space (space) to the tenant for occupancy by the tenant's family with assistance for a tenancy under the Section 8 housing choice voucher program (voucher program) of the United States Department of Housing and Urban Development (HUD). During the term of the lease, a manufactured home owned by the family will be located on the space. The family will reside in the manufactured home with assistance under the voucher program.

   b. The owner has entered into a Housing Assistance Payments Contract (HAP contract) with the PHA under the voucher program. Under the HAP contract, the PHA will make housing assistance payments to the owner to help the family pay the rent for the space.

2. **Lease**

   a. The owner has given the PHA a copy of the lease, including any revisions agreed by the owner and the tenant. The owner certifies that the terms of the lease are in accordance with all provisions of the HAP contract, and that the lease includes the tenancy addendum.

   b. The tenant shall have the right to enforce the tenancy addendum against the owner. If there is any conflict between the tenancy addendum and any other provisions of the lease, the language of the tenancy addendum shall control.

3. **Use of Manufactured Home**

   a. During the lease term, the family will reside in the manufactured home located on the space with assistance under the voucher program.

   b. The composition of the household must be approved by the PHA. The family must promptly inform the PHA of the birth, adoption or court-awarded custody of a child. Other persons may not be added to the household without prior written approval of the owner and the PHA.

   c. The manufactured home space may only be used for residence by the PHA-approved household members. The manufactured home must be the family's only residence. Members of the family may engage in legal profit-making activities incidental to primary use of the manufactured home and space for residence by members of the family.

   d. The tenant may not sublease or let the manufactured home or the space.

   e. The tenant may not assign the lease or transfer the space.

4. **Rent to Owner**

   a. The initial rent to owner for the space may not exceed the amount approved by the PHA in accordance with HUD requirements.

   b. Changes in the rent to owner for the space shall be determined by the provisions of the lease. However, the owner may not raise the rent during the initial term of the lease.

   c. During the term of the lease (including the initial term of the lease and any extension term), the rent to owner for the space may at no time exceed:

      (1) The reasonable rent for the space as most recently determined or redetermined by the PHA in accordance with HUD requirements, or

      (2) Rent charged by the owner for comparable unassisted spaces in the manufactured home park.

5. **Family Payment to Owner**

   a. The family is responsible for paying the owner any portion of the rent to owner that is not covered by the PHA housing assistance payment.

   b. Each month, the PHA will make a housing assistance payment to the owner on behalf of the family in accordance with the HAP contract. The amount of the monthly housing assistance payment will be determined by the PHA in accordance with HUD requirements for a manufactured home space tenancy under the Section 8 voucher program.

   c. The monthly housing assistance payment shall be credited against the monthly rent to owner for the space.

   d. The tenant is not responsible for paying the portion of rent to owner covered by the PHA housing assistance payment under the HAP contract between the owner and the PHA. A PHA failure to pay the housing assistance payment to the owner is not a violation of the lease. The owner may not terminate the tenancy for nonpayment of the PHA housing assistance payment.

   e. The owner may not charge or accept, from the family or from any other source, any payment for rent of the space in addition to the rent to owner. The rent to owner for the space includes owner management and maintenance charges for the space, and owner-paid utilities. However, rent to owner does not include tenant-paid utilities.

   f. The owner must immediately return any excess rent payment to the tenant.

6. **Other Fees and Charges**

   a. Rent to owner does not include cost of any meals or supportive services or furniture which may be provided by the owner.

   b. The owner may not require the tenant or family members to pay charges for any meals or supportive services or furniture which may be provided by the owner. Nonpayment of any such charges is not grounds for termination of tenancy.

   c. The owner may not charge the tenant extra amounts for items customarily included in rent to owner in the locality, or provided at no additional cost to unsubsidized tenants in the premises.

7. **Maintenance, Utilities, and Other Services**

a. **Maintenance**

(1) The manufactured home park and the space shall be operated in accordance with the housing quality standards (HQS). The owner shall provide all maintenance and management services and facilities necessary for compliance with the HQS, including: trash collection and facilities for disposal of waste and refuse. However, the owner is not required to maintain or repair the family's manufactured home.

(2) The owner shall provide adequate maintenance of roads, walkways and other common areas and facilities, and shall assure that the family has adequate access to the space.

b. **Utilities and appliances**

(1) The owner must provide sources and lines for supply of all utilities needed to comply with the HQS, including water, electricity and other necessary utilities.

(2) The owner is not responsible for a breach of the HQS caused by the tenant's failure to:

(a) Pay for any utilities that are to be paid by the tenant.

(b) Provide and maintain any appliances that are to be provided by the tenant.

c. **Family damage**. The owner is not responsible for a breach of HQS because of damages to the manufactured home by a member of the household.

8. **Termination of Tenancy by Owner**

a. **Requirements.** The owner may only terminate the tenancy in accordance with the lease and HUD requirements.

b. **Grounds.** During the term of the lease (the initial term of the lease or any extension term), the owner may only terminate the tenancy because of:

(1) Serious or repeated violation of the lease;

(2) Violation of Federal, State, or local law that imposes obligations on the tenant in connection with the occupancy or use of the space and the manufactured home park;

(3) Criminal activity or alcohol abuse (as provided in paragraph c); or

(4) Other good cause (as provided in paragraph d).

c. **Criminal activity or alcohol abuse**.

(1) The owner may terminate the tenancy during the term of the lease if any member of the household, a guest or another person under a resident's control commits any of the following types of criminal activity:

(a) Any criminal activity that threatens the health or safety of, or the right to peaceful enjoyment of the manufactured home park by, other residents (including property management staff residing in the manufactured home park);

(b) Any criminal activity that threatens the health or safety of, or the right to peaceful enjoyment of their residences by, persons residing in the immediate vicinity of the manufactured home park;

(c) Any violent criminal activity on or near the manufactured home park; or

(d) Any drug-related criminal activity on or near the manufactured home park.

(2) The owner may terminate the tenancy during the term of the lease if any member of the household is:

(a) Fleeing to avoid prosecution, or custody or confinement after conviction, for a crime, or attempt to commit a crime, that is a felony under the laws of the place from which the individual flees, or that, in the case of the State of New Jersey, is a high misdemeanor; or

(b) Violating a condition of probation or parole under Federal or State law.

(3) The owner may terminate the tenancy for criminal activity by a household member in accordance with this section if the owner determines that the household member has committed the criminal activity, regardless of whether the household member has been arrested or convicted for such activity.

(4) The owner may terminate the tenancy during the term of the lease if any member of the household has engaged in abuse of alcohol that threatens the health, safety or right to peaceful enjoyment of the manufactured home park by other residents.

d. **Other good cause for termination of tenancy**

(1) During the initial lease term, other good cause for termination of tenancy must be something the family did or failed to do.

(2) During the initial lease term or during any extension term, other good cause includes:

(a) Disturbance of neighbors,

(b) Destruction of property, or

(c) Living or housekeeping habits that cause damage to the manufactured home, the space or the manufactured home park.

(3) After the initial lease term, such good cause includes:

(a) The tenant's failure to accept the owner's offer of a new lease or revision;

(b) The owner's desire to use the space for personal or family use or for a purpose other than residential rental use; or

(c) A business or economic reason for termination of the tenancy (such as sale of the property, renovation of the manufactured home park, the owner's desire to rent the space for a higher rent).

e. **Eviction by court action**. The owner may only evict the tenant from the space by a court action.

f. **Owner notice of grounds**

(1) The owner must give the tenant a notice that specifies the grounds for termination of tenancy during the term of the lease. The tenancy does not terminate before the owner has given this notice to the tenant.

(2) The notice must be given at or before commencement of the eviction action. The notice may be included in or combined with any owner eviction notice.

(3) The owner must give the PHA a copy of any owner eviction notice at the same time the owner notifies the tenant.

(4) Eviction notice means a notice to vacate, or a complaint or other initial pleading used to begin an eviction action under State or local law.

9. **Lease: Relation to HAP Contract**. If the HAP contract terminates for any reason, the lease terminates automatically.

10. **PHA Termination of Assistance**. The PHA may terminate program assistance for the family for any grounds authorized in accordance with HUD requirements. If the PHA terminates program assistance for the family, the lease terminates automatically.

11. **Family Move-Out**. The tenant must notify the PHA and the owner before the family moves out of the space.

12. **Security Deposit**

   a. The owner may collect a security deposit from the tenant. (However, the PHA may prohibit the owner from collecting a security deposit in excess of private market practice, or in excess of amounts charged by the owner to unassisted tenants. Any such PHA-required restriction must be specified in the HAP contract.)

   b. When the family moves out of the space, the owner, subject to State and local law, may use the security deposit, including any interest on the deposit, as reimbursement for any unpaid rent payable by the tenant, any damages or any other amounts that the tenant owes under the lease.

   c. The owner must give the tenant a list of all items charged against the security deposit, and the amount of each item. After deducting the amount, if any, used to reimburse the owner, the owner must promptly refund the full amount of the unused balance to the tenant.

   d. If the security deposit is not sufficient to cover amounts the tenant owes under the lease, the owner may collect the balance from the tenant.

13. **Prohibition of Discrimination**. In accordance with applicable equal opportunity statutes, Executive Orders, and regulations, the owner must not discriminate against any person because of race, color, religion, sex, national origin, age, familial status or disability in connection with the lease.

14. **Conflict with Other Provisions of Lease**

   a. The terms of the tenancy addendum are prescribed by HUD in accordance with Federal law and regulation, as a condition for Federal assistance to the tenant and tenant's family under the Section 8 voucher program.

   b. In case of any conflict between the provisions of the tenancy addendum as required by HUD, and any other provisions of the lease or any other agreement between the owner and the tenant, the requirements of the HUD-required tenancy addendum shall control.

15. **Changes in Lease or Rent**

   a. The tenant and the owner may not make any change in the tenancy addendum. However, if the tenant and the owner agree to any other changes in the lease, such changes must be in writing, and the owner must immediately give the PHA a copy of such changes. The lease, including any changes, must be in accordance with the requirements of the tenancy addendum.

   b. In the following cases, tenant-based assistance shall not be continued unless the PHA has approved a new tenancy in accordance with program requirements and has executed a new HAP contract with the owner:

      (1) If there are any changes in lease requirements governing tenant or owner responsibilities for utilities or appliances;

      (2) If there are any changes in lease provisions governing the term of the lease;

      (3) If the family moves to a new unit, even if the unit is in the same building or complex.

   c. PHA approval of the tenancy, and execution of a new HAP contract, are not required for agreed changes in the lease other than as specified in paragraph b.

   d. The owner must notify the PHA of any changes in the amount of the rent to owner at least sixty days before any such changes go into effect, and the amount of the rent to owner following any such agreed change may not exceed the reasonable rent for the space as most recently determined or redetermined by the PHA in accordance with HUD requirements.

16. **Notices**. Any notice under the lease by the tenant to the owner or by the owner to the tenant must be in writing.

17. **Definitions**

Family. The persons who may reside in the manufactured home located on the space with assistance under the program.

HAP contract. The housing assistance payments contract between the PHA and the owner. The PHA pays housing assistance payments to the owner in accordance with the HAP contract.

Household. The persons who may reside in the manufactured home located on the space. The household consists of the family and any PHA-approved live-in aide. (A live-in aide is a person who resides in the unit to provide necessary supportive services for a member of the family who is a person with disabilities.)

Housing quality standards (HQS). The HUD minimum quality standards for manufactured housing assisted under the Section 8 tenant-based programs.

HUD. The U.S. Department of Housing and Urban Development.

HUD requirements. HUD requirements for the Section 8 program. HUD requirements are issued by HUD headquarters, as regulations, Federal Register notices or other binding program directives.

Lease. The written agreement between the owner and the tenant for the lease of the space to the tenant. The lease includes the tenancy addendum prescribed by HUD.

Manufactured home park. The property on which the space is located, including common areas and grounds.

PHA. Public Housing Agency.

Program. The Section 8 housing choice voucher program.

Rent to owner. The total monthly rent payable to the owner for the space. The rent to owner is the sum of the portion of rent payable by the tenant plus the PHA housing assistance payment to the owner.

Section 8. Section 8 of the United States Housing Act of 1937 (42 United States Code 1437f).

Space (manufactured home space). The manufactured home space rented by the tenant with assistance under the program.

Tenant. The family member (or members) who leases the space from the owner.

Voucher program. The Section 8 housing choice voucher program. Under this program, HUD provides funds to a PHA for rent subsidy on behalf of eligible families. The tenancy under the lease will be assisted with rent subsidy for a tenancy under the voucher program.

Landlord-Tenant Laws:
A Summary of State Guidelines

This Appendix Includes:

★ **Returned Check Fees**

★ **Security Deposit Limits**

★ **Deadlines for Returning Security Deposits**

★ **Notice of Entry Requirements**

★ **Late Fees**

The guidelines contained in this appendix are provided to assist you in drafting and enforcing your lease agreement. While this information is deemed accurate, you are encouraged to **consult an expert in the area of landlord-tenant law** – or at least contact your state's equivalent to a **"Department of Real Estate,"** to make sure the information provided in this appendix is still current at the time you are referencing it.

If you require a more comprehensive legal resource regarding your rights and responsibilities as an **American Landlord** (as opposed to a brief appendix on the subject), we recommend, *American Landlord Law: Everything U Need to Know about Landlord Tenant Laws* – available at book retailers nationwide or through **www.EverythingUNeedToKnow.com**. This essential companion explains in great detail *the most critical aspects of landlord-tenant law* in an easy-to-read format, so you will be able to understand all the fine details in order to adequately **protect yourself from the commonly encountered unforeseen legal pitfalls**.

Returned Check Fees

Alabama	$30 - Check writer is also responsible for all other costs of collection.
Alaska	$30
Arizona	$25
Arkansas	$25
California	$25
Colorado	$20 - Check writer is also responsible for all other costs of collection.
Connecticut	$20 - Check writer is also responsible for all other costs of collection.
Delaware	$40
District of Columbia	$25
Florida	Checks from (1) $0.01-$50.00=$25.00 fee, (2) $50.01-$300.00=$30.00 fee, (3) $300.01 and over = the greater of $40.00 fee or 5% of the face amount of the check. Check writer is also responsible for all other costs of collection.
Georgia	$30 or 5% of the face amount of the check, whichever is greater.
Hawaii	$30 - Check writer is also responsible for all other costs of collection.
Idaho	$20 - Check writer is also responsible for all other costs of collection.
Illinois	$25 - Check writer is also responsible for all other costs of collection.
Indiana	$20 - Check writer is also responsible for all other costs of collection.
Iowa	$30
Kansas	$30
Kentucky	$25
Louisiana	$25 or 5% of the face amount of the check, whichever is greater.
Maine	$25
Maryland	$35
Massachusetts	$25
Michigan	$25
Minnesota	$30 - Check writer is also responsible for all other costs of collection and civil penalties may be imposed for nonpayment.

Mississippi	$40
Missouri	$25
Montana	$30
Nebraska	$35
Nevada	$25
New Hampshire	$25
New Jersey	$30
New Mexico	$30
New York	$20 - Check writer is also responsible for all other costs of collection.
North Carolina	$25
North Dakota	$30
Ohio	$30 or 10% of the face amount of the check, whichever is greater.
Oklahoma	$25
Oregon	$25
Pennsylvania	$30
Rhode Island	$25
South Carolina	$30
South Dakota	$40
Tennessee	$30 - Check writer is also responsible for all other costs of collection.
Texas	$30 - Other costs of collection may be charged.
Utah	$20 - Check writer is also responsible for all other costs of collection.
Vermont	$25
Virginia	$35
Washington	$30 - This amount is assessed as a Handling Fee for returned checks.
West Virginia	$25
Wisconsin	$20 - Check writer is also responsible for all other costs of collection.
Wyoming	$30

Security Deposit Limits

Alabama	1 month's rent
Alaska	2 months' rent unless monthly rent exceeds $2,000
Arizona	1 ½ months' rent unless both parties agree to more
Arkansas	2 months' rent
California	2 months' rent if unfurnished unit, 3 months' rent if furnished unit, extra ½ month's rent if tenant has waterbed
Colorado	No statute
Connecticut	2 months' rent or 1 month's rent if tenant over 62 years old
Delaware	No limit if month-to-month tenancy, 1 month's rent if year or longer lease
District of Columbia	1 month's rent
Florida	No statute
Georgia	No statute
Hawaii	1 month's rent
Idaho	No statute
Illinois	No statute
Indiana	No statute
Iowa	2 months' rent
Kansas	1 month's rent if unfurnished unit, 1 ½ months' rent if furnished unit
Kentucky	No statute
Louisiana	No statute
Maine	2 months' rent
Maryland	2 months' rent
Massachusetts	1 month's rent
Michigan	1 ½ months' rent
Minnesota	No statute
Mississippi	No statute

Missouri	2 months' rent
Montana	No statute
Nebraska	1 month's rent if tenant has no pet(s), 1 ¼ months' rent if tenant has pet(s)
Nevada	3 months' rent
New Hampshire	$100 or 1 month's rent, whichever greater, no limit if landlord and tenant share facilities
New Jersey	1 ½ months' rent
New Mexico	1 month's rent if less than 1 year lease, no limit if year or longer lease
New York	No limit unless covered by local rent control regulations
North Carolina	1 ½ months' rent if month to month tenancy, 2 months' rent if lease term longer than 2 months
North Dakota	1 month's rent or $1,500 if tenant has pet(s)
Ohio	No statute
Oklahoma	No statute
Oregon	No statute
Pennsylvania	2 months' rent first year of tenancy, 1 month's rent all future years
Rhode Island	1 month's rent
South Carolina	No statute
South Dakota	1 month's rent, larger deposit allowed if special conditions create a danger to the maintenance of the unit
Tennessee	No statute
Texas	No statute
Utah	No statute
Vermont	No statute
Virginia	2 months' rent
Washington	No statute
West Virginia	No statute
Wisconsin	No statute
Wyoming	No statute

Deadlines for Returning Security Deposits

Alabama	35 days
Alaska	14 days if proper termination notice given, 30 days if not
Arizona	14 days
Arkansas	30 days
California	3 weeks
Colorado	1 month unless lease provides for longer period up to 60 days, 72 weekday non-holiday hours if emergency termination due to gas equipment hazard
Connecticut	30 days or within 15 days of receipt of forwarding address from tenant, whichever is later
Delaware	20 days
District of Columbia	45 days
Florida	15 days if no deductions, 30 days to give notice of what deductions will be made then tenant has 15 days to dispute any deduction and remaining deposit must be returned within 30 days of initial deduction notification
Georgia	1 month
Hawaii	14 days
Idaho	21 days unless both parties agree, then up to 30 days
Illinois	45 days if no deductions, 30 days to itemize deductions
Indiana	45 days
Iowa	30 days
Kansas	30 days
Kentucky	No statute
Louisiana	1 month
Maine	21 days if tenancy at will, 30 days if written lease
Maryland	45 days, 10 days to itemize deductions if tenant utilizes a surety bond
Massachusetts	30 days
Michigan	30 days
Minnesota	3 weeks, 5 days if termination due to condemnation

Mississippi	45 days
Missouri	30 days
Montana	10 days if no deductions, 30 days if deductions
Nebraska	14 days
Nevada	30 days
New Hampshire	30 days, if shared facilities and deposit is more than 30 days' rent then 20 days unless written agreement otherwise
New Jersey	30 days, 5 days if termination due to fire, flood, condemnation, evacuation
New Mexico	30 days
New York	Reasonable time
North Carolina	30 days
North Dakota	30 days
Ohio	30 days
Oklahoma	30 days
Oregon	31 days
Pennsylvania	30 days
Rhode Island	20 days
South Carolina	30 days
South Dakota	2 weeks
Tennessee	No statute, 10 days to itemize deductions
Texas	30 days
Utah	30 days or within 15 days of receipt of forwarding address from tenant, whichever is later
Vermont	14 days
Virginia	45 days
Washington	14 days
West Virginia	No statute
Wisconsin	21 days
Wyoming	30 days or within 15 days of receipt of forwarding address from tenant, whichever is later, 60 days if unit has damage

Notice of Entry Requirements

Alabama	2 days
Alaska	24 hours
Arizona	2 days
Arkansas	No statute
California	48 hours for move out inspection, 24 hours otherwise
Colorado	No statute
Connecticut	Reasonable time
Delaware	2 days
District of Columbia	No statute
Florida	12 hours
Georgia	No statute
Hawaii	2 days
Idaho	No statute
Illinois	No statute
Indiana	No statute
Iowa	24 hours
Kansas	Reasonable time
Kentucky	2 days
Louisiana	No statute
Maine	24 hours
Maryland	No statute
Massachusetts	No statute
Michigan	No statute
Minnesota	Reasonable time
Mississippi	No statute
Missouri	No statute

Montana	24 hours
Nebraska	1 day
Nevada	24 hours
New Hampshire	Adequate notice under the circumstances
New Jersey	No statute
New Mexico	24 hours
New York	No statute
North Carolina	No statute
North Dakota	Reasonable time
Ohio	24 hours
Oklahoma	1 day
Oregon	24 hours
Pennsylvania	No statute
Rhode Island	2 days
South Carolina	24 hours
South Dakota	No statute
Tennessee	No statute
Texas	No statute
Utah	No statute
Vermont	48 hours
Virginia	24 hours
Washington	2 days
West Virginia	No statute
Wisconsin	12 hours
Wyoming	No statute

Late Fees

Alabama	No statute
Alaska	No statute
Arizona	Late fees must be reasonable and indicated in the lease agreement
Arkansas	No statute
California	Late fees must be close to the landlord's actual losses and indicated in the lease agreement as follows: "Because landlord and tenant agree that actual damages for late rent payments are very difficult or impossible to determine, landlord and tenant agree to the following stated late charge as liquidated damages."
Colorado	No statute
Connecticut	Late fees can be charged when rent is nine days late
Delaware	Late fees cannot be more than 5% of the rent amount due and can be charged when the rent is more than 5 days late. If the landlord does not have an office within the rental property's county the tenant has an additional three days before late fees can be charged.
District of Columbia	No statute
Florida	No statute
Georgia	No statute
Hawaii	No statute
Idaho	No statute
Illinois	No statute
Indiana	No statute
Iowa	Late fees cannot be more than $10 a day with a maximum of $40 a month allowed
Kansas	No statute
Kentucky	No statute
Louisiana	No statute
Maine	Late fees cannot be more than 4% of the rent amount due for a 30 day period and must be indicated in writing to the tenant at the start of their tenancy. Late fees can be charged when rent is 15 days late.
Maryland	Late fees cannot be more than 5% of the rent amount due

Massachusetts	Late fees can be charged when rent is 30 days late
Michigan	No statute
Minnesota	No statute
Mississippi	No statute
Missouri	No staute
Montana	No statute
Nebraska	No statute
Nevada	Late fees must be indicated in the lease agreement
New Hampshire	No statute
New Jersey	Late fees can be charged when rent is 5 days late
New Mexico	Late fees cannot be more than 10% of the rent amount due per rental period. Tenant must be notified of the late fee charged by the end of the next rental period.
New York	No statute
North Carolina	Late fees cannot be more than 5% of the rent amount due or $15, whichever is greater, and can be charged when rent is 5 days late
North Dakota	No statute
Ohio	No statute
Oklahoma	No statute
Oregon	Late fees cannot be more than a reasonable amount charged by others in the same market if a flat fee is utilized, if a daily charge is utilized it cannot be more than 6% of the reasonable flat fee with a maximum of 5% of the rent amount due per rental period allowed. Late fees can be charged when rent is four days late and must be indicated in the lease agreement.
Pennsylvania	No statute
Rhode Island	No statute
South Carolina	No statute
South Dakota	No statute
Tennessee	Late fees can be charged when rent is 5 days late and cannot be more than 10% of the late amount. However, if the fifth day is a weekend or holiday and the tenant pays the rent amount due on the following business day, a late fee cannot be charged.
Texas	No statute

Utah	No statute
Vermont	No statute
Virginia	No statute
Washington	No statute
West Virginia	No statute
Wisconsin	No statute
Wyoming	No statute

Rental Forms and Agreements: Miscellaneous Tools of the Trade

---

This Appendix Includes:

- ★ **Rental Application (single)**
- ★ **Rental Application (co-tenants)**
- ★ **Co-Signer/Guarantor Application**
- ★ **Verification of Employment (VOE)**
- ★ **Verification of Rent (VOR)**
- ★ **Statement of Credit Denial**
- ★ **Lease Agreement**
- ★ **Modification of Lease**
- ★ **Sublease Agreement**
- ★ **Assignment of Lease**
- ★ **Option to Purchase**
- ★ **Pet Agreement**
- ★ **Assessment of Condition**
- ★ **Property Management Agreement**
- ★ **Residential Sales Contract**
- ★ **Quit-Claim Deed**

All rental forms and agreements in this appendix can be printed from the CD-ROM located in the very back of this book. *[See Appendix F for installation instructions]*

Rental Application (single)

Instructions:
1. Insert your IMAGE or LOGO (optional)
2. Enter 'PROPERTY ADDRESS APPLYING FOR'
3. REPLACE ALL of this text with YOUR contact info
4. Click on 'PRINT FORM' when finished

Everything U Need to Know...

Click here to insert image/logo

Residential Rental Application

Applicant Information

Property address applying for:

Name:

Date of birth:	SSN:	Phone:

Current address:

City:	State:	ZIP Code:

Own Rent (Please circle)	Monthly payment or rent:	How long?

Previous address:

City:	State:	ZIP Code:

Owned Rented (Please circle)	Monthly payment or rent:	How long?

Employment Information

Current employer:

Employer address:	How long?

City:	State:	ZIP Code:

Phone:	E-mail:	Fax:

Position:	Hourly Salary (Please circle)	Annual income:

Emergency Contact

Name of a person not residing with you:

Address:

City:	State:	ZIP Code:	Phone:

Relationship:

References

Name:	Address:	Phone:

Have you ever been convicted of a crime? (yes / no) If so, please explain all offenses including where, when and why:

Have you ever been evicted? (yes / no) If so, please explain where, when and why:

I acknowledge that falsification or omission of any information on this rental application may result in the immediate dismissal or retraction of an offer of tenancy. I hereby voluntarily consent to and authorize the AmerUSA Corporation ("AmerUSA"), acting as the landlord's designated screening organization for the above referenced rental property, to obtain my consumer report and render a credit decision. I further authorize all persons and organizations that may have information relevant to this research to disclose such information to the landlord's authorized agent, AmerUSA. I hereby release the landlord and its authorized agent, AmerUSA, from all claims and liabilities of any nature in connection with this research, results and decision. A photocopy of this authorization will be considered valid. I understand that I have specific prescribed rights as a consumer under the federal Fair Credit Reporting Act ('FCRA') and have received a copy of those rights titled "FCRA Summary of Rights."

Signature of applicant:	Date:

This form provided by USLandlord.com

Rental Application (co-tenants)

Instructions:
1. Insert your IMAGE or LOGO (optional)
2. Enter 'PROPERTY ADDRESS APPLYING FOR'
3. REPLACE ALL of this text with YOUR contact info
4. Click on 'PRINT FORM' when finished

Everything U Need to Know...

Click here to insert image/logo

Residential Rental Application

Applicant Information

Property address applying for:		
Name:		
Date of birth:	SSN:	Phone:
Current address:		
City:	State:	ZIP Code:
Own Rent (Please circle)	Monthly payment or rent:	How long?
Previous address:		
City:	State:	ZIP Code:
Owned Rented (Please circle)	Monthly payment or rent:	How long?

Employment Information

Current employer:		
Employer address:		How long?
City:	State:	ZIP Code:
Phone:	E-mail:	Fax:
Position:	Hourly Salary (Please circle)	Annual income:

Emergency Contact

Name of a person not residing with you:			
Address:			
City:	State:	ZIP Code:	Phone:
Relationship:			

References

Name:	Address:	Phone:

Have you ever been convicted of a crime? (yes / no) If so, please explain all offenses including where, when and why:

Have you ever been evicted? (yes / no) If so, please explain where, when and why:

Co-Applicant Information

Property address applying for:		
Name:		
Date of birth:	SSN:	Phone:
Current address:		
City:	State:	ZIP Code:
Own Rent (Please circle)	Monthly payment or rent:	How long?
Previous address:		
City:	State:	ZIP Code:
Owned Rented (Please circle)	Monthly payment or rent:	How long?

Co-Applicant Employment Information

Current employer:			
Employer address:			How long?
City:	State:		ZIP Code:
Phone:	E-mail:		Fax:
Position:	Hourly Salary (Please circle)		Annual income:

Co-Applicant Emergency Contact

Name of a person not residing with you:			
Address:			
City:	State:	ZIP Code:	Phone:
Relationchip:			

Co-Applicant References

Name:	Address:	Phone:

Have you ever been convicted of a crime? (yes / no) If so, please explain all offenses including where, when and why:

Have you ever been evicted? (yes / no) If so, please explain where, when and why:

I/We acknowledge that falsification or omission of any information on this rental application may result in the immediate dismissal or retraction of an offer of tenancy. I/We hereby voluntarily consent to and authorize the AmerUSA Corporation ("AmerUSA"), acting as the landlord's designated screening organization for the above referenced rental property, to obtain my consumer report and render a credit decision. I/We further authorize all persons and organizations that may have information relevant to this research to disclose such information to the landlord's authorized agent, AmerUSA. I/We hereby release the landlord and its authorized agent, AmerUSA, from all claims and liabilities of any nature in connection with this research, results and decision. A photocopy of this authorization will be considered valid. I/We understand that I/we have specific prescribed rights as a consumer under the federal Fair Credit Reporting Act ('FCRA') and have received a copy of those rights titled "FCRA Summary of Rights."

Signature of applicant:	Date:
Signature of co-applicant:	Date:

This form provided by USLandlord.com

Co-Signer/Guarantor Application

Instructions:
1. Insert your IMAGE or LOGO (optional)
2. Enter 'PROPERTY ADDRESS APPLYING FOR'
3. REPLACE ALL of this text with YOUR contact info
4. Click on 'PRINT FORM' when finished

Everything U Need to Know...

Click here to insert image/logo

Co-Signer/Guarantor Application

Co-Signer/Guarantor Information		
Property address applying for:		
Name:		
Date of birth:	SSN:	Phone:
Current address:		
City:	State:	ZIP Code:
Own Rent (Please circle) Monthly payment or rent:		How long?
Previous address:		
City:	State:	ZIP Code:
Owned Rented (Please circle) Monthly payment or rent:		How long?

Employment Information		
Current employer:		
Employer address:		How long?
City:	State:	ZIP Code:
Phone:	E-mail:	Fax:
Position:	Hourly Salary (Please circle)	Annual income:

Emergency Contact			
Name of a person not residing with you:			
Address:			
City:	State:	ZIP Code:	Phone:
Relationship:			

References		
Name:	Address:	Phone:

Have you ever been convicted of a crime? (yes / no) If so, please explain all offenses including where, when and why:

Have you ever been evicted? (yes / no) If so, please explain where, when and why:

I acknowledge that falsification or omission of any information on this rental application may result in the immediate dismissal or retraction of an offer of tenancy. I hereby voluntarily consent to and authorize the AmerUSA Corporation ("AmerUSA"), acting as the landlord's designated screening organization for the above referenced rental property, to obtain my consumer report and render a credit decision. I further authorize all persons and organizations that may have information relevant to this research to disclose such information to the landlord's authorized agent, AmerUSA. I hereby release the landlord and its authorized agent, AmerUSA, from all claims and liabilities of any nature in connection with this research, results and decision. A photocopy of this authorization will be considered valid. I understand that I have specific prescribed rights as a consumer under the federal Fair Credit Reporting Act ('FCRA') and have received a copy of those rights titled "FCRA Summary of Rights."

Signature of co-signer/guarantor:	Date:

This form provided by USLandlord.com

Verification of Employment (VOE)

Instructions:
1. Insert your IMAGE or LOGO (optional)
2. Enter EMPLOYER & APPLICANT information
3. REPLACE ALL of this text with YOUR contact info
4. Click on 'PRINT FORM' when finished

Everything U Need to Know...

Click here to insert image/logo

Request for Verification of Employment

Part I - Request

Employer - Please complete either Part II or Part III as applicable. Complete Part IV and return directly to management listed above.

To: (Name and Address of Employer)

Attn:
Company:
Address:
City: State: ZIP Code:
Ph: Fax:

Applicant Information

Name:

Address:

City: State: ZIP Code:

Employee ID: Department: Badge #:

I have applied for residency and stated that I am now or was formerly employed by you. My signature below (*or accompanying Applicant Signature Authorization) authorizes verification of this information.

*Signature of applicant: Date:

Part II - Verification of Present Employment

Applicant's Present Position:

Probability of Continued Employment: Hire Date:

Gross Base Pay: $ Hourly   Weekly Annually (Please circle)   Bonus Income: $

For Military Personnel Only (Monthly Amounts)

Base Pay: $ Rations: $ Clothing: $

Quarters: $ Flight or Hazard: $ Variable Housing Allowance: $

Remarks:

Part III - Verification of Previous Employment

Position Held: Hire Date:

Reason for Leaving: Termination Date:

Gross Base Pay: $ Hourly   Weekly Annually (Please circle)   Bonus Income: $

Part IV - Authorized Signature

Name: Title: Phone:

Signature of employer: Date:

This form provided by USLandlord.com

Verification of Rent (VOR)

Instructions:
1. Insert your IMAGE or LOGO (optional)
2. Enter LANDLORD & APPLICANT information
3. REPLACE ALL of this text with YOUR contact info
4. Click on 'PRINT FORM' when finished

Everything U Need to Know...

Click here to insert image/logo

Request for Verification of Rent

Part I - Request
Landlord - Please complete either Part II or Part III as applicable. Complete Part IV and return directly to management listed above.
To: (Name and Address of Landlord)

Attn:
Company:
Address:
City: State: ZIP Code:
Ph: Fax:

Applicant Information

Name:

Address:

City:	State:	ZIP Code:

I have applied for residency and stated that I am now or was formerly your tenant. My signature below (*or accompanying Applicant Signature Authorization) authorizes verification of this information.

*Signature of applicant:	Date:

Part II - Verification of Present Tenancy

Tenant has rented since (month/day/year):

Rent Amount: $	Weekly Monthly (Please circle)	Pets?: Yes No (Please circle)

Number of times 30 days past due in last 12 months:

Remarks:

Part III - Verification of Previous Tenancy

Tenant has rented from (month/day/year):   to (month/day/year):

Rent Amount: $	Weekly Monthly (Please circle)	Pets?: Yes No (Please circle)

Number of times 30 days past due in last 12 months (if applicable):

Remarks:

Part IV - Authorized Signature

Name:	Title:	Phone:

Signature of landlord:	Date:

This form provided by USLandlord.com

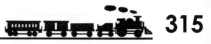

Statement of Credit Denial

Instructions:
1. Insert your IMAGE or LOGO (optional)
2. Enter APPLICANT & REASON(s) for denial
3. REPLACE ALL of this text with YOUR contact info
4. Click on 'PRINT FORM' when finished

Everything U Need to Know...

Click here to insert image/logo

Statement of Credit Denial

Applicant

Name:

Address:

City: State: ZIP code:

Reason for Denial

Thank you for your recent application.

At this time, we regret we are unable to offer you tenancy for the following reason(s):

Consumer Credit Reporting Agencies

Our decision was based in whole or in part on information obtained in a report from the consumer reporting agency listed below. You have a right under the Fair Credit Reporting Act to know the information contained in your credit file at the consumer reporting agency. The reporting agency played no part in our decision and is unable to supply specific reasons why we have denied credit to you.

Experian P.O. Box 949 Allen, TX 75013-0949 www.experian.com	Trans Union Post Office Box 2000 Chester, PA 19022 www.transunion.com	Equifax, Inc. P.O. Box 740123 Atlanta, GA 30374-0123 www.equifax.com

Equal Credit Opportunity

The Federal Equal Credit Opportunity Act prohibits creditors from discriminating against credit applicants on the basis of race, color, religion, national origin, sex, marital status, age (provided that the applicant has the capacity to enter into a binding contract), because all or part of the applicant's income derives from any public assistance program, or because the applicant has in good faith exercised any right under the Consumer Credit Protection Act. The Federal agency that administers compliance with this law concerning this creditor is, Equal Credit Opportunity, Federal Trade Commission, Washington, D.C. 20580.

Management signature: Date:

This form provided by USLandlord.com

Lease Agreement

Instructions:
1. Insert your IMAGE or LOGO (optional)
2. Highlight & complete LEASE AGREEMENT FIELDS
3. REPLACE ALL of this text with YOUR contact info
4. Click on 'PRINT FORM' when finished

Residential Lease Agreement

AGREEMENT TO LEASE

This agreement is entered into between _____, of
_____, _____ County,
_____, referred to as "lessor," and _____, of
_____, _____ County,
_____, referred to as "lessee."

RECITALS

A. Lessor is the owner and/or manager of real property that is available for lease.

B. Lessee desires to lease residential property to occupy and use as their residence.

C. The parties desire to establish an agreement to ensure a future lease of the residential property described in this agreement.

In consideration of the matters described above, and of the mutual benefits and obligations set forth in this agreement, the parties agree as follows:

SECTION I - SUBJECT OF LEASE

Lessor shall lease to prospective lessee the residential property owned by prospective lessor located at
_____, _____, _____County,
_____, for lessee and their family to occupy and use as their residence.

SECTION II - TERM OF LEASE

The premises shall be leased to lessee for a period of _____ starting from
_____. Any option to renew, extend or modify this lease shall require the approval of both the lessee and lessor.

SECTION III - MONTHLY RENTAL

Lessee shall pay $ _____ per month as the monthly rental for the term of the lease with the first payment due on or before _____, and subsequent payments on the ____ day of each succeeding month. This rental payment shall be subject to renegotiation by the parties at any time either of the parties exercises the option to renew the lease under the provisions of any subsequent lease agreement. It is agreed that if the rental payment is not received by the ____ day of the month, then a late fee of ____ shall be assessed and due immediately. Additional terms (optional): _____
_____

SECTION IV - SECURITY DEPOSIT

On the execution of this lease, lessee deposits with lessor $ _____, receipt of which is acknowledged by lessor, as security for the faithful performance by lessee of the terms of this lease agreement, to be returned to lessee, without interest (unless required by law), on the full and faithful performance by lessee of the provisions of this residential lease agreement.

SECTION V - NUMBER OF OCCUPANTS

Lessee agrees that the leased apartment shall be occupied by no more than _____ adults and _____ children under the age of 18 years without the prior, express, and written consent of lessor.

SECTION VI - ASSIGNMENT AND SUBLETTING

Without the prior, express, and written consent of lessor, lessee shall not assign this lease, or sublet the premises or any part of the premises. A consent by lessor to one assignment or subletting shall not be deemed to be a consent to any subsequent assignment or subletting.

SECTION VII - SHOWING PROPERTY FOR RENTAL

Lessee grants permission to lessor to show the property to new rental applicants with reasonable advance notice and during reasonable hours of the day, within 30 days of the expiration of the term of this lease.

SECTION VIII - ENTRY FOR INSPECTION, REPAIRS AND ALTERATIONS

Lessor shall have the right to enter the leased premises with reasonable advance notice for inspection and whenever necessary to make repairs and alterations of the property.

SECTION IX - REDECORATION AND ALTERATIONS

It is agreed that lessee will not make or permit to be made any alterations, additions, improvements, or changes in the leased property without in each case first obtaining the written consent of lessor. A consent to a particular alteration, addition, improvement, or change shall not be deemed a consent to or a waiver of restrictions against alterations, additions, improvements, or changes for the future. All alterations, changes, and improvements built, constructed, or placed in the leased property by lessee, with the exception of fixtures removable without damage to the apartment and movable personal property, shall, unless otherwise provided by written agreement between lessor and lessee, be the property of lessor and remain in the leased apartment at the expiration or earlier termination of this lease.

SECTION X - TAXES AND UTILITIES

A. Prospective lessor shall be liable for the payment of all real property taxes assessed against the residential premises as well as the following:

_____

B. Prospective lessee shall be liable for all personal property taxes as well as the following:

_____

SECTION XI - MAINTENANCE/REPAIRS

A. Prospective lessor shall be responsible for the following types of maintenance or repairs on the premises:

_____

B. Prospective lessee shall be responsible for the following types of maintenance or repairs on the premises:

_____

SECTION XII - ANIMALS

Lessee shall keep no domestic or other animals in or about the property or on the property premises without the prior, express, and written consent of lessor.

SECTION XIII - WASTE, NUISANCE OR UNLAWFUL USE

Lessee agrees that they will not commit waste on the premises, or maintain or permit to be maintained a nuisance on the premises, or use or permit the premises to be used in an unlawful manner.

SECTION XIV - LESSEE'S HOLDING OVER

The parties agree that any holding over by lessee under this lease, without lessor's written consent, shall be a tenancy at will which may be terminated by lessor on 30 days' notice in writing.

SECTION XV - REDELIVERY OF PREMISES

At the end of the term of this lease, lessee shall quit and deliver up the premises to lessor in as good condition as they are now, ordinary wear, decay, and damage by the elements excepted.

SECTION XVI - DEFAULT

If lessee defaults in the payment of rent or any part of the rent at the times specified above, or if lessee defaults in the performance of or compliance with any other term or condition of this lease agreement *[or of the regulations attached to and made a part of this lease agreement, which regulations shall be subject to occasional amendment or addition by lessor]*, the lease, at the option of lessor, shall terminate and be forfeited, and lessor may reenter the premises and retake possession and recover damages, including costs and attorney fees. Lessee shall be given 30 days *[written]* notice of any default or breach. Termination and forfeiture of the lease shall not result if, within 15 days of receipt of such notice, lessee has corrected the default or breach or has taken action reasonably likely to effect correction within a reasonable time.

SECTION XVII - DESTRUCTION OF PREMISES AND EMINENT DOMAIN

In the event the leased premises are destroyed or rendered untenantable by fire, storm, or earthquake, or other casualty not caused by the negligence of lessee, or if the leased premises are taken by eminent domain, this lease shall be at an end from such time except for the purpose of enforcing rights that may have then accrued under this lease agreement. The rental shall then be accounted for between lessor and lessee up to the time of such injury or destruction or taking of the premises, lessee paying up to such date and lessor refunding the rent collected beyond such date. Should a part only of the leased premises be destroyed or rendered untenantable by fire, storm, earthquake, or other casualty not caused by the negligence of lessee, the rental shall abate in the proportion that the injured part bears to the whole leased premises. The part so injured shall be restored by lessor as speedily as practicable, after which the full rent shall recommence and the lease continue according to its terms. Any condemnation award concerning the leased premises shall belong exclusively to lessor.

SECTION XVIII - DELAY IN OR IMPOSSIBILITY OF DELIVERY OF POSSESSION

In the event possession cannot be delivered to lessee on commencement of the lease term, through no fault of lessor or lessor's agents, there shall be no liability on lessor or lessor's agents, but the rental provided in this lease agreement shall abate until possession is given. Lessor or lessor's agents shall have 30 days in which to give possession, and if possession is tendered within that time, lessee agrees to accept the leased premises and this lease agreement. In the event possession cannot be delivered within that time, through no fault of lessor or lessor's agents, then this lease and all rights under this lease agreement shall be at an end.

SECTION XIX - BINDING EFFECT

The covenants and conditions contained in this lease agreement shall apply to and bind the heirs, legal representatives, and assigns of the parties to this lease agreement, and all covenants are to be construed as conditions of this lease.

SECTION XX - GOVERNING LAW

It is agreed that this agreement shall be governed by, construed, and enforced in accordance with the laws of the State of _____.

SECTION XXI - ATTORNEY FEES

In the event that any action is filed in relation to this agreement, the unsuccessful party in the action shall pay to the successful party, in addition to all the sums that either party may be called on to pay, a reasonable sum for the successful party's attorney fees.

SECTION XXII - ENTIRE AGREEMENT

This agreement shall constitute the entire agreement between the parties. Any prior understanding or representation of any kind preceding the date of this agreement shall not be binding upon either party except to the extent incorporated in this agreement.

SECTION XXIII - MODIFICATION OF AGREEMENT

Any modification of this agreement or additional obligation assumed by either party in connection with this agreement shall be binding only if evidenced in a writing signed by each party or an authorized representative of each party.

SECTION XXIV - PARAGRAPH HEADINGS

The titles to the paragraphs of this agreement are solely for the convenience of the parties and shall not be used to explain, modify, simplify, or aid in the interpretation of the provisions of this agreement.

In witness of the above, each party to this agreement has caused it to be executed on the date indicated below.

Signature of lessor: _____ Date: _____

Signature of lessee: _____ Date: _____

Signature of lessee: _____ Date: _____

This form provided by USLandlord.com

Modification of Lease

Instructions:
1. Insert your IMAGE or LOGO (optional)
2. Complete AMENDMENT FIELDS
3. REPLACE ALL of this text with YOUR contact info
4. Click on 'PRINT FORM' when finished

Everything U Need to Know...

Click here to insert image/logo

Modification of Lease Agreement

AMENDMENT TO LEASE

For valuable consideration, receipt of which is hereby acknowledged, _____ ,
"Lessor" and _____ , "Lessee", parties to the Lease Agreement made
for premises located at _____ , _____ ,
_____ County, _____ and dated _____ agree
to modify and amend said Lease Agreement in the following way(s):

_____

_____

_____

_____

ORIGINAL LEASE AGREEMENT

All other terms and covenants of the original Lease Agreement shall remain in full force and effect.

In witness of the above, each party to this agreement has caused it to be executed on the date indicated below.

Signature of lessor: _____ Date: _____

Signature of lessee: _____ Date: _____

Signature of lessee: _____ Date: _____

This form provided by USLandlord.com

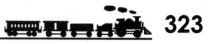

Sublease Agreement

Instructions:
1. Insert your IMAGE or LOGO (optional)
2. Highlight & complete LEASE AGREEMENT FIELDS
3. REPLACE ALL of this text with YOUR contact info
4. Click on 'PRINT FORM' when finished

Everything U Need to Know...

Click here to insert image/logo

Residential Sublease Agreement

AGREEMENT TO SUBLEASE

This agreement is entered into between _____, of
_____, _____, _____ County,
_____, referred to as "sublessor," and _____, of
_____, _____, _____ County,
_____, referred to as "sublessee."

RECITALS

A. Sublessor is the lessee of real property that is available for subleasing.

B. Sublessee desires to sublease residential property to occupy and use as their residence.

C. Lessor of the master lease agreement described in Section VI desires to permit the sublessor the right to sublease the residential property described in Section I.

In consideration of the matters described above, and of the mutual benefits and obligations set forth in this agreement, the parties agree as follows:

SECTION I - SUBJECT OF SUBLEASE

Sublessor shall sublease to prospective sublessee the residential property leased by sublessor located at
_____, _____, _____ County,
_____, for sublessee and their family to occupy and use as their residence.

SECTION II - TERM OF LEASE

The premises shall be subleased to lessee for a period of _____ starting from
_____. Any option to renew, extend or modify this lease shall require the approval of the lessor.

SECTION III - MONTHLY RENTAL

Sublessee shall pay $ _____ per month as the monthly rental for the term of the sublease with the first payment due on or before _____, and subsequent payments on the ____ day of each succeeding month. This rental payment shall be subject to renegotiation by the sublessee and the lessor under the master lease agreement. It is agreed that if the rental payment is not received by the ____ day of the month, then a late fee of ____ shall be assessed and due immediately. Additional terms (optional):

_____
_____

SECTION IV - SECURITY DEPOSIT

On the execution of this sublease, sublessee deposits with sublessor $ _____, receipt of which is acknowledged by lessor, as security for the faithful performance by sublessee of the terms of this lease agreement, to be returned to sublessee, without interest (unless required by law), on the full and faithful performance by lessee of the provisions of the originial master lease agreement.

SECTION V - NUMBER OF OCCUPANTS

Sublessee agrees that the leased apartment shall be occupied by no more _____ adults and _____ children under the age of 18 years without the prior, express, and written consent of sublessor.

SECTION VI - MASTER LEASE AGREEMENT

The sublease agreement incorporates and is subject to the master lease agreement between the sublessor and lessor, a copy of which is attached hereto, and which is hereby referred to and incorporated as if it wereset out here at length. The sublessee agrees to assume all of the obligations and responsibilities of the sublessor under the master lease agreement for the duration of the sublease agreement.

SECTION VII - BINDING EFFECT

The covenants and conditions contained in this lease agreement shall apply to and bind the heirs, legal representatives, and assigns of the parties to this lease agreement, and all covenants are to be construed as conditions of this lease.

SECTION VIII - GOVERNING LAW

It is agreed that this agreement shall be governed by, construed, and enforced in accordance with the laws of the State of _____.

SECTION IX - ATTORNEY FEES

In the event that any action is filed in relation to this agreement, the unsuccessful party in the action shall pay to the successful party, in addition to all the sums that either party may be called on to pay, a reasonable sum for the successful party's attorney fees.

SECTION X - ENTIRE AGREEMENT

This agreement shall constitute the entire agreement between the parties. Any prior understanding or representation of any kind preceding the date of this agreement shall not be binding upon either party except to the extent incorporated in this agreement.

SECTION XI - MODIFICATION OF AGREEMENT

Any modification of this agreement or additional obligation assumed by either party in connection with this agreement shall be binding only if evidenced in a writing signed by each party or an authorized representative of each party.

In witness of the above, each party to this agreement has caused it to be executed on the date indicated below.

Signature of sublessor: _____ Date:_____

Signature of sublessee: _____ Date:_____

As lessor of the attached master lease agreement, I hereby give my consent to the above described provisions as set out in this sublease agreement.

Signature of lessor: _____ Date:_____

This form provided by USLandlord.com

Assignment of Lease

Instructions:
1. Insert your IMAGE or LOGO (optional)
2. Highlight & complete LEASE ASSIGNMENT FIELDS
3. REPLACE ALL of this text with YOUR contact info
4. Click on 'PRINT FORM' when finished

Residential Lease Assignment

AGREEMENT TO ASSIGN

This agreement is entered into between _____, of
_____, _____, _____County,
_____, referred to as "assignor," and _____, of
_____, _____, _____County,
_____, referred to as "assignee."

RECITALS

A. Assignor has entered into a lease agreement, as lessor, with _____,
of _____, _____,
County, _____, referred to as "lessee." A copy of the lease agreement, containing a
description of the premises, is attached to this agreement as Exhibit A.

B. Prospective assignor desires to assign the lease agreement to prospective assignee, who will assume all
liabilities and duties as well as all rights of prospective assignor pertaining to the collection of all rents to
become due under the lease agreement after the effective date of the assignment.

In consideration of the mutual covenants contained in this agreement, the parties agree as follows:

     1.   Assignor will transfer and assign to assignee all right to the collection of all rents
required under the lease agreement provisions in the lease dated _____ on
the premises described as follows: _____.

     2.   The assignment shall become effective on _____, and shall apply
to all rents due thereafter until expiration of the lease agreement term.

In witness of the above, each party to this agreement has caused it to be executed on the date indicated below.

Signature of assignor: _____   Date: _____

Signature of assignee: _____   Date: _____

Option to Purchase

Instructions:
1. Insert your IMAGE or LOGO (optional)
2. Highlight & complete AGREEMENT FIELDS
3. REPLACE ALL of this text with YOUR contact info
4. Click on 'PRINT FORM' when finished

Everything U Need to Know...

Click here to insert image/logo

Option to Purchase Leased Property

OPTION TO PURCHASE

This agreement is entered into between _____, of
_____, _____, _____ County,
_____, referred to as "lessor," and _____, of
_____, _____, _____ County,
_____, referred to as "lessee."

Lessor agrees to sell to lessee, at their option, the following property owned by lessor, namely:
_____, _____ County,
_____, subject to the following terms and conditions:

1. This option to purchase will expire on _____ .

2. Notice of election to purchase by lessee shall be in writing and given to lessor by _____ .

3. The price to be paid for the property, if this option is exercised, is $ _____ dollars.
After payment is made to lessor in full, lessor agrees to execute and deliver to lessee a deed conveying the property to lessee, and to deliver possession of property free of all liens and encumbrances.

4. _____
_____

5. _____
_____

ORIGINAL LEASE AGREEMENT

All other terms and covenants of the original Lease Agreement shall remain in full force and effect.

In witness of the above, each party to this agreement has caused it to be executed on the date below.

Signature of lessor:_____   Date:_____

Signature of lessee:_____   Date:_____

Signature of lessee:_____   Date:_____

This form provided by USLandlord.com

Pet Agreement

Instructions:
1. Insert your IMAGE or LOGO (optional)
2. Complete PET AGREEMENT FIELDS
3. REPLACE ALL of this text with YOUR contact info
4. Click on 'PRINT FORM' when finished

Everything U Need to Know...

Click here to insert image/logo

Pet Agreement

AMENDMENT TO LEASE

For valuable consideration, receipt of which is hereby acknowledged, _____ , "Lessor" and _____ , "Lessee", parties to the Lease Agreement made for property located at _____ , _____ , _____ County, _____ and dated on _____ agree to modify and amend said Lease Agreement in the following way(s):

Lessee desires to keep the following described pet in the dwelling referred to above:

Type: _____

Breed: _____

Weight: _____

TERMS AND CONDITIONS

1. Lessee agrees that they are solely responsible for the maintenance of the above described pet, and agree to keep their pet under control at all times.

2. Lessee agrees to keep their pet restrained, but not tethered, when it is outside their dwelling.

3. Lessee agrees to adhere to local ordinances, including leash and licensing requirements.

4. Lessee agrees not to leave their pet unattended for unreasonable periods.

5. Lessee agrees to clean up after their pet and to dispose of their pet's waste properly and quickly.

6. Lessee agrees not to leave food or water for their pet or any other animal outside their dwelling where it may attract other animals.

7. Lessee agrees to keep their pet from being unnecessarily noisy or aggressive and causing any annoyance or discomfort to others and will remedy immediately any complaints made.

8. Lessee agrees to provide their pet with an identification tag while on the premises.

9. Lessee agrees not to breed or allow the pet to reproduce. If this should occur, the pet's offspring must be placed within 10 weeks of birth.

10. Lessee agrees to immediately pay for any damage, loss, or expense caused by their pet, and in addition, they will add $ _____ to their security/cleaning deposit, which may be used for cleaning, repairs or delinquent rent when Lessee vacates. This added deposit, or what remains of it when pet damages have been assessed, will be returned to Lessee within 10 days after they have proved that they no longer keep this pet.

11. Lessee agrees that this Agreement applies only to the specific pet described above.

12. Lessee agrees that the Lessor reserves the right to revoke permission to keep the pet should the Lessee break this agreement. Lessee will be given 10 days to remove the pet from the premises.

TERMS AND CONDITIONS (Continued)

13. Any animals on the property not registered under this agreement will be presumed to be strays and will be removed according to law, at the option of the Lessor.

ORIGINAL LEASE AGREEMENT

All other terms and covenants of the original Lease Agreement shall remain in full force and effect.

In witness of the above, each party to this agreement has caused it to be executed on the date below.

Signature of lessor:_____ Date:_____

Signature of lessee:_____ Date:_____

Signature of lessee:_____ Date:_____

This form provided by USLandlord.com

Assessment of Condition

Assessment of Condition of Rental Property

This checklist will help you protect your initial deposit. Using the key below, fill in the letter that best describes the condition of your unit when you begin your lease, and then return a copy of this checklist within 3 days. When you move out, request this checklist, fill in the "End of Lease" column and then return it so we may corroborate your assessment using the "Landlord's end-of-lease assessment" column.

Key	
Missing	M
Good condition	G
Scratched	S
Damaged	D
Broken	B
Repair needed	R

Exterior	Beginning of lease	End of lease	Landlord's end-of-lease assessment	Comments
Front door				
Front screen door				
Back door				
Back screen door				
Screens and storm windows				
Windows and frames				
Mailbox				
Doorbell				
Apartment number				
Garbage container				
Recycling containers				
Security intercom				
Other				

Kitchen	Beginning of lease	End of lease	Landlord's end-of-lease assessment	Comments
Windows				
Blinds/curtains				
Floor				
Walls				
Ceiling				
Lights and switches				
Outlets				
Stove				
Refrigerator				
Dishwasher				
Garbage disposal				
Sink				
Cabinets and counter				
Baseboards				
Trim				
Other				

Dining room	Beginning of lease	End of lease	Landlord's end-of-lease assessment	Comments
Windows				
Blinds/curtains				
Carpet or floor				
Walls				
Ceiling				
Lights and switches				
Outlets				
Baseboards				
Trim				
Other				

Living room	Beginning of lease	End of lease	Landlord's end-of-lease assessment	Comments
Windows				
Blinds/curtains				
Carpet or floor				
Walls				
Ceilings				
Outlets				
Lights and switches				
Baseboards				
Trim				
Cable outlet				
Other				

Hallway and stairwell	Beginning of lease	End of lease	Landlord's end-of-lease assessment	Comments
Carpet or floor				
Walls				
Ceiling				
Lights and switches				
Outlets				
Baseboards				
Trim				
Stair treads				
Landing and handrail				
Other				

Everything Ⓤ Need to Know...

Bedroom #1	Beginning of lease	End of lease	Landlord's end-of-lease assessment	Comments
Door				
Windows				
Blinds/curtains				
Carpet or floor				
Walls				
Ceiling				
Lights and switches				
Outlets				
Closet				
Baseboards				
Trim				
Other				

Bedroom #2	Beginning of lease	End of lease	Landlord's end-of-lease assessment	Comments
Door				
Windows				
Blinds/curtains				
Carpet or floor				
Walls				
Ceiling				
Lights and switches				
Outlets				
Closet				
Baseboards				
Trim				
Other				

Bedroom #3	Beginning of lease	End of lease	Landlord's end-of-lease assessment	Comments
Door				
Windows				
Blinds/curtains				
Carpet or floor				
Walls				
Ceiling				
Lights and switches				
Outlets				
Closet				
Baseboards				
Trim				
Other				

Bathroom #1	Beginning of lease	End of lease	Landlord's end-of-lease assessment	Comments
Door				
Window				
Blinds/curtains				
Floor				
Walls				
Ceiling				
Sink				
Tub and/or shower				
Toilet				
Cabinet, shelves, closet				
Towel bars				
Lights and switches				
Outlets				
Baseboards				
Trim				
Other				

Bathroom #2	Beginning of lease	End of lease	Landlord's end-of-lease assessment	Comments
Door				
Window				
Blinds/curtains				
Floor				
Walls				
Ceiling				
Sink				
Tub and/or shower				
Toilet				
Cabinet, shelves, closet				
Towel bars				
Lights and switches				
Outlets				
Baseboards				
Trim				
Other				

Furniture	Beginning of Lease	End of Lease	Landlord's end-of-lease assessment	Comments
Kitchen chairs				
Tables				
End tables				
Lounge chairs				
Couches				
Lamps				
Desks				
Desk chairs				
Bookshelves				
Beds				
Mattresses				
Dressers				
Other				

Furniture	Beginning of Lease	End of Lease	Landlord's end-of-lease assessment	Comments

Property Management Agreement

Instructions:
1. Insert your IMAGE or LOGO (optional)
2. Highlight & complete MGMT AGREEMENT FIELDS
3. REPLACE ALL of this text with YOUR contact info
4. Click on 'PRINT FORM' when finished

Everything U Need to Know...

Click here to insert image/logo

Property Management Agreement

AGREEMENT TO MANAGE

This agreement is entered into between _____ , of
_____ , _____ , _____ County,
_____ , referred to as "owner," and _____ , of
_____ , _____ , _____ County,
_____ , referred to as "agent."

RECITALS

A. Owner holds title to the following premises located at _____ ,
_____ , _____ County, _____ also described as
_____ , here referred to as property.

B. Agent is experienced in the business of operating and managing real estate similar to the above-described property.

C. Owner desires to engage the services of agent to manage and operate the property, and agent desires to provide such services on the following terms and conditions.

In consideration of the mutual covenants contained herein, the parties agree:

SECTION I - EMPLOYMENT OF AGENT

Agent shall act as the exclusive agent of owner to manage, operate, and maintain the property.

SECTION II - BEST EFFORTS OF AGENT

On assuming the management and operation of the property, agent shall thoroughly inspect the property and submit a written report to owner. The written report shall contain the opinion of agent concerning the present efficiency under which the property is being managed and operated, and recommended changes, if necessary, in the management structure of the property, in the rehabilitation of the property, and any other matters that will improve the efficient management and operation of the property. After conferring with owner and obtaining approval to make any necessary improvements, agent shall undertake completion of the improvements.

SECTION III - LEASING OF PROPERTY

Agent shall make reasonable efforts to lease available space of the property, and shall be responsible for the advertising of vacancies by reasonable and proper means. Agent shall also have the right to negotiate, execute and enter into, on behalf of owner, month-to-month tenancies of units of the property. Agent may negotiate all extensions and renewals of such month-to-month tenancies and leases. Agent shall not, without the prior written consent of owner, enter into any lease for a term less than _____ months or more than _____ months. Agent shall have the right to make concessions, including rental concessions, as inducements to prospective tenants to occupy the property.

SECTION IV - MAINTENANCE, REPAIRS, AND OPERATIONS

Agent shall use its best efforts to insure that the property is maintained in an attractive condition and in a good state of repair. In this regard, agent shall use its best skills and efforts to serve the tenants of the property and shall purchase necessary supplies, make contracts for, or otherwise furnish, electricity, gas, fuel, water, telephone, window cleaning, refuse disposal, pest control, and any other utilities or services required for the operation of the property. Agent shall make or cause to be made and supervise necessary repairs and alterations and shall decorate and furnish the property. Expenditures for repairs, alterations, decorations or furnishings in excess of $ _____ shall not be made without prior written consent of owner, except in t he case of emergency, or if agent in good faith determines that such expenditures are necessary to protect the property from damage, to prevent injury to persons or loss of life, or to maintain services to tenants.

SECTION V - EMPLOYEES

5.1.   Agent shall employ, discharge, and supervise all on-site employees or contractors required for the efficient operation and maintenance of the property. All on-site personnel, except independent contractors and employees of independent contractors, shall be the employees of agent. Agent shall pay the salaries of such on-site employees and, to the extent there are revenues from the property available, pay all charges for services rendered by independent contractors and the employees of independent contractors.

5.2.   All salaries (including all contributions of employer not listed in the paycheck) of such on-site employees shall be charged to owner. To the extent there are insufficient funds available from revenues received from the operation of the property to reimburse agent for such salaries, owner shall directly reimburse agent within 15 days after demand by agent for reimbursement. Agent shall not be responsible or liable to owner for any act, default, or negligence of on-site personnel, or for any error of judgment or mistake of law or fact in connection with their employment, conduct, or discharge, except that agent shall be responsible for any such act, default, or negligence that is due directly or indirectly to its own negligent act or omission in the hiring or supervision of any such on-site personnel.

5.3.   On-site personnel shall include all resident personnel, including, but not limited to, managers and maintenance personnel, all recreational personnel (whether part-time or full-time), day-care center personnel, and all other individuals located, rendering services, or performing activities on the property in connection with its operation.

SECTION VI - GOVERNMENT REGULATIONS

Agent shall manage the property in full compliance with all laws and regulations of any federal, state, county, or municipal authority having jurisdiction over the property.

SECTION VII - COLLECTION OF INCOME; INSTITUTION OF LEGAL ACTION

7.1.   Agent shall use its best efforts to collect promptly all rents and other income issuing from the property when such amounts become due. It is understood that agent does not guarantee the collection of rents.

7.2.   Agent shall, in the name of owner, execute and serve such notices and demands on delinquent tenants as agent may deem necessary or proper. Agent, in the name of owners, shall institute, settle, or compromise any legal action and make use of such methods of legal process against a delinquent tenant or the property of a delinquent tenant as may be necessary to enforce the collection of rent or other sums due from the tenant, to enforce any covenants or conditions of any lease or month-to-month rental agreement, and to recover possession of any part of the property. No other form of legal action will be instituted and no settlement, compromise, or adjustment of any matters involved therein shall be made without the prior written consent of owner, except when agent determines that immediate action is necessary.

SECTION VIII - BANK ACCOUNTS

Agent shall deposit (either directly or in a depositary bank for transmittal) all revenues from the property into the general property management trust fund of agent, here referred to as the trust account. The trust account shall be maintained at all times in a national or state member bank that is a member of the Federal Deposit Insurance Corporation. Agent shall not commingle any of the above-described revenues with any funds or other property of agent. From the revenues deposited in the trust account, agent shall pay all items with respect to the property for which payment is provided in this agreement, including the compensation of agent and deposits to the reserve accounts as provided for in Section Eleven. After such payments agent shall remit any balance of any monthly revenues to owner concurrently with the delivery of the monthly report referred to in Section X.

SECTION IX - RESERVE ACCOUNT

9.1.   Agent shall establish a reserve account for the following items: taxes, assessments, debt service, insurance premiums, repairs (other than normal maintenance), replacement of personal property, and refundable deposits. Agent shall use its best judgment in transferring adequate funds from the trust account to the reserve account in order to pay the above items without incurring late pay interest fees, cancellations, or forfeitures. If the reserve account contains inadequate funds to pay any of the above items, agent must obtain approval from owner before paying the items directly from the trust account. If owner determines that the funds in the reserve account are excessive, owner shall direct that agent return such excess funds to the trust account. The reserve account shall be maintained in an interest-bearing savings account in a national or state bank that is a member of the Federal Deposit Insurance Corporation.

9.2.   Anything in this agreement to the contrary notwithstanding, agent shall not be liable for any failure or bankruptcy of any bank used as a depository of any funds maintained in the reserve account.

SECTION X - RECORDS AND REPORTS

10.1.   Agent will keep books, accounts, and records that reflect all revenues and all expenditures incurred in connection with the management and operation of the property. The books, accounts, and records shall be maintained at the principal place of business of agent. Agent shall, during regular business hours, make the books, accounts, and records required to be maintained hereunder available to owner or the representatives of owner for examination and audit by appointment on no less than 3 days' prior notice. All such audits shall be at the expense of owner.

10.2.   Agent shall furnish owner, no later than the end of the next succeeding month, a detailed statement of all revenues and expenditures for each preceding month, a summary of all concessions and rental concessions given to induce prospective tenants to occupy the property, the original copy of all invoices, statements, purchase orders, and billings received and paid during such preceding month, as well as such other information relating to the operation or management of the property that, in the opinion of agent, requires the attention of owner. Owner shall retain for safekeeping and store all original invoices, statements, purchase orders, billings, and other documents delivered by agent with respect to the property. Owner, on payment of reasonable costs incurred by it, shall make available to agent copies of all or any portion of any invoice, statement, purchase order, billing report, or other document received from agent with respect to the property.

10.3.   Within 30 days after the end of each calendar year, agent shall prepare and deliver to owner a detailed statement of revenues received and expenditures incurred and paid during the calendar year that result from operations of the property. Within 10 days, following expiration or termination of this agreement, agent shall deliver to owner all books, accounts, and records pertaining to the property.

SECTION XXVII - ENTIRE AGREEMENT

This lease agreement shall constitute the entire agreement between the parties. Any prior understanding or representation of any kind preceding the date of this lease agreement shall not be binding upon either party except to the extent incorporated in this lease agreement.

SECTION XXVIII - MODIFICATION OF AGREEMENT

Any modification of this property management agreement or additional obligation assumed by either party in connection with this agreement shall be binding only if evidenced in a writing signed by each party or an authorized representative of each party.

SECTION XXIX - NOTICES

A. All notices, demands, or other writings that this agreement requires to be given, or which may be given, by either party to the other, shall be deemed to have been fully given when made in writing and deposited in the United States mail, registered and postage prepaid, and addressed as follows:

To owner: _____

To agent: _____

B. The address to which any notice, demand, or other writing may be given or made or sent to any party as above provided may be changed by written notice given by such party as above provided.

SECTION XXX - TIME OF THE ESSENCE

It is specifically declared and agreed that time is of the essence of this lease agreement.

SECTION XXXI - PARAGRAPH HEADINGS

The titles to the paragraphs of this agreement are solely for the convenience of the parties and shall not be used to explain, modify, simplify, or aid in the interpretation of the provisions of this agreement.

In witness of the above, each party to this agreement has caused it to be executed on the date indicated below.

Signature of owner: _____   Date: _____

    Print name: _____   Title: _____

Signature of agent: _____   Date: _____

    Print name: _____   Title: _____

Residential Sales Contract

Instructions:
1. Insert your IMAGE or LOGO (optional)
2. Highlight & complete SALES CONTRACT FIELDS
3. REPLACE ALL of this text with YOUR contact info
4. Click on 'PRINT FORM' when finished

Everything U Need to Know...

Click here to insert image/logo

Residential Sales Contract

AGREEMENT TO PURCHASE REAL PROPERTY

This agreement is entered into between _____, of
_____, _____ County,
_____, referred to as "seller," and _____, of
_____, _____ County,
_____, referred to as "buyer."

In consideration of the mutual covenants and agreements contained in this agreement, the parties agree as follows:

SECTION I - PROPERTY DESCRIPTION

Buyers agree to buy the property located at _____,
_____, _____ County, _____.
This described property is referred to as property. Property is sold subject to applicable ordinances, restrictions, and easements of record. The following items owned by seller are included with this property:
_____.

SECTION II - SALES PRICE

The sales price is $ _____.

SECTION III - DEPOSIT

Buyers will deposit $ _____ with sellers as a good faith deposit, which will be applied against the sales price at the closing on property. If the sale does not close for any reason by
_____ as specified in Section IX, except on a default by sellers for any of the reasons provided in Sections V and XIV below, buyers will forfeit the deposit, and the deposit will become the property of sellers.

SECTION IV - METHOD OF PAYMENT

The sales price will be paid in cash, or by cashier's check or certified check. Buyers represent that buyers have the financial means needed to purchase property.

SECTION V - INSPECTIONS

Buyers have personally inspected property, and accept property in its present condition, as is, subject only to buyers' approval of an inspection report within 10 days after the effective date of this agreement. Buyers will obtain and pay for all inspections and reports. If the inspection report on property indicates a material defect, buyers must notify sellers within 5 days and sellers will have a reasonable time to cure the defect. If sellers are unable or unwilling to cure the defect, and buyers and sellers are unable to negotiate mutually acceptable alternate terms, sellers may elect to terminate this agreement by giving notice to buyers, and buyers' good faith deposit will be returned to buyers.

SECTION VI - TITLE EVIDENCE

Prior to closing, sellers will provide buyers with a title insurance commitment for property. Buyers may object to any matters shown on the title commitment by giving sellers written notice within 5 days of receipt of the commitment. If sellers are unwilling or unable to satisfy buyers' objections, sellers may elect to terminate this agreement by giving notice to buyers or may eliminate any defects and close the transaction. At closing, sellers will pay for an owner's title policy to be issued after closing, insuring buyers in the amount of the purchase price.

SECTION VII - ASSESSMENTS AND TAXES

Sellers will pay special assessments that are a lien on property up to the closing date. Sellers will also pay all property taxes that became a lien before the year of closing. Taxes that become a lien in the year of closing will be shared so that sellers pay a prorated amount for each day from January 1st to the closing date. Taxes will be prorated on a calendar year basis, based on the most recent assessed value and tax rate.

SECTION VIII - PRORATIONS

Interest, insurance, rents, assessments, association fees, and other items, as applicable, will be prorated to the closing day. Buyers will be responsible for the day of closing.

SECTION IX - CLOSING DAY

The sale will be closed on _____. If the sale does not close on or before _____, sellers may notify buyers that this agreement is terminated and retain buyers' good faith deposit. Sellers will then be free to dispose of property. Sellers will also have the right to pursue all remedies available against buyers for their breach of this agreement.

SECTION X - OCCUPANCY

Sellers will give occupancy to buyers immediately at closing. Sellers will remove all personal property, except items being conveyed at closing, and will leave property in a clean and neat condition.

SECTION XI - MEDIATION

Any dispute related to this agreement will be submitted to mediation. The mediation will be conducted according to the rules and procedures of the National Association of Realtors Homesellers/Homebuyers Dispute Resolution System. If the parties cannot reach a binding agreement in mediation, they may use other available remedies.

SECTION XII - HEIRS AND SUCCESSORS

This agreement binds sellers, sellers' heirs and personal representatives, and anyone succeeding to sellers' interest in property. Buyers may not assign this agreement without sellers' written permission.

SECTION XIII - GOVERNMENT REQUIREMENTS

Sellers agree that property will meet all _____ and _____ County building and zoning requirements at closing.

SECTION XIV - FINANCING

Within 10 days of the effective date of this agreement, buyers will provide sellers either with a letter of commitment from a licensed mortgage company or proof of assets totaling at least the remaining amount of the sales price in Section II minus the deposit in Section III. If buyers are unable or unwilling to provide such documentation, sellers may elect to terminate this agreement by giving notice to buyers, and buyers' good faith deposit will be returned to them.

SECTION XV - NO COMMISSION

Buyers and sellers acknowledge that no broker or agent has been retained by either of them and that no commission or fee is or will be owed to any third party in connection with the sale and purchase of property.

SECTION XVI - EFFECTIVE DATE

The effective date of this agreement will be the date of buyers' signing. If buyers do not sign this agreement within 5 days of the date of sellers' signing, this agreement will terminate and become null and void.

SECTION XVII - PARAGRAPH HEADINGS

The titles to the paragraphs of this agreement are solely for the convenience of the parties and shall not be used to explain, modify, simplify, or aid in the interpretation of the provisions of this agreement.

In witness of the above, each party to this agreement has caused it to be executed on the date indicated below.

Signature of seller:_____ Date:_____

Signature of buyer:_____ Date:_____

Signature of buyer:_____ Date:_____

Quit-Claim Deed

Instructions:
1. Insert your IMAGE or LOGO (optional)
2. Complete QUIT-CLAIM FIELDS
3. REPLACE ALL of this text with YOUR contact info
4. Click on 'PRINT FORM' when finished

Everything U Need to Know...

Click here to insert image/logo

Quit-Claim Deed

QUIT-CLAIM DEED

THIS QUIT-CLAIM DEED, is executed _____ by _____ , hereinafter
referred to as "Grantor(s)", whose address is _____ , _____ ,
_____ County, _____ to _____ ,
hereinafter referred to as "Grantee(s)", whose address is _____ ,
_____ , _____ County, _____ ;

WITNESSETH, that the Grantor(s), for and in consideration of the sum of $ _____
in hand paid by the said Grantee(s), the receipt whereof is hereby acknowledged, does hereby remise, release
and quit-claim unto the Grantee(s), all right, title, interest, and claim which the Grantor(s) has in and to the
following property located at _____ , _____ ,
_____ County, _____ ;

TO HAVE AND HOLD the same, together with all and singular the appurtenances thereunto, of all
interest, equity and claim whatsoever the Grantor(s) may have, either in law or equity, for the proper use,
benefit and behalf of the Grantee(s) forever.

IN WITNESS WHEREOF, the Grantor(s) has signed and sealed these presents on _____ .

Signature of grantor(s): _____

Signature of grantee(s): _____

NOTARY PUBLIC

STATE OF _____)

COUNTY OF _____)

The foregoing instrument was acknowledged before me this _____ day of _____ ,
20 _____ , by the Grantor referred to above.

_____
Notary Public Signature

_____
Notary Public Printed

_____
My commission expires

Appendix E

Government Forms and Publications: Landlord Responsibilities

This Appendix Includes:

★ **Lead–Based Paint Disclosure**

★ **Lead–Based Paint Pamphlet**

★ **FCRA Summary of Rights**

he following forms and publications were produced by the **Department of Housing and Urban Development** and the **Federal Trade Commission** for your use as an **American Landlord**. Unlike many of the government forms that can be easily tossed aside and ignored, *these documents are actually worth examining* – if for no reason other than to educate yourself… *especially* if you plan on investing in some of the older homes around town that were constructed prior to 1978.

And let's not forgot about the **Fair Credit Reporting Act** and its companion, the **FCRA Summary of Rights**. As you may recall, this **Federal Trade Commission disclosure** was mentioned a few times in the **"Tenant Screening" chapters**. It has been **magnified here** for your convenience in reading. Remember – required disclosures should *always* be examined *prior to using them*. **Never** take your rights and responsibilities as an **American Landlord** for granted.

Lead-Based Paint Disclosure

Disclosure of Information on Lead-Based Paint and/or Lead-Based Paint Hazards

Lead Warning Statement

Housing built before 1978 may contain lead-based paint. Lead from paint, paint chips, and dust can pose health hazards if not managed properly. Lead exposure is especially harmful to young children and pregnant women. Before renting pre-1978 housing, lessors must disclose the presence of known lead-based paint and/or lead-based paint hazards in the dwelling. Lessees must also receive a federally approved pamphlet on lead poisoning prevention.

Lessor's Disclosure

(a) Presence of lead-based paint and/or lead-based paint hazards (check (i) or (ii) below):

    (i) _____ Known lead-based paint and/or lead-based paint hazards are present in the housing (explain).

    _____

    _____

    (ii) _____ Lessor has no knowledge of lead-based paint and/or lead-based paint hazards in the housing.

(b) Records and reports available to the lessor (check (i) or (ii) below):

    (i) _____ Lessor has provided the lessee with all available records and reports pertaining to lead-based paint and/or lead-based paint hazards in the housing (list documents below).

    _____

    _____

    (ii) _____ Lessor has no reports or records pertaining to lead-based paint and/or lead-based paint hazards in the housing.

Lessee's Acknowledgment (initial)

(c) _____ Lessee has received copies of all information listed above.

(d) _____ Lessee has received the pamphlet *Protect Your Family from Lead in Your Home.*

Agent's Acknowledgment (initial)

(e) _____ Agent has informed the lessor of the lessor's obligations under 42 U.S.C. 4852d and is aware of his/her responsibility to ensure compliance.

Certification of Accuracy

The following parties have reviewed the information above and certify, to the best of their knowledge, that the information they have provided is true and accurate.

Lessor	Date	Lessor	Date
Lessee	Date	Lessee	Date
Agent	Date	Agent	Date

Lead-Based Paint Pamphlet

Protect Your Family From Lead In Your Home

 EPA United States
Environmental
Protection Agency

United States
Consumer Product
Safety Commission

United States
Department of Housing
and Urban Development

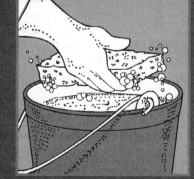

Are You Planning To Buy, Rent, or Renovate a Home Built Before 1978?

Many houses and apartments built before 1978 have paint that contains high levels of lead (called lead-based paint). Lead from paint, chips, and dust can pose serious health hazards if not taken care of properly.

OWNERS, BUYERS, and RENTERS are encouraged to check for lead (see page 6) before renting, buying or renovating pre-1978 housing.

Federal law requires that individuals receive certain information before renting, buying, or renovating pre-1978 housing:

LANDLORDS have to disclose known information on lead-based paint and lead-based paint hazards before leases take effect. Leases must include a disclosure about lead-based paint.

SELLERS have to disclose known information on lead-based paint and lead-based paint hazards before selling a house. Sales contracts must include a disclosure about lead-based paint. Buyers have up to 10 days to check for lead.

RENOVATORS disturbing more than 2 square feet of painted surfaces have to give you this pamphlet before starting work.

IMPORTANT!

Lead From Paint, Dust, and Soil Can Be Dangerous If Not Managed Properly

FACT: Lead exposure can harm young children and babies even before they are born.

FACT: Even children who seem healthy can have high levels of lead in their bodies.

FACT: People can get lead in their bodies by breathing or swallowing lead dust, or by eating soil or paint chips containing lead.

FACT: People have many options for reducing lead hazards. In most cases, lead-based paint that is in good condition is not a hazard.

FACT: Removing lead-based paint improperly can increase the danger to your family.

If you think your home might have lead hazards, read this pamphlet to learn some simple steps to protect your family.

1

Lead Gets in the Body in Many Ways

Childhood lead poisoning remains a major environmental health problem in the U.S.

People can get lead in their body if they:

◆ Breathe in lead dust (especially during renovations that disturb painted surfaces).

◆ Put their hands or other objects covered with lead dust in their mouths.

◆ Eat paint chips or soil that contains lead.

Lead is even more dangerous to children under the age of 6:

◆ At this age children's brains and nervous systems are more sensitive to the damaging effects of lead.

Even children who appear healthy can have dangerous levels of lead in their bodies.

◆ Children's growing bodies absorb more lead.

◆ Babies and young children often put their hands and other objects in their mouths. These objects can have lead dust on them.

Lead is also dangerous to women of childbearing age:

◆ Women with a high lead level in their system prior to pregnancy would expose a fetus to lead through the placenta during fetal development.

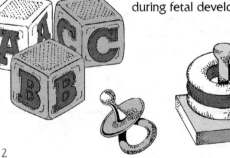

Lead's Effects

It is important to know that even exposure to low levels of lead can severely harm children.

In children, lead can cause:

◆ Nervous system and kidney damage.

◆ Learning disabilities, attention deficit disorder, and decreased intelligence.

◆ Speech, language, and behavior problems.

◆ Poor muscle coordination.

◆ Decreased muscle and bone growth.

◆ Hearing damage.

While low-lead exposure is most common, exposure to high levels of lead can have devastating effects on children, including seizures, unconsciousness, and, in some cases, death.

Although children are especially susceptible to lead exposure, lead can be dangerous for adults too.

In adults, lead can cause:

◆ Increased chance of illness during pregnancy.

◆ Harm to a fetus, including brain damage or death.

◆ Fertility problems (in men and women).

◆ High blood pressure.

◆ Digestive problems.

◆ Nerve disorders.

◆ Memory and concentration problems.

◆ Muscle and joint pain.

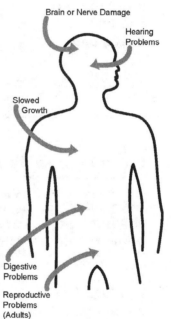

Brain or Nerve Damage

Hearing Problems

Slowed Growth

Digestive Problems

Reproductive Problems (Adults)

Lead affects the body in many ways.

3

Where Lead-Based Paint Is Found

In general, the older your home, the more likely it has lead-based paint.

Many homes built before 1978 have lead-based paint. The federal government banned lead-based paint from housing in 1978. Some states stopped its use even earlier. Lead can be found:

◆ In homes in the city, country, or suburbs.

◆ In apartments, single-family homes, and both private and public housing.

◆ Inside and outside of the house.

◆ In soil around a home. (Soil can pick up lead from exterior paint or other sources such as past use of leaded gas in cars.)

Checking Your Family for Lead

Get your children and home tested if you think your home has high levels of lead.

To reduce your child's exposure to lead, get your child checked, have your home tested (especially if your home has paint in poor condition and was built before 1978), and fix any hazards you may have. Children's blood lead levels tend to increase rapidly from 6 to 12 months of age, and tend to peak at 18 to 24 months of age.

Consult your doctor for advice on testing your children. A simple blood test can detect high levels of lead. Blood tests are usually recommended for:

◆ Children at ages 1 and 2.

◆ Children or other family members who have been exposed to high levels of lead.

◆ Children who should be tested under your state or local health screening plan.

Your doctor can explain what the test results mean and if more testing will be needed.

4

Identifying Lead Hazards

Lead-based paint is usually not a hazard if it is in good condition, and it is not on an impact or friction surface, like a window. It is defined by the federal government as paint with lead levels greater than or equal to 1.0 milligram per square centimeter, or more than 0.5% by weight.

Deteriorating lead-based paint (peeling, chipping, chalking, cracking or damaged) is a hazard and needs immediate attention. It may also be a hazard when found on surfaces that children can chew or that get a lot of wear-and-tear, such as:

◆ Windows and window sills.

◆ Doors and door frames.

◆ Stairs, railings, banisters, and porches.

> **Lead from paint chips, which you can see, and lead dust, which you can't always see, can both be serious hazards.**

Lead dust can form when lead-based paint is scraped, sanded, or heated. Dust also forms when painted surfaces bump or rub together. Lead chips and dust can get on surfaces and objects that people touch. Settled lead dust can re-enter the air when people vacuum, sweep, or walk through it. The following two federal standards have been set for lead hazards in dust:

◆ 40 micrograms per square foot ($\mu g/ft^2$) and higher for floors, including carpeted floors.

◆ 250 $\mu g/ft^2$ and higher for interior window sills.

Lead in soil can be a hazard when children play in bare soil or when people bring soil into the house on their shoes. The following two federal standards have been set for lead hazards in residential soil:

◆ 400 parts per million (ppm) and higher in play areas of bare soil.

◆ 1,200 ppm (average) and higher in bare soil in the remainder of the yard.

The only way to find out if paint, dust and soil lead hazards exist is to test for them. The next page describes the most common methods used.

5

Checking Your Home for Lead

Just knowing that a home has lead-based paint may not tell you if there is a hazard.

You can get your home tested for lead in several different ways:

◆ A paint **inspection** tells you whether your home has lead-based paint and where it is located. It won't tell you whether or not your home currently has lead hazards.

◆ A **risk assessment** tells you if your home currently has any lead hazards from lead in paint, dust, or soil. It also tells you what actions to take to address any hazards.

◆ A combination risk assessment and inspection tells you if your home has any lead hazards and if your home has any lead-based paint, and where the lead-based paint is located.

Hire a trained and certified testing professional who will use a range of reliable methods when testing your home.

◆ Visual inspection of paint condition and location.

◆ A portable x-ray fluorescence (XRF) machine.

◆ Lab tests of paint, dust, and soil samples.

There are state and federal programs in place to ensure that testing is done safely, reliably, and effectively. Contact your state or local agency (see bottom of page 11) for more information, or call **1-800-424-LEAD (5323)** for a list of contacts in your area.

Home test kits for lead are available, but may not always be accurate. Consumers should not rely on these kits before doing renovations or to assure safety.

What You Can Do Now To Protect Your Family

If you suspect that your house has lead hazards, you can take some immediate steps to reduce your family's risk:

◆ **If you rent, notify your landlord of peeling or chipping paint.**

◆ **Clean up paint chips immediately.**

◆ **Clean floors, window frames, window sills, and other surfaces weekly.** Use a mop or sponge with warm water and a general all-purpose cleaner or a cleaner made specifically for lead. REMEMBER: NEVER MIX AMMONIA AND BLEACH PRODUCTS TOGETHER SINCE THEY CAN FORM A DANGEROUS GAS.

◆ **Thoroughly rinse sponges and mop heads after cleaning dirty or dusty areas**.

◆ **Wash children's hands often, especially before they eat and before nap time and bed time.**

◆ **Keep play areas clean.** Wash bottles, pacifiers, toys, and stuffed animals regularly.

◆ **Keep children from chewing window sills or other painted surfaces.**

◆ **Clean or remove shoes before entering your home to avoid tracking in lead from soil.**

◆ **Make sure children eat nutritious, low-fat meals high in iron and calcium,** such as spinach and dairy products. Children with good diets absorb less lead.

7

Reducing Lead Hazards In The Home

Removing lead improperly can increase the hazard to your family by spreading even more lead dust around the house.

Always use a professional who is trained to remove lead hazards safely.

In addition to day-to-day cleaning and good nutrition:

◆ You can **temporarily** reduce lead hazards by taking actions such as repairing damaged painted surfaces and planting grass to cover soil with high lead levels. These actions (called "interim controls") are not permanent solutions and will need ongoing attention.

◆ To **permanently** remove lead hazards, you should hire a certified lead "abatement" contractor. Abatement (or permanent hazard elimination) methods include removing, sealing, or enclosing lead-based paint with special materials. Just painting over the hazard with regular paint is not permanent removal.

Always hire a person with special training for correcting lead problems—someone who knows how to do this work safely and has the proper equipment to clean up thoroughly. Certified contractors will employ qualified workers and follow strict safety rules as set by their state or by the federal government.

Once the work is completed, dust cleanup activities must be repeated until testing indicates that lead dust levels are below the following:

◆ 40 micrograms per square foot ($\mu g/ft^2$) for floors, including carpeted floors;

◆ 250 $\mu g/ft^2$ for interior windows sills; and

◆ 400 $\mu g/ft^2$ for window troughs.

Call your state or local agency (see bottom of page 11) for help in locating certified professionals in your area and to see if financial assistance is available.

Remodeling or Renovating a Home With Lead-Based Paint

Take precautions before your contractor or you begin remodeling or renovating anything that disturbs painted surfaces (such as scraping off paint or tearing out walls):

◆ **Have the area tested for lead-based paint.**

◆ **Do not use a belt-sander, propane torch, high temperature heat gun, dry scraper, or dry sandpaper** to remove lead-based paint. These actions create large amounts of lead dust and fumes. Lead dust can remain in your home long after the work is done.

◆ **Temporarily move your family** (especially children and pregnant women) out of the apartment or house until the work is done and the area is properly cleaned. If you can't move your family, at least completely seal off the work area.

◆ **Follow other safety measures to reduce lead hazards.** You can find out about other safety measures by calling 1-800-424-LEAD. Ask for the brochure "Reducing Lead Hazards When Remodeling Your Home." This brochure explains what to do before, during, and after renovations.

If you have already completed renovations or remodeling that could have released lead-based paint or dust, get your young children tested and follow the steps outlined on page 7 of this brochure.

If not conducted properly, certain types of renovations can release lead from paint and dust into the air.

9

Other Sources of Lead

While paint, dust, and soil are the most common sources of lead, other lead sources also exist.

◆ **Drinking water.** Your home might have plumbing with lead or lead solder. Call your local health department or water supplier to find out about testing your water. You cannot see, smell, or taste lead, and boiling your water will not get rid of lead. If you think your plumbing might have lead in it:

- Use only cold water for drinking and cooking.

- Run water for 15 to 30 seconds before drinking it, especially if you have not used your water for a few hours.

◆ **The job.** If you work with lead, you could bring it home on your hands or clothes. Shower and change clothes before coming home. Launder your work clothes separately from the rest of your family's clothes.

◆ Old painted **toys** and **furniture.**

◆ Food and liquids stored in **lead crystal** or **lead-glazed pottery or porcelain.**

◆ **Lead smelters** or other industries that release lead into the air.

◆ **Hobbies** that use lead, such as making pottery or stained glass, or refinishing furniture.

◆ **Folk remedies** that contain lead, such as "greta" and "azarcon" used to treat an upset stomach.

For More Information

The National Lead Information Center

Call **1-800-424-LEAD (424-5323)** to learn how to protect children from lead poisoning and for other information on lead hazards. To access lead information via the web, visit **www.epa.gov/lead** and **www.hud.gov/offices/lead/**.

EPA's Safe Drinking Water Hotline

Call **1-800-426-4791** for information about lead in drinking water.

Consumer Product Safety Commission (CPSC) Hotline

To request information on lead in consumer products, or to report an unsafe consumer product or a product-related injury call **1-800-638-2772**, or visit CPSC's Web site at: **www.cpsc.gov.**

Health and Environmental Agencies

Some cities, states, and tribes have their own rules for lead-based paint activities. Check with your local agency to see which laws apply to you. Most agencies can also provide information on finding a lead abatement firm in your area, and on possible sources of financial aid for reducing lead hazards. Receive up-to-date address and phone information for your local contacts on the Internet at **www.epa.gov/lead** or contact the National Lead Information Center at **1-800-424-LEAD.**

For the hearing impaired, call the Federal Information Relay Service at **1-800-877-8339** to access any of the phone numbers in this brochure.

11

EPA Regional Offices

Your Regional EPA Office can provide further information regarding regulations and lead protection programs.

EPA Regional Offices

Region 1 (Connecticut, Massachusetts, Maine, New Hampshire, Rhode Island, Vermont)

> Regional Lead Contact
> U.S. EPA Region 1
> Suite 1100 (CPT)
> One Congress Street
> Boston, MA 02114-2023
> 1 (888) 372-7341

Region 2 (New Jersey, New York, Puerto Rico, Virgin Islands)

> Regional Lead Contact
> U.S. EPA Region 2
> 2890 Woodbridge Avenue
> Building 209, Mail Stop 225
> Edison, NJ 08837-3679
> (732) 321-6671

Region 3 (Delaware, Maryland, Pennsylvania, Virginia, Washington DC, West Virginia)

> Regional Lead Contact
> U.S. EPA Region 3 (3WC33)
> 1650 Arch Street
> Philadelphia, PA 19103
> (215) 814-5000

Region 4 (Alabama, Florida, Georgia, Kentucky, Mississippi, North Carolina, South Carolina, Tennessee)

> Regional Lead Contact
> U.S. EPA Region 4
> 61 Forsyth Street, SW
> Atlanta, GA 30303
> (404) 562-8998

Region 5 (Illinois, Indiana, Michigan, Minnesota, Ohio, Wisconsin)

> Regional Lead Contact
> U.S. EPA Region 5 (DT-8J)
> 77 West Jackson Boulevard
> Chicago, IL 60604-3666
> (312) 886-6003

Region 6 (Arkansas, Louisiana, New Mexico, Oklahoma, Texas)

> Regional Lead Contact
> U.S. EPA Region 6
> 1445 Ross Avenue, 12th Floor
> Dallas, TX 75202-2733
> (214) 665-7577

Region 7 (Iowa, Kansas, Missouri, Nebraska)

> Regional Lead Contact
> U.S. EPA Region 7
> (ARTD-RALI)
> 901 N. 5th Street
> Kansas City, KS 66101
> (913) 551-7020

Region 8 (Colorado, Montana, North Dakota, South Dakota, Utah, Wyoming)

> Regional Lead Contact
> U.S. EPA Region 8
> 999 18th Street, Suite 500
> Denver, CO 80202-2466
> (303) 312-6021

Region 9 (Arizona, California, Hawaii, Nevada)

> Regional Lead Contact
> U.S. Region 9
> 75 Hawthorne Street
> San Francisco, CA 94105
> (415) 947-4164

Region 10 (Alaska, Idaho, Oregon, Washington)

> Regional Lead Contact
> U.S. EPA Region 10
> Toxics Section WCM-128
> 1200 Sixth Avenue
> Seattle, WA 98101-1128
> (206) 553-1985

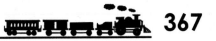

CPSC Regional Offices

Your Regional CPSC Office can provide further information regarding regulations and consumer product safety.

Eastern Regional Center
Consumer Product Safety Commission
201 Varick Street, Room 903
New York, NY 10014
(212) 620-4120

Western Regional Center
Consumer Product Safety Commission
1301 Clay Street, Suite 610-N
Oakland, CA 94612
(510) 637-4050

Central Regional Center
Consumer Product Safety Commission
230 South Dearborn Street, Room 2944
Chicago, IL 60604
(312) 353-8260

HUD Lead Office

Please contact HUD's Office of Healthy Homes and Lead Hazard Control for information on lead regulations, outreach efforts, and lead hazard control and research grant programs.

U.S. Department of Housing and Urban Development
Office of Healthy Homes and Lead Hazard Control
451 Seventh Street, SW, P-3206
Washington, DC 20410
(202) 755-1785

U.S. EPA Washington DC 20460
U.S. CPSC Washington DC 20207
U.S. HUD Washington DC 20410

EPA747-K-99-001
June 2003

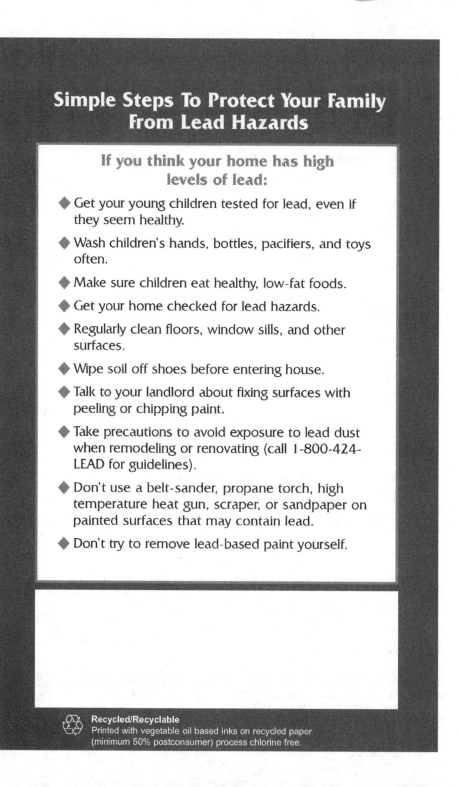

Simple Steps To Protect Your Family From Lead Hazards

If you think your home has high levels of lead:

◆ Get your young children tested for lead, even if they seem healthy.

◆ Wash children's hands, bottles, pacifiers, and toys often.

◆ Make sure children eat healthy, low-fat foods.

◆ Get your home checked for lead hazards.

◆ Regularly clean floors, window sills, and other surfaces.

◆ Wipe soil off shoes before entering house.

◆ Talk to your landlord about fixing surfaces with peeling or chipping paint.

◆ Take precautions to avoid exposure to lead dust when remodeling or renovating (call 1-800-424-LEAD for guidelines).

◆ Don't use a belt-sander, propane torch, high temperature heat gun, scraper, or sandpaper on painted surfaces that may contain lead.

◆ Don't try to remove lead-based paint yourself.

Recycled/Recyclable
Printed with vegetable oil based inks on recycled paper (minimum 50% postconsumer) process chlorine free.

FCRA Summary of Rights

AmerUSA Corporation
3665 East Bay Drive #204-183
Largo, Florida 33771
Ph 727.467.0908 Fx 727.467.0918

FCRA Summary of Rights

A Summary of Your Rights - Under the Fair Credit Reporting Act

The federal Fair Credit Reporting Act (FCRA) is designed to promote accuracy, fairness, and privacy of information in the files of every "consumer reporting agency" (CRA). Most CRAs are credit bureaus that gather and sell information about you -- such as if you pay your bills on time or have filed bankruptcy -- to creditors, employers, landlords, and other businesses. You can find the complete text of the FCRA, 15 U.S.C. §§1681-1681u, by visiting www.ftc.gov. The FCRA gives you specific rights, as outlined below. You may have additional rights under state law. You may contact a state or local consumer protection agency or a state attorney general to learn those rights.

- **You must be told if information in your file has been used against you.** Anyone who uses information from a CRA to take action against you -- such as denying an application for credit, insurance, or employment -- must tell you, and give you the name, address, and phone number of the CRA that provided the consumer report.

- **You can find out what is in your file.** At your request, a CRA must give you the information in your file, and a list of everyone who has requested it recently. There is no charge for the report if a person has taken action against you because of information supplied by the CRA, if you request the report within 60 days of receiving notice of the action. You also are entitled to one free report every twelve months upon request if you certify that (1) you are unemployed and plan to seek employment within 60 days, (2) you are on welfare, or (3) your report is inaccurate due to fraud. Otherwise, a CRA may charge you up to eight dollars.

- **You can dispute inaccurate information with the CRA.** If you tell a CRA that your file contains inaccurate information, the CRA must investigate the items (usually within 30 days) by presenting to its information source all relevant evidence you submit, unless your dispute is frivolous. The source must review your evidence and report its findings to the CRA. (The source also must advise national CRAs -- to which it has provided the data -- of any error.) The CRA must give you a written report of the investigation, and a copy of your report if the investigation results in any change. If the CRA's investigation does not resolve the dispute, you may add a brief statement to your file. The CRA must normally include a summary of your statement in future reports. If an item is deleted or a dispute statement is filed, you may ask that anyone who has recently received your report be notified of the change.

- **Inaccurate information must be corrected or deleted.** A CRA must remove or correct inaccurate or unverified information from its files, usually within 30 days after you dispute it. **However, the CRA is not required to remove accurate data from your file unless it is outdated (as described below) or cannot be verified.** If your dispute results in any change to your report, the CRA cannot reinsert into your file a disputed item unless the information source verifies its accuracy and completeness. In addition, the CRA must give you a written notice telling you it has reinserted the item. The notice must include the name, address and phone number of the information source.

- **You can dispute inaccurate items with the source of the information.** If you tell anyone -- such as a creditor who reports to a CRA -- that you dispute an item, they may not then report the information to a CRA without including a notice of your dispute. In addition, once you've notified the source of the error in writing, it may not continue to report the information if it is, in fact, an error.

- **Outdated information may not be reported.** In most cases, a CRA may not report negative information that is more than seven years old; ten years for bankruptcies.

- **Access to your file is limited.** A CRA may provide information about you only to people with a need recognized by the FCRA -- usually to consider an application with a creditor, insurer, employer, landlord, or other business.

- **Your consent is required for reports that are provided to employers, or reports that contain medical information.** A CRA may not give out information about you to your employer, or prospective employer, without your written consent. A CRA may not report medical information about you to creditors, insurers, or employers without your permission.

- **You may choose to exclude your name from CRA lists for unsolicited credit and insurance offers.** Creditors and insurers may use file information as the basis for sending you unsolicited offers of credit or insurance. Such offers must include a toll-free phone number for you to call if you want your name and address removed from future lists. If you call, you must be kept off the lists for two years. If you request, complete, and return the CRA form provided for this purpose, you must be taken off the lists indefinitely.

- **You may seek damages from violators.** If a CRA, a user or (in some cases) a provider of CRA data, violates the FCRA, you may sue them in state or federal court.

FOR QUESTIONS OR CONCERNS PLEASE CONTACT

Federal Trade Commission
Consumer Response Center- FCRA
Washington, DC 20580 * 202-326-3761

Bonus CD-ROM:
The American Landlord Resource Center

System Requirements:

★ **Windows 2000, XP or Vista (with CD-ROM Drive)**
★ **Adobe Reader (Version 7 or Higher - Available as a Free Download)**
★ **Internet Connection (Recommended)**

The enclosed CD-ROM is outfitted with rental forms, agreements and publications, among many other invaluable resources *[some forms and agreements may need to be modified (or amended) to accommodate new or existing laws in your state]*. Each form comes equipped with fields that can be highlighted and then hovered with your mouse for pop-up instructions. You can even personalize each form and agreement with your contact information and logo *[see the illustrations on the following pages]*.

Installation Instructions

Insert the CD into your CD-ROM drive and follow the onscreen instructions. If the installation process does not automatically begin, click the **START** button, then click **RUN** and type in the following: **D:\americanlandlord.exe** and click **OK** to begin following the onscreen instructions. *(If the location of your CD-ROM begins with a letter other than **D**, you must replace it with the proper drive letter.)*

Terms of Use

All copyrighted forms are provided for your personal use only and may not be redistributed or sold. Note: The contents of this CD-ROM are not intended as a substitute for the advice of an attorney.

How to Personalize a Rental Form

The End Result

JOHN Z. DOE RENTAL PROPERTY LLC
2008 Western Avenue
Anytown, USA 12345
PH (555) 555-1212
FX (555) 555-1313

Residential Rental Application

Applicant Information

Property address applying for: 1002 North Canyon Rd , Unit #3, Anytown, USA 12345

Name:

Date of birth:	SSN:	Phone:

Current address:

City:	State:	ZIP Code:

Own	Rent	(Please circle)	Monthly payment or rent:	How long?

Previous address:

City:	State:	ZIP Code:

Owned	Rented	(Please circle)	Monthly payment or rent:	How long?

Employment Information

Current employer:

Employer address:	How long?

City:	State:	ZIP Code:

Phone:	E-mail:	Fax:

Position:	Hourly	Salary	(Please circle)	Annual income:

Emergency Contact

Name of a person not residing with you:

Address:

City:	State:	ZIP Code:	Phone:

Relationship:

References

Name:	Address:	Phone:

Have you ever been convicted of a crime? (yes / no) If so, please explain all offenses including where, when and why:

Have you ever been evicted? (yes / no) If so, please explain where, when and why:

I acknowledge that falsification or omission of any information on this rental application may result in the immediate dismissal or retraction of an offer of tenancy. I hereby voluntarily consent to and authorize the AmerUSA Corporation ("AmerUSA"), acting as the landlord's designated screening organization for the above referenced rental property, to obtain my consumer report and render a credit decision. I further authorize all persons and organizations that may have information relevant to this research to disclose such information to the landlord's authorized agent, AmerUSA. I hereby release the landlord and its authorized agent, AmerUSA, from all claims and liabilities of any nature in connection with this research, results and decision. A photocopy of this authorization will be considered valid. I understand that I have specific prescribed rights as a consumer under the federal Fair Credit Reporting Act ('FCRA') and have received a copy of those rights titled "FCRA Summary of Rights."

Signature of applicant:	Date:

This form provided by USLandlord.com

Index

Also available:

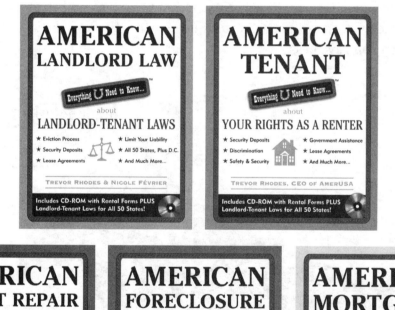

Everything U Need to Know...™

We would like to hear from you!

Please email us your comments or suggestions about **American Landlord** or any other volume from the Everything U Need to Know... series. Whether it's an idea for a new volume or a comment about an existing one, it's always a distinct pleasure to listen to what *you* have to say...

feedback@euntk.com